Oldsmobile V-8 ENGINES
How to Build
MAX PERFORMANCE

Bill Trovato

CarTech®

CarTech®

CarTech®, Inc.
838 Lake Street South
Forest Lake, MN 55025
Phone: 651-277-1200 or 800-551-4754
Fax: 651-277-1203
www.cartechbooks.com

© 2015 by Bill Trovato
1st Edition Published in 2010

All rights reserved. No part of this publication may be reproduced or utilized in any form or by any means, electronic or mechanical, including photocopying, recording, or by any information storage and retrieval system, without prior permission from the Author. All text, photographs, and artwork are the property of the Author unless otherwise noted or credited.

The information in this work is true and complete to the best of our knowledge. However, all information is presented without any guarantee on the part of the Author or Publisher, who also disclaim any liability incurred in connection with the use of the information.

All trademarks, trade names, model names and numbers, and other product designations referred to herein are the property of their respective owners and are used solely for identification purposes. This work is a publication of CarTech, Inc., and has not been licensed, approved, sponsored, or endorsed by any other person or entity.

Edit by Paul Johnson
Layout by Monica Seiberlich

ISBN 978-1-61325-495-0
Item No. SA172P

Library of Congress Cataloging-in-Publication Data
Trovato, Bill.
 [How to build max-performance Oldsmobile V-8s]
 Oldsmobile V-8 engines : how to build max performance (updated) / author, Bill Trovato.
   pages cm
 Revised edition of: How to build max-performance Oldsmobile V-8s. 2010.

 1. Oldsmobile automobile--Motors--Maintenance and repair.
 2. Oldsmobile automobile--Performance. I. Title.

TL215.O4T76 2015
629.25'040288--dc23

2015010528

Written, edited, and designed in the U.S.A.
Printed in U.S.A.
10 9 8 7 6 5 4 3 2

Front Cover: This ever-popular 496 pump-gas Oldsmobile street engine custom built for Adam Wahl has excellent street manners and an abundance of low-end torque. This particular engine has many accessories, including a March Performance Pulleys serpentine conversion kit. Inside, the engine has basic popular bolt-on parts. This engine produces 560 reliable horsepower and a whopping 650 ft-lbs of torque, which can easily spin the tires.

Title Page: The finished BTR billet tunnel ram helped make 780 hp out of Turner's 417-ci BTR-prepared DX Olds.

Back Cover Photos

Top Left: At full lift, the pushrod is at the other side of the pushrod cup, but is fully contacting the entire pushrod cup in the rocker body. This style and shape of rocker body allows this to take place.

Top Right: CP custom pistons are manufactured accurately enough so that if you want to hone the bores to a particular size, you can then order the piston in that size. You don't want to use a micrometer to measure the skirt and set clearance as with some other pistons. First, the skirt is not straight or round, and chances are you cannot measure the exact spot accurately. Second, the skirt clearance is set for you, so don't reinvent the wheel and change it from the designed clearance. I have followed this method with 100-percent success.

Middle Left: When oil gets to the front of the passenger-side oil gallery and feeds the front main and cam bearing like the other four, it then transfers through that common passage and feeds the driver-side oil gallery.

Middle Right: This is a Stage-3 Batten cylinder head and can, which can be identified by the rocker stud pads being all tied in together, unlike on the Stage-1 and Stage-2 castings.

Bottom: This is the author's 1970 442, running low 11-second quarter-mile times and chasing the NHRA E/Stock Automatic-Class World Record.

CONTENTS

Acknowledgments 4
Introduction 5

Chapter 1: Engine Blocks 7
Small-Blocks 7
Big-Blocks 11
Engine Block Filler 13
Lifter Bore Bank Angles 14
Engine Block Machining 14
Bottom-End Girdles 17

Chapter 2: Crankshafts 20
Factory Small-Block Crank
  Identification and Application 20
Factory Big-Block Crank
  Identification and Application 20
Aftermarket Crankshafts 23
Bearing Clearance 24
Crank Grinding 26
Stroking 30
Magnafluxing 30
Engine Bearings 31
Anti-Friction Coatings 32
Crankshaft Balancing 33
Harmonic Balancers 35
Rear Main Bearing Seals 38

Chapter 3: Camshafts and Valvetrain 39
Rocker Arms 39
Pushrods 44
Timing Chains 45
Roller-Bearing Cam Bolt and Camshaft Walk 46
Camshafts and Camshaft Selection 47
Camshaft Specifications 51
Lifters 51
Valvesprings, Retainers and Locks 53

Chapter 4: Connecting Rods 56
Factory Connecting Rods 56
Aftermarket Steel Connecting Rods 58
Aluminum Connecting Rods 59
Connecting-Rod Side Clearance 60
Rod-to-Stroke Ratio 61

Chapter 5: Pistons, Rings and Pins 62
Factory Cast Pistons 62
Aftermarket Forged Pistons 64
Off-the-Shelf Pistons 64
Custom Pistons 65
Piston Domes and Compression Ratio 66
Piston Rings 68
Gapless Rings 70
Piston Clearances 71
Piston Pins 71
Coatings 75
Ring Gaps 76

Chapter 6: Oiling System 78
Oiling-System Flow Path 78
Oil Restrictors 80
Main-Bearing Modifications 81
Lifter Gallery Plugs 81
Oil Pumps 82
Oil-Filter Adapters and Oil Filters 84
Oil Pans 85
Windage Trays 87
Engine Oils 87
Vacuum Pumps 88

Chapter 7: Cylinder Heads and Induction 90
Factory Small-Block Cylinder Heads 90
Factory Big-Block Cylinder Heads 91
Head Gaskets 92
The Milling Process 94
Aftermarket Cylinder Heads 95
Porting Tips and Tricks 102
Valveguides 106
The Valve Job 107
The Flow Bench 109
CNC-Ported Cylinder Heads 110
Valves 111
Intake Manifolds 113
Carburetors 122

Chapter 8: Exhaust System 127
Factory Cast-Iron Manifolds 127
Center Divider on Factory Heads 129
Header Sizing 130
Full-Size Headers 131
Low-Cost Headers 131
Merge Collectors 131
Painted versus Coated versus Stainless 132
Crank Case Evacuation 132
Exhaust Gaskets 132
Mufflers and Exhaust Pipes 133

Chapter 9: Ignition System 134
Ignition Boxes 134
Advance Curves 136
Crank Triggers and Magnetic Pickups 136
Distributors 136
Distributor Gears 137
Ignition Coils 138
Spark Plugs 138
Spark Plug Wires 139
Setting Ignition Timing 139

Appendix A: Assembly Tips and Techniques 140
Appendix B: Popular BTR Performance Combinations ... 142
Source Guide 143

ACKNOWLEDGMENTS

Several people shaped and molded me as a young Oldsmobile enthusiast. It is my pleasure to give them credit. The very first time I ever went to a drag strip as a teenager with my first car (a white 1970 Cutlass S), I saw George Howcroft leave the starting line with the front wheels in the air, running some 11.40-second ETs in his black-and-gold, NHRA E/Stock Automatic (E/SA) class, 1970 442 W-30.

At that moment, my future was determined; I decided to do whatever it took to run that fast one day. George took me under his wing and continuously helped me to progress; he possessed tremendous knowledge and had raced Oldsmobiles since the 1950s. In the mid-1980s, George convinced me to compete in NHRA Stock Eliminator with his old W-30 that was for sale. Eventually, I purchased the black-and-gold car that I first saw him race when I was a teenager. I decided that if I was going to race in the NHRA, I was not going to show up unless I could come close to setting a national record. This mindset motivated me, during my early years as a garage/backyard engine builder and racer, to chase that NHRA E/SA record. George helped me as much as he possibly could until he was stricken with cancer and passed away at age 62 in the late 1980s. If he could see what he helped me to achieve, I think he would be proud.

Another person who deserves credit as one of my mentors is Dave Smith of Dave Smith Engineering. As a young Oldsmobile racer, I looked up to him; he was a high-profile, accomplished Oldsmobile racer. I can remember calling him, buying parts and asking for advice on many Olds-specific subjects that I so desperately wanted to learn about, and he always took the time to help me. I also offer this written apology for calling him and taking up way too much of his time. As a shop owner now, I know how difficult it is to spend time on the phone. He helped pave the way to my future.

A special thanks goes to my auto tech teacher Paul Reynolds and my machine shop teacher Bob Finnegan. These guys educated and molded me as a young man in high school and I always looked up to them. I was fortunate recently to have both of them visit the shop; time traveled 30 years in an instant. They were able to see what their hard work in education had created. I was also able to thank them personally, something that I had wanted to do in recent years.

F. J. Smith is another gentleman whom I always admired, respected, and wanted to be like when I read about him in the *Oldsmobile in Action* publications of the early 1980s. He is very well respected in the performance industry, contributing his great knowledge of race car design and safety to the SFI Foundation. Many of the chassis safety regulations that we all have to follow are the result of much of his work. He contributed a great deal to Oldsmobile racing in the 1980s when it was at an all-time high. He set many records during Oldsmobile Racing's development years, and was a major contributor to the design of many of Oldsmobile's racing parts and engine building methods that we all still use today.

INTRODUCTION

This is my 1970 442, running low 11-second quarter-mile times and chasing the NHRA E/Stock Automatic-class World Record.

In this revised edition of *Oldsmobile V-8 Engines: How to Build Max Performance*, I am sharing more than 30 years of accumulated Oldsmobile knowledge to help in your Oldsmobile performance endeavors. I began working on the first edition of this book in 2008 and have learned much since then. My most popular builds are, by far, pump-gas street-driven big-block engines. So now, with this extra information, you can successfully build your own pump-gas street engine, or at least educate yourself so that an expert can build it for you properly.

This journey began for me at age 16, when I rebuilt my first 455-ci Olds engine for a 1970 Cutlass S.

I've never believed in following the masses; I tend to do things considered "outside the box." In this book I explain why I do some of the things that I do and, I hope, help you to step up a notch in the Oldsmobile performance world. You may find that some of my techniques are about as far from building a small-block Chevy as you can get. I tend to go down the road less traveled, but I don't just give good advice. I only give advice that I've physically proved to be good.

My goal in sharing this knowledge with Oldsmobile enthusiasts is that this book results in faster ET slips at the racetrack and more usable power on the street. I remember my early days with Oldsmobile performance and the feeling of hunger for this knowledge. I'm also here to save you from dropping your engine off at your local machine shop and having it built with conventional techniques that result in premature engine wear and ultimately engine failure. I can help you save a bunch of money, but you have to understand that high-performance Oldsmobiles are inherently more expensive to build than a Chevy or a Ford engine.

Almost every topic in this book could have a book written about it to cover every detail. Here, I share my experience in power and longevity techniques that are unique to high-performance Oldsmobiles.

My working career started on my 16th birthday, as a heliarc welder at a sheet-metal fabrication shop. Next, I worked at the Delco Products General Motors plant in Rochester, New York, for 19 years and served a five-year apprenticeship as an automation mechanic. As a journeyman automation mechanic, I worked repairing, troubleshooting, and redesigning automated equipment.

While employed at the Delco Products division of General Motors Corporation, I also worked weekends, from 1997 to 2001, as a tech official for the National Muscle Car Association (NMCA). At the time, Petersen Publishing owned NMCA, and it was best known for *Hot Rod* magazine. It was a great experience, flying around to races working as a tech official, writing and enforcing rules, and helping host the events. During that time, I became race director for the brand-new (at that time) National Mustang Racers Association (NMRA) and was one of the people who helped get that organization started on the right foot.

INTRODUCTION

When I first started at Delco Products in 1986, fewer than 4,000 people worked there. Around the turn of the century, I noticed that there was a mass exodus of manufacturing plants from the United States, headed for Mexico. Our plant was sending manufacturing assembly lines there one by one. In 2003, the building had a lot of empty space and only about 1,200 people were employed there. That was enough to show where it was all heading. So, in 2004, I decided to leave factory life and start my own business, which is now known as BTR Performance. If you ever visit my facility, you'll see evidence of my CNC machine background throughout the shop. I even have a CNC machine from the old plant. I believe that meticulous machining techniques and precise tolerance control are the foundation for all brands of high-performance engines.

By the early 1990s, I had the car running within a few hundredths of the national record. I attended a few NHRA divisional points meets, but quickly decided that it wasn't for me. Even if I could set the record, low-11-second ETs just were not going to cut it for me, having raced my street-driven 1970 Cutlass with nitrous oxide and run 9-second ETs. Some friends from the Chicago area (including Mike Glasby, Chuck Samuel, Nick Scavo, and Ronnie Mroz) were racing in the newly formed NMCA and I really liked the heads-up–style drag racing, where the fastest guy was to have the advantage! This was for me.

I first started racing the street-legal drag racing scene in what was called the EZ Street class at NMCA in 1996. I ran my red (formerly white) 442-ci, DX-based, small-block 1970 Cutlass. I had fun and turned a best of 9.41 in the class, which was very respectable for that time. But, I knew that racing a 3,800-pound car was not going to do the job, so I set out to build the 1978 Olds Starfire. I knew it would be light, and designed the combination to run into the high 8s at 150 mph, never even considering that the car would eventually run in the high 7s at more than 175 mph.

My original combination for this EZ Street class (at the lighter weight) was a flat-tappet, 337-ci Oldsmobile DX-based small-block with cast-iron Batten heads and a single-stage nitrous plate. This combination was competitive in 2003, going a best of 8.70 at 157 mph, but by this time participation in the EZ Street class that I built the car around had begun to dwindle. 2004, I built a new 403-ci, NASCAR block-based small-block Olds engine, and set the car up to race in the National Street Car Association (NSCA) Limited Street class. I was successful at setting the Limited Street record at 7.90 seconds at 175 mph and winning two consecutive National Championships (2005 and 2006). In 2007, I decided to compete in the NMCA's no-wheelie-bar Xtreme Street class. Since the start of competition, the Starfire always qualified on top of the ladder and set the national record in 2009 with a 7.97-second pass at 172 mph.

This Oldsmobile Starfire set another NMCA Extreme Street record in 2010; it ran a personal best 7.85 at 175 mph, 3,035 pounds. It continued to win races until I retired the car at the end of the 2012 season.

During nearly 30 years of building Oldsmobile engines, I have had plenty of successes and failures; both have led me to where I am today. I've always used the common-sense approach to engine building rather than what was the common and/or accepted current practice. When competing at a national level, you are running against people who are all talented, or else they would not be there.

Given that, this type of competition forces you to do your best and make enough horsepower with your engine combination to compete. Racing against Fords and Chevrolets with an Oldsmobile forces you to design and fabricate nearly the entire engine, rather than just going out and buying the latest performance cylinder head or intake manifold and bolting it on.

I hope you enjoy what I've learned from those years of hard work, hard thinking, and great mentors!

CHAPTER 1

ENGINE BLOCKS

Oldsmobile engine blocks, as far as most Olds enthusiasts are concerned, started in 1965. The first V-8s in this new-style Oldsmobile engine line started as the 330-ci models for the small-block family and the 400- and 425-ci models for the big-block family. The engine-block designs remained virtually unchanged right up to the last Olds engine that came off the assembly line in the late 1980s. Olds blocks are very easy to identify. A letter cast into the front of the engine block under the intake manifold sealing rail identifies a small-block. A letter in the same place identifies a big-block.

Small-Blocks

Oldsmobile small-block V-8s consisted of a variety of cubic-inch models, including the 260-, 307-, 330-, 350-, and 403-ci engines. For high-performance use, the 350- and 403-ci versions are the most popular with Olds enthusiasts.

Oldsmobile small-blocks share many features. The bore spacing (defined as the center-to-center distance between the cylinders) was set at 4.625 inches, which is shared with the Olds big-block. The main bearing bores are set at 2.687 inches on all small-blocks with the exception of the diesels. The diesel block main-bearing bores are the same diameter as the big-block Olds, which are measured at 3.189 inches. The deck height, measured from the crankshaft centerline to the cylinder head mounting surface, is set at 9.330 inches on all small-block Oldsmobile V-8s. The lower portion of the block

The Sunnen CK 10 cylinder hone does a great job of honing cylinders round and with little distortion. Newer, more advanced honing machines are available, but many top engine builders prefer this machine.

The letter at the end of the casting number indicates which big-block engine it is. An "A" casting is the 1965 425-ci engine, a "D" casting is the later 425-ci engine, a "G" casting is the long-stroke 400-ci engine, and an "F" casting is the 455 engine. Here, the little "A" next to the "F" means that this block has no provisions for a 4-speed.

CHAPTER 1

The large numeral after the casting number indicates which small-block engine it is. A "2" is a 350-ci engine, a "4A" or "4B" is a 403-ci engine. Blocks with these numbers are about the only ones you want use for serious high-performance.

has only subtle differences, with the exception of the main-bearing webs. The lifter-valley areas in all the small-blocks are very similar and are not considered to be a weak spot. I have never seen a failure in this area. The lifter bores on all small-blocks are .842 inch in diameter and were all designed for use with flat-tappet hydraulic lifters. The exceptions are the later diesel blocks and late-model 307 gas engines, which had .921-inch-diameter lifter bores for use with hydraulic-roller lifters.

As mentioned, the first of the Olds small-blocks was the 330-ci model, which was produced from 1965 to 1967. These engines have a 3.937-inch bore and a stroke of 3.385 inches. I have sonic tested a few of these blocks and you can safely overbore the cylinders .060 inch (or 4.000 inches) at best. The 330 blocks are, in my opinion, only good for restoration pieces. Although they appear to be as strong as any of the newer 350 blocks, the small bore size makes it an undesirable choice for high-performance use.

In 1968, the introduction of the 350-ci Olds engine stepped up the performance of the small-block by increasing the bore size to 4.057 inches. I have always wondered why Olds engineers chose such an oddball bore size. The 350 blocks share most of the features of the 330-ci block, with this notable exception. I have sonic tested some of the 1968–1974 blocks and have not found any whose cylinders couldn't be safely overbored .060 inch. Most of the high-performance 350 engines that I build use a 4.125-inch bore with a custom-made piston. The 4.125-inch size is the best you can use to obtain the most horsepower in these engines. The cylinder wall thickness

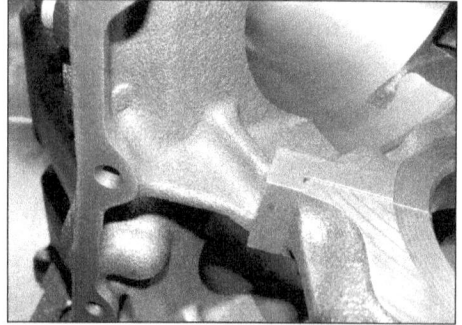

The main webbing on a gasoline small-block engine is even thinner than on the Olds big-block. How much stress can it handle? Who really knows? It depends on the weight of the rotating assembly, RPM, crank stiffness, detonation, static compression, and numerous other factors. Oldsmobile racers have pushed these blocks pretty far, but it's only a matter of time before you run over the crankshaft when pushed to the limit.

The main webs in this 403 block don't have a whole lot of material to hold the crankshaft in the block. Some have had success in 12-second quarter-mile cars for a while, but I have seen them fail also. My opinion: Why go there? An engine failure is too costly. It's too bad that Olds engineers lightened the structure; there would be an awful lot of these out there racing.

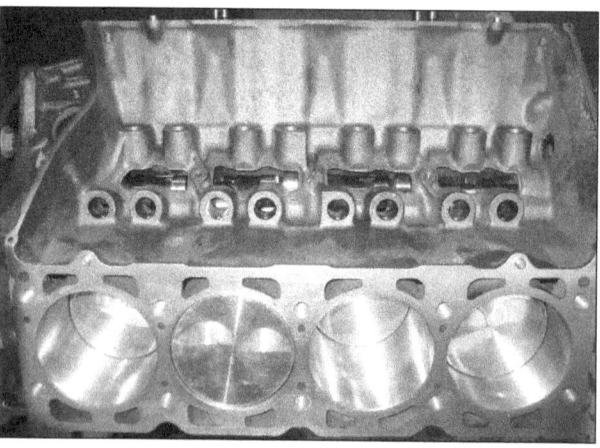

I have seen numerous performance Olds engines over the years and have yet to see a lifter bore failure. There is no need for modifications here.

at this bore on these blocks is enough to allow the bore to remain round at all but the highest horsepower levels. I estimate that to be at 650 hp or less.

In 1975, Oldsmobile introduced the 403-ci engine. This block shared a redesign with the 350 block to include a weight savings. One of these changes was the removal of the already thin main-bearing webs that tie into the main-bearing bores from the oil pan rails. Do not use one of these later-model 350 blocks for any high-performance build because the beefier pre-1975 blocks are still readily available.

The 403-ci small-block has the largest bore of any Olds engine, set at 4.350 inches. The cylinder walls are not that thick, however, and the best method of keeping a round bore is to keep the walls as thick as possible by honing the existing bore until it is perfectly straight and round, and then using a custom piston with file-to-fit rings. The maximum amount I would ever consider for an overbore on a 403 is .030-inch oversize. Forget any more than that. This block has siamesed cylinders that strengthen the area by tying the bores together side to side, but the rest of the cylinder thickness is borderline too thin due to the weight-saving redesign.

With the large-bore design, this block sounds like a great deal. Unfortunately, another way the Olds engineers saved weight in this block was by removing material and effectively adding windows to the already-weak main bearing webs. When looking at one of these blocks on the engine stand, it is plain to see that there is not much material to hold the spinning crank assembly in the block. You'd be lucky if the crankshaft doesn't fall on the floor when you turn the engine stand over to bolt the heads on, let alone spin some RPM with rods and pistons connected! I'm exaggerating here, of course, but the main bearing webs are one of the important areas of strength in an engine block design. The Olds designers missed the boat on this one. There are, however, some alternatives.

One way of reducing some bottom-end stress with these engine blocks is to reduce the weight of the rotating and reciprocating lower-end components. Another way to help these engines is to use a main-bearing girdle (like the part made by J&S). It has been debated whether the girdle helps or doesn't help, but I can say that the 403 engines that I have built with the girdle in place have not failed. The main-bearing girdle cannot weaken the lower end, so I put it on.

One particular 403 engine that I built for a customer has used the girdle and lightweight components with great success. This particular street-and-strip engine has aluminum connecting rods and lightweight custom pistons. The street-driven 1987 Cutlass in which the engine was installed ran 12.30-second passes at the quarter-mile drag strip (at full street weight and naturally aspirated) and 11.50-second times with a small amount of nitrous oxide. Yes, I said

The Mondello engine-block girdle is a welded-together unit. I have seen numerous high-horsepower Oldsmobile engines perform reliably with it.

nitrous oxide. This 403-ci "bomb" is still ticking some four years later.

In 1977, the Oldsmobile Division decided to produce a diesel engine for the full-size Delta 88s. These Oldsmobile diesel engines were not necessarily good when new, and had a variety of warranty issues. However, it gave Olds racing enthusiasts a good block to convert into a bulletproof gasoline-powered high-performance engine.

Three versions of these blocks were available: the "D" casting block with .842-inch-diameter lifter bores, or the "DX" block with either .842-inch or .921-inch-diameter lifter bores. These blocks had the same deck

The BTR girdle bolts are torqued to the pan rails with 3/8-inch grade-8 bolts. This ties the pan rail to the main caps and replaces the lack of sufficient thickness in the main webbing. It also ties together the three center caps and studs.

CHAPTER 1

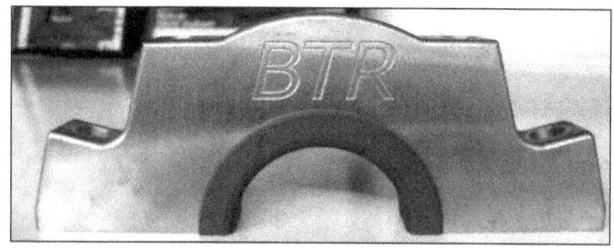

This four-bolt billet-steel main cap is designed for use in small-block diesel conversions. These caps are available for 2.5- and 3-inch main crankshafts. Generally, you only need the four-bolt caps for mains number-2, -3, and -4. One of the purposes of the four-bolt main cap is to keep the side of the block from spreading. I do not recommend four-bolt caps for thin main-web engines.

Small-block diesel engines are relatively easy to spot. They have a "-D3" code on the block behind the timing cover, along with a rather large "D" or "DX" on the side of the block near the freeze plug area.

The injector-pump boss on a diesel block hits the timing chain unless it is cleared by grinding or some other method.

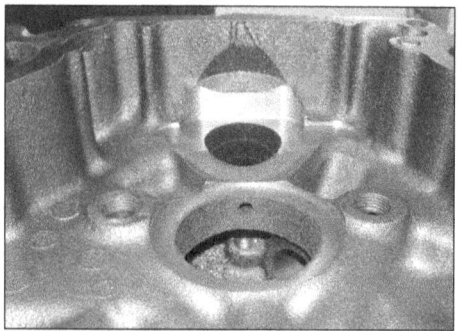

A neat little program on the Cincinnati CNC machine mills the injector pump area. It also mills a pocket in front of the number-1 cam bearing so that a capsulated thrust bearing can be installed to prevent wear between the camshaft and the cast-iron block. Not only does the thrust bearing prevent wear, it allows you to set the lifter-to-lobe relationship exactly where you want it.

height (9.330 inches) as all the gasoline Olds small-blocks. The main bearing bore used big-block dimensions (3.189 inches), which accepted a 3-inch main bearing journal big-block crankshaft, or the standard cast diesel crankshaft. The cylinder wall is much thicker than the gasoline small-blocks, and a diesel block's cylinders can be bored to as much as 4.250-inch, although there are some parts of the bore that start getting thin at that size. Half-inch-diameter head bolts were used on these engines for improved head gasket sealing and will not have to be upgraded. The oiling system remains unchanged on these blocks.

To convert one of these engines for gasoline use, there are only a few minor modifications required. The diesel fuel-injector pump boss must be cleared, due to interference with standard timing chains. This task can be accomplished either by grinding the boss away by hand, machining it away on a mill, or (as I do) milling the area away on the CNC machine for maximum weight removal and the best-possible appearance. All above methods will get the job done.

The diesel timing chain cover may have to be changed to a standard-type gasoline engine piece; the seal area interferes with some harmonic balancers. Additionally, if a back-grooved cam bearing is to be used, the passage that connects the top of the cam bearing bore to the injector pump hole must be plugged with a .250-inch-diameter dowel. The length of the dowel is unimportant as long as it seals the passage and doesn't move. I've found that 1/2- to 3/4-inch lengths are fine. Chances are you will be making a dowel on the lathe out of a piece of aluminum that will fit the hole exactly, as this is a drilled hole and is not necessarily a precise diameter. This dowel plug has a .001-inch or so press-fit clearance, and is installed in the passage with the cam bearing removed. The dowel is typically driven into position with a long drift punch through the connecting passage in the number-1 cam-bearing oil-feed hole. If a conventional (non-back-grooved) cam bearing is to be utilized, this passage can remain open, because the cam-bearing shell seals the hole.

Oldsmobile also made a special high-performance engine block commonly referred to as the "NASCAR block." These high-performance blocks can still be found, but are very rare. There are many different variations of these, but there are basically two different models. One carries Olds PN 22528096 and

ENGINE BLOCKS

The pocket that is cut into the camshaft thrust area is cut precisely so that the thrust bearing stays in place. Because approximately .140 inch is machined out of the block to retain the thrust bearing, the cam bearing needs to be driven into the block by that amount minus about .030 inch.

The endmill machines a pocket that is 2.930 x .140 inches deep to allow the Cloyes roller thrust bearing to sit in the pocket without falling out. This DX block has main-bearing spacers. It is best to use a main cap that is the proper size so that the only spacer needed is in the block.

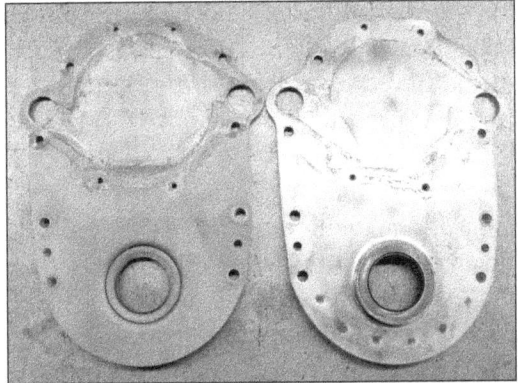

The timing cover on the left is the stock version found on every gasoline-powered Oldsmobile engine. The timing cover on the right is from a diesel engine. The harmonic-balancer seal protrudes from the front of the timing cover. It is best to check for interference before you glue this cover on. This hits some harmonic balancers, and does not hit others.

This late 39-degree 425 block used .921-inch lifter bores and had bronze lifter bore bushings installed that were finish machined to .842 diameter for use with more readily available parts.

features coolant-flow passages between the cylinders. The other carries Olds PN 22527735 and has siamesed cylinder bores, which have no coolant-flow passages between the cylinders and allow for larger bore diameters. The siamesed NASCAR blocks can handle bore sizes as large as 4.350 and still retain ample cylinder-wall thickness. The only concern at that point is the lack of space between the cylinders; this is where head gaskets are challenged to seal, as horsepower and cylinder pressure get higher.

The siamesed-cylinder NASCAR blocks are the rarest, strongest, and most desirable of these high-performance castings. I have seen many of the special high-performance Olds blocks and there seems to be so many variations and inconsistencies, so it isn't worth discussing them all. I have seen the PN 22528096 "non-siamesed" block have siamesed cylinders. I have seen blocks with 2.500-, 2.750-, and 3.000-inch main-bearing diameters. I have seen each of these blocks with .842-, .875-, and .921-inch-diameter lifter bores, etc. The only way to determine if the block has siamesed cylinder bores is to visually inspect them through the freeze-plug holes. Each block, regardless of part number, must be visually inspected to see exactly what features and dimensions it truly has.

Big-Blocks

Oldsmobile big-block engines also consisted of three different cubic-inch displacements. They were offered at 400, 425, and 455 ci. With regard to high-performance use, the 455 is the most popular and is used most by Olds enthusiasts.

Oldsmobile big-blocks have many shared features and dimensions. The bore spacing between the cylinders is the same as all Olds engines at 4.625 inches. The main-housing bores are all set at 3.189 inches on all big-block engines. The deck height (measured from the crankshaft centerline to

CHAPTER 1

This number designates a siamesed NASCAR block.

The main webs are considerably thicker on this NASCAR block, compared to a production diesel block. Other than the main bearing bore diameter, the bottom side of the blocks is the same.

the cylinder-head mounting surface) is set at 10.625 inches on all of the big Oldsmobile blocks. Most of the factory blocks measure right on that dimension too. The lifter-valley areas in all the big-blocks are very similar and are not considered to be a weak spot. I have never seen a failure in this area. The lifter bores on the 400/425 engines could be .842 or .921 diameter, depending on the application. The 455 engines all retained the .842-diameter lifter bores, and all were designed for hydraulic flat-tappet lifters. The main webs are quite thin and are virtually the same on all models. Forget about four-bolt main-bearing caps; there is nothing to bolt to.

Older 1968–1970 model-year engine blocks had a casting designation at the rear of the engine, near the bellhousing area, of 68F, F1, F2, or F3. It has been circulated that these blocks had higher nickel content, and are therefore more desirable. I consider this to be a myth. I have honed many blocks with high nickel content, and soft honing stones are always required to finish high-nickel content blocks. But I have never had to use a soft stone on an Olds block. I have never found much of a difference at all between later-model and earlier-model blocks. I have also sonic tested many Oldsmobile big-blocks and actually found some later blocks to have thicker cylinder walls than some older models. Some of the thickest cylinder walls I have seen on 455 blocks are the later F6 blocks. It's easy to see if you look through the water jacket holes in the deck at the backside of the cylinders. If you look at one of these blocks next to any of the others, it's easy to see the difference.

With all that being stated, the best way to select a good Oldsmobile big-block core is to simply look over the entire casting. This includes inspecting inside the water jackets from the deck and freeze-plug area. Some blocks have thicker walls than others, and this can typically be seen by the naked eye. A block that has had antifreeze in it all its usable life ultimately has thicker cylinder walls, due to less deterioration from rust. Rust is most common on cooling systems serviced with water alone. The thinnest spots in the cylinder walls are in the area between the cylinders. Sonic testing, or measuring the space between the cylinder walls through the freeze-plug holes, can determine this thickness.

If you know the amount of space between the cylinders, you can determine the approximate cylinder wall thickness at that point by subtracting the distance between the cylinder walls from the bore-spacing dimension (4.625 inches) and dividing by 2. The average big-block can be bored safely to 4.185 inches and maintain round cylinders with as much power as the block can handle. A 4.200-inch bore can work well on a good core with about 600 hp. Some builders go to 4.250-inch bore, but this leaves the cylinder wall thickness about .090-inch thick at the thinnest area. I do not recommend this. Good piston-ring seal and oil control far

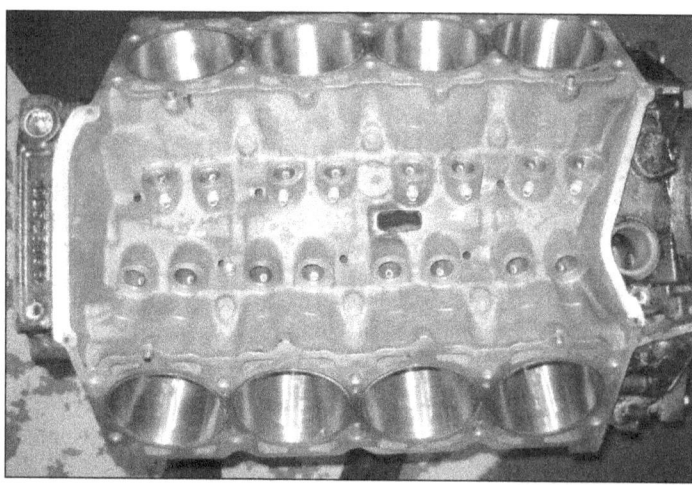

NASCAR blocks (shown) are essentially the same in the lifter valley as diesel blocks, other than the lack of the injector-pump boss.

ENGINE BLOCKS

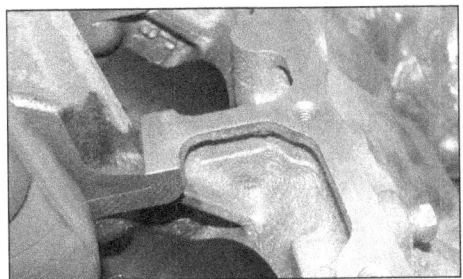

The main webs on big-block Olds engines are very thin and need some sort of a girdle instead.

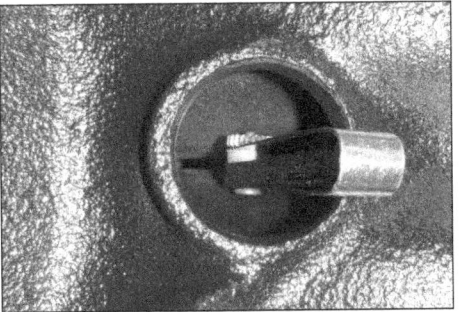

I call this the poor man's sonic test. The thinnest parts of the cylinder walls are in the 9-o'clock and 3-o'clock position as you are facing the block decks. So if you measure the space between the cylinders and subtract the bore spacing (4.625 inches) and divide by 2, you get the approximate cylinder wall thickness in the thinnest areas.

outweigh the small cubic-inch and potential cylinder-head flow gain the bigger bore brings with it.

The latest long-stroke 400 G block can be bored and honed to 4.000 inches safely in limited horsepower applications. This bore generally leaves about .250-inch wall thickness everywhere at that size, which is acceptable in the 400- to 500-hp range, which is all you would ever ask for in one of these situations anyway.

Engine Block Filler

I have half-filled Olds blocks with cement-type products (Hard-Block or similar) that occupy the water jackets for the purpose of tying in the cylinder walls for strength. I have not found that it helps ring seal significantly; I don't use it unless the customer requests it specifically. The negative effect

A typical cylinder wall thickness for a 4.185-inch-bore big-block in the 9-o'clock position is about .200 inch. This one is on the thick side.

of block filling is that there is less cooling of the crankcase oil, which can cause high oil temperatures while driving on the street or when making back-to-back passes during round-robin bracket racing.

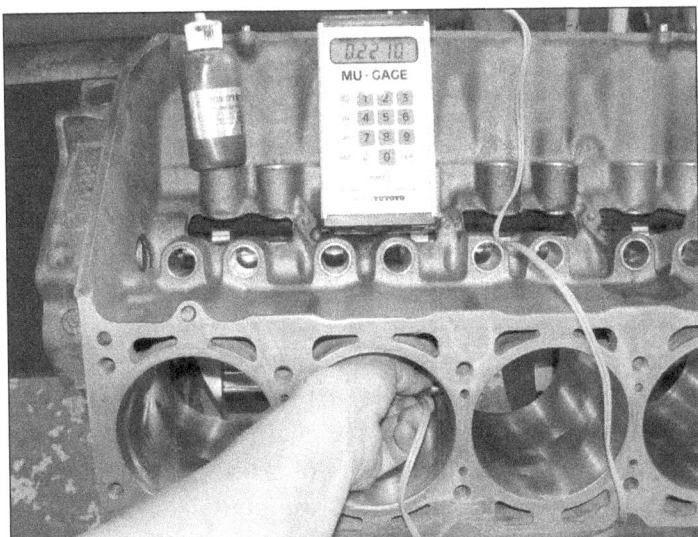

This same "D" 425 block sonic tested in the 3-o'clock position is still plenty thick to hold a round bore.

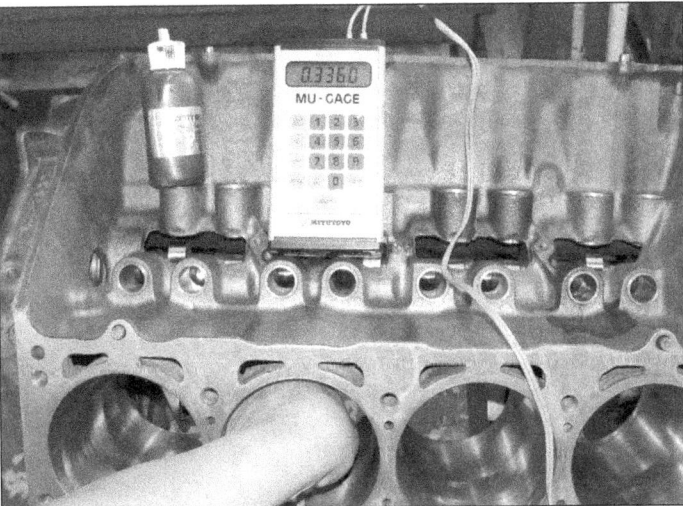

Cylinder-wall thickness in the 6-o'clock and 12-o'clock positions is almost not even worth checking. I have always found them to be very thick.

CHAPTER 1

If you must half-fill your Oldsmobile block, make sure that the fill is not so high that the water cannot transfer from cylinder to cylinder. Generally, if you fill to the bottom of the water pump holes, it is too high. Look through the water holes in the deck and plan the amount of fill before you pour. If your block is already filled to the base of the water pump holes, look through the deck at the water passages to verify that water is able to transfer from cylinder to cylinder. If the water cannot transfer, the only way to fix it is to fabricate an external manifold, or use a combination of pipe fittings and hoses to return or feed the water from each cylinder.

My 1,250-hp nitrous, siamese NASCAR small-block build is all-out max-effort build. I have completely filled the block; I use no water for cooling. I have found that this method seems to hold the cylinder walls in shape even with the abuse of detonation and burning pistons. This technique is good for builds such as mine but is also good for any Oldsmobile engine block. However, you have to pay attention to the way you race with this type of block and how much heat you put into the engine prior to the run. Forget bracket racing in round-robin situations; I don't recommend it.

Lifter Bore Bank Angles

There are two lifter-bank angles in the Oldsmobile engine, commonly referred to as the 39-degree and the 45-degree blocks. The older 400- and 425-ci engines could be either, depending on their production year and model. All 330-ci Olds engines have a 45-degree bank angle, and all 1968-and-newer Olds engines have the 39-degree bank. What most people don't know is that the actual bank angle on the 39-degree block is 42 degrees, meaning that the lifters are actually 42 degrees apart from each other.

The easiest way to determine which block you have is to install something (like a straight edge) into the lifter bore and determine if it is parallel to the cylinder wall or not. The cylinder bores are cast at a 45-degree angle, so if the lifter bores align with them, you have a 45-degree block. It should be plain to see one way or the other.

The camshaft cores are sometimes more difficult to find (and may be more expensive) for the 45-degree block. If you have a choice, the 39-degree block is more desirable. I have found that the 45-degree blocks cannot be converted to a 39-degree (42-degree) bank angle by boring and bushing due to the lack of sufficient material in the lifter-bore bosses. I did try.

Engine Block Machining

The days of "hot tanking" a block are gone. Heating a large vat of some form of acid is just not feasible in business, due to cost and toxicity. As far as I'm concerned, the only proper way to clean cast-iron engine blocks is to use the bake/blast/wash process. In this process, the block is stripped of all the plug and cam bearings, placed in an oven, and baked at 700 degrees F for two to three hours. Whatever oil, grease, and dirt that is on the block or hiding in oil passages is turned to ash.

The next step is to place the block in the blast machine. The block is fastened inside a rotating fixture and steel shot is thrown around by a high-speed paddle wheel. The ash and rust is completely removed in about 10 minutes of run time. Jet washing with hot soapy water after that removes the rust residue and leftover shot. The engine block looks brand new at this point and the machining process can begin.

The first machining operation to do on the engine block is the main bearing bore work. If the block is machined properly, most of the block-machining operations were referenced off the main bearing bores. You can check main bearing bore size

Lifter Diameter

Year	Displacement	Model	Lifter Diameter	Cam Bank Angle (degrees)
1964	330	All	.842	45
1965	330	All	.842	45
1965	400	All	.842	45
1965	425	All	.842	45
1966	330	All	.842	45
1966	400	All	.921	39
1966	425	All except Toronado	.842	45
1966	425	Toronado	.921	39
1967	330	All	.842	45
1967	400	All	.921	39
1967	425	All except Toronado	.842	39
1967	425	Toronado	.921	39
1968+	All	All	All	39

by torquing the main caps and measuring roundness and diameter by using a dial bore gauge. It is not quite as easy to check for alignment. Some old-school books show the use of a straightedge and feeler gauges, but I consider this method to be a waste of time. I have set some factory blocks on a mill and indicated the end main journals until they read zero on each, and run the indicator along the center three mains and found some to be within a few tenths, and some to be off by .002!

Some people wonder why they wipe out main bearings with a .0025 main bearing clearance. If you want to avoid a future headache, just have the mains align honed and be done with it. This process is one that requires some skill and experience; be sure to select the right shop to do the job. I have seen many blocks that were line honed and were far from "aligned." If you are installing aftermarket caps, the block must be align bored and align honed anyway, so you are good to go.

Boring the cylinders is simply a method of sizing the cylinders for an oversize piston. The cylinders at my shop are bored .005 to .008 under final size. Some literature specifies that you can bore within .003 and then final hone, but depending on the finish after the boring operation, that amount may not be enough to remove tooling marks. It takes more time in the hone, but you are guaranteed the proper finish with the extra material. Engine blocks at my shop are bored on a very large Cincinnati CNC machine. A precision bar goes through the main journals and cam tunnel. When the block is set on the machine fixture, each bore is machined exactly 45 degrees from main/camshaft centerline, and parallel to them. The bore locations are referenced off the cylinder-head dowel pins, and bore spacing is set at 4.625 inches in the boring program. This ensures that all of the machine work of the block is "blueprinted."

Block Decking

The next block machining operation is to deck the block for the purpose of making the surface flat for head-gasket sealing and machining a predetermined deck height. Deck height is referred to as the distance from the crankshaft centerline to the cylinder-head gasket surface of the engine block. I make the surface absolutely smooth and am convinced that a smooth surface seals the best on any gasket. Rough finishes to "bite" the gasket simply leave peaks and valleys. I'm sorry, but I don't want any valleys in a sealing surface. The deck surfaces are cut immediately after the boring operation without the block being moved from the fixture; therefore, the deck surface has to be perpendicular to the bores and parallel to the main journals. The cutter is referenced (or zeroed) from the main-journal centerline. And if a deck height of 10.600 inches is desired, then the cutter is raised to 10.600 inches and the deck is cut.

Honing

The honing process is one that seems to attract many different opinions on how it should be performed. I have tried many procedures and found that they all seem to work about the same as long as the cylinder is straight and round. Some finishes seem to help on different tension rings but, in general, I wouldn't worry

The blasting unit houses the previously thermal-cleaned, completely dry engine blocks or cylinder heads. They are fastened inside and rotate 360 degrees while a high-speed paddlewheel throws steel shot at the parts. Five minutes later, a previously rusty engine block looks like brand new and is ready for machining.

A thermal cleaning oven does a great job of cleaning all of the oil and grease from an engine block, cylinder heads, or parts. It is not a good idea to thermal clean aluminum heads or parts. The amount of heat required to clean properly affects the heat treatment of the part and can soften it considerably.

CHAPTER 1

At BTR the block is set up on a precision fixture that holds it at 45 degrees to engine centerline. The block is bored and decked in one operation; therefore, the decks have to be parallel to the mains and perpendicular to the bores. With the cutter referencing off the precision main bar, deck heights can be cut very easily to any desired dimension.

The Sunnen CK 10-cylinder hone does a great job of honing cylinders round and with little distortion. Newer, more advanced honing machines are available, but many top engine builders prefer this machine.

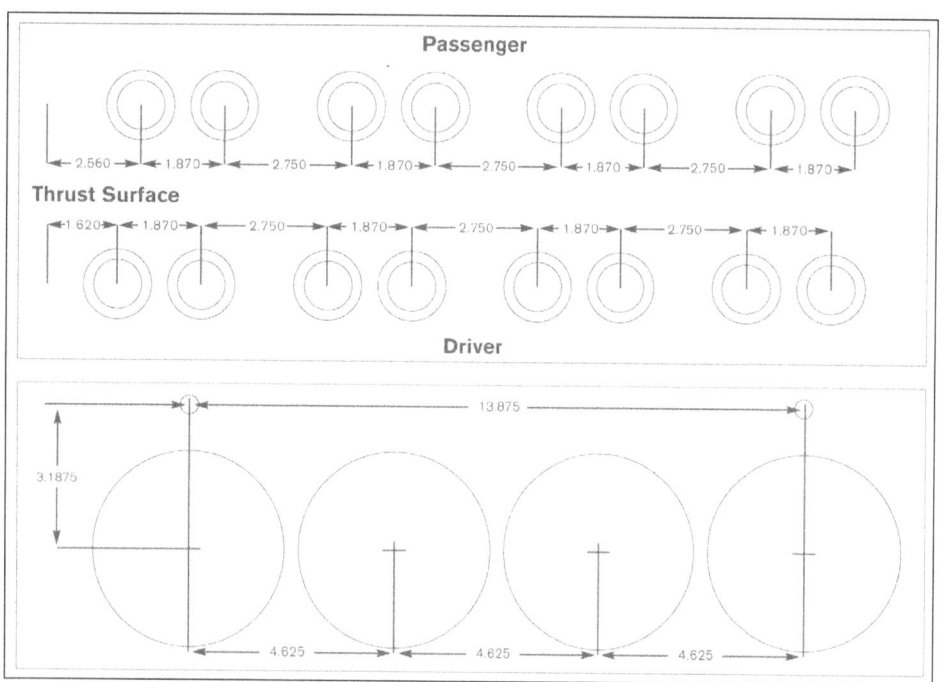

Blueprint specifications for small- and big-block Oldsmobile engines.

about the different finishes that some engine builders prefer to create. I also stress that you can't get the bores too straight or too round. This is the single most important part of the honing process. When I hone cylinders, I install a 2-inch-thick torque plate. I have not found different results between a steel torque plate and an aluminum plate. I simply use the aluminum plate for everything.

I use a 150-grit stone and bring the bore to .0025 to .003 inch of the final dimension. A 220-grit stone can be used to finish also, but the 150-grit stone simply reduces honing time and heat. I hone .0003 inch under the final dimension with the 220-grit stone. The final step is to give each cylinder three up-and-down strokes with a 280-grit stone; the same with the 400-grit stone.

There are disagreements about whether diamond stones should or shouldn't be used for performance applications. My feeling is that the stone is the better process, because as the stone wears, you get fresh stone to cut with. The diamond really doesn't wear away much, which leaves a rounded grit over time. I can't say it is wrong to use the diamond abrasives; it's just my preference to use the stones and it works for me.

Camshaft Thrust Surface

All Olds blocks have the same thrust-pad dimensions, with the notable exception of diesel blocks. The thrust pad for these blocks is .050 inch deeper than for gas blocks. Less material is machined on that thrust surface to maintain proper lifter-to-cam lobe relationship when

ENGINE BLOCKS

using a conventional non-diesel Oldsmobile camshaft. A common procedure that I use is to machine the camshaft thrust surface into the front of the block for a roller thrust bearing, otherwise known as a Torrington bearing. Over the years, I have seen many blocks scored in this area.

The reverse rotation of the distributor gear forces the camshaft against the block and can sometimes wear in this area. The ultimate solution is to machine a pocket into the block that allows a one-piece thrust bearing to fit snugly into the front of the block, so that the camshaft rides on that roller surface and cannot wear. The bearing to use is the Cloyes PN 9-220 roller thrust bearing, and the pocket needs to be machined 2.930 inches around and .140 inch deep for the bearing to fit properly. The .140-inch depth is critical, mostly because of the lobe-to-lifter relationship.

On a roller-cam application the lifter should be in the center of the camshaft lobe. It is critical to have the lifter positioned correctly when the cam and lifter are the flat-tappet type of design to ensure rotation of the lifter during operation. The centerline of the camshaft lobe should be offset .060 inch to the rear of the block from the centerline of the lifter. By machining the thrust pocket to the same depth as the thickness of the bearing, that stock relationship is maintained. The front cam bearing needs to be installed farther rearward to prevent contact with the roller bearing. It can extend slightly into that pocket without hitting the inner race of the bearing. When the front cam bearing is installed, the oil hole (or groove) is blocked slightly and does not create an issue.

You must also consider the upper and lower timing gear relationship and distributor gear and camshaft gear relationship when adding these thrust washers or thrust bearings. Many novice Oldsmobile engine builders take shortcuts and add only the bearing or bronze thrust washer behind the camshaft to move it forward. When the camshaft is moved forward by this method, the two gears do not mesh properly and can wear prematurely. If you maintain the OEM thrust surface location with proper machining, you should have no issues.

Thrust Washers

Competition Cams manufactures a .041-inch-thick bronze thrust washer (PN 225) that protects the engine's camshaft thrust surface when it is not feasible to machine your block for a roller thrust bearing. You do, however, need to machine that thrust washer thickness off the thrust face of the camshaft to provide the proper alignment between the timing chain set and the distributor gear to maintain the proper lifter-to-lobe relationship. I do not recommend installing bronze thrust washers without machining the block or camshaft. This is especially critical with flat-tappet camshafts.

This .041-inch-thick bronze spacer is available through many Oldsmobile vendor sources and from Comp Cams. It is always a good idea to use a thrust bearing or thrust washer to protect the front of the block from wearing.

Proper lifter rotation does not occur if the .060 lifter-to-lobe offset is not maintained.

Head Bolts

I convert from the factory 7/16-inch-diameter head bolts to 1/2-inch-diameter head bolts (or studs) whenever the customer allows. There is plenty of material in the block to do so, and this adds valuable clamping force to the 10-head bolt design, which makes this modification a no-brainer. Drilling by hand is not generally acceptable unless you've made a tool to keep the drill perfectly square to the deck. To do it yourself, you could make a tool that bolts to the deck of the block and allows you to drill and tap the hole absolutely straight. As long as the hole is on location and is perpendicular to the deck, it doesn't matter if you use a hammer and a chisel to do the job. I prefer to do the job on the precision CNC milling machine, though.

Bottom-End Girdles

Big-block Oldsmobile engine blocks are generally pretty reliable for engines making between 600 and 650 hp. After that, you should consider a bottom-end girdle. I have seen many block failures, and with a little Internet research you can find many Olds engine-block failure photos that can help you draw some of your own conclusions. Olds experts agree that the most common failures occur at the number-4 main-web areas. The use of solid motor mounts, which are fastened to the block in this area, is the leading cause for failure. All of the engine's torque and vehicle weight is transmitted in this motor-mount area via two 7/16-inch-diameter bolts.

CHAPTER 1

The use of front-mounted motor plates and rubber mounts with engine torque limiters should help. The main reason for the failure is the design of the block. There is simply not enough material in critical areas to hold the crankshaft in place and resist block flexing. A number of girdles from different manufacturers can stiffen the block. Some of these girdle manufacturers made them at one time and do not make them anymore, some have them in stock, and some are made only to order.

These girdles all have a slightly different design. These main girdles have been available through such companies as Mondello Performance, Product Engineering, J&S Machine, Rocket Racing, Product Engineering, Dick Miller Racing, Jeff Smith Racing, and Noel Engineering. The goal of these girdles is to reduce block flex and keep the oil-pan rails from spreading due to the thin main webs.

The first type of girdle, the "halo" girdle, is available through both Dick Miller Racing and J&S Machine and bolts onto the block with very little (if any) modifications to block

The Program Engineering girdle (shown) uses steel inner caps, but my preference is the stock caps with a billet girdle surrounding the three main caps and tying everything together.

The Noel Engineering girdle is the strongest girdle made for an Oldsmobile engine. Notice the keyed main caps. Once this whole thing is bolted together, the block and the caps cannot move in any direction. The quality of these girdles is impeccable. Quite a bit of time is involved in making them and they are not cheap, but if you want the best, this is it.

The Noel Engineering girdle has cross-bolted mains, and the 3/4-inch-thick girdle pan rails are torqued to the engine-block pan rails with a nut and stud in every bolt hole. These are the strongest of all the girdles, but unfortunately, there were only a few made, due to the expense in small-run manufacturing.

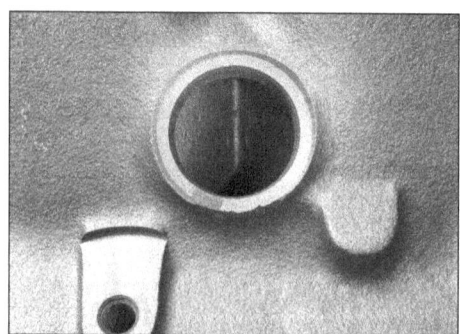

To determine if an engine block has siamesed cylinders, look through the freeze plug holes to see if the cylinders are connected. A standard non-siamesed block has a space between the cylinders to allow coolant to pass through.

Jeff Smith made only a few girdles, but the design worked well and is a proven piece.

ENGINE BLOCKS

This is the beginning stage of the BTR one-piece billet engine-block girdle. It starts out as a 150-pound piece of steel; when finished it weighs a mere 18 pounds.

The finished BTR engine-block girdle is one of the few Oldsmobile girdles that are often kept in stock. This style of girdle is a proven piece, and I have seen it help hold together engines making about 900 hp on big-block Oldsmobile engines.

or oil pan, unlike the so-called pan rail-type girdles. It bolts on top of the numbers-1 to -4 main caps and ties them together. Most 403-ci-engine enthusiasts use this style of girdle for ease of installation and cost. I have seen many 403 engines destroyed due to block breakage, but fewer if the halo girdle had been installed on them. I consider this modification cheap insurance for these engines.

The second category of block girdle is a one-piece unit, either manufactured from a single piece of billet or a series of welded-together parts to make it a one-piece unit. This girdle bolts to the oil pan rails of the block and the girdle material ties the two rails together by crossing over the main caps and tying everything together. Many 800- to 900-hp Olds engines have successfully used this style of girdle. These have been made through Jeff Smith Racing, BTR Performance, Rocket Racing, and Mondello Performance.

The third category of girdle is a bolt-together design that is available through Product Engineering and sometimes available through Noel Engineering. The Product Engineering girdle kit comes supplied with steel main caps for numbers-1 to -4, pan rails, and fasteners. The pan rails bolt in place and bolt into the -1 to -4 main caps through the side. The girdle sold by Noel Engineering is a little more sophisticated. It is installed in the same manner, but the supplied main caps are tightly keyed and bolted to the pan rail sections. I think this is the strongest unit made. The main caps cannot walk or move because they are keyed vertically and bolted. This is an extremely high-quality unit, and in my opinion is the most desirable.

The bad news is there were only a few made and no more will be made unless enough orders are taken for a higher production run. Keep in mind that the pan-rail girdles are considered the strongest of the breed, but require oil-pan modifications. Aluminum oil pans made by Moroso are available for the BTR Performance, Product Engineering, Jeff Smith, and Mondello girdles through me at BTR Performance.

In general, it is best to use the 1968–1976 Olds blocks for most high-performance applications up to about 650 hp. If your engine-project goal is above that level, choose a gasoline block with an aftermarket girdle or use a 350 D or DX block with a four-bolt main-bearing-cap conversion for your high-performance project. You could try to find a suitable NASCAR block. They are out there if you are willing to pay the high price for them.

BTR girdle bolts are torqued to the pan rails with 3/8-inch Grade-8 bolts. This ties the pan rail to the main caps and replaces the lack of sufficient thickness in the main webbing. It also ties together the three center caps and studs.

CHAPTER 2

CRANKSHAFTS

The crankshaft transfers all the power made in the combustion chamber to the transmission. In high-performance applications, it needs to be incredibly strong. This chapter will be your guide to the best-possible crankshaft choices for your particular engine build.

Factory Small-Block Crank Identification and Application

All 330-ci Olds engines (1964–1967 model years) were produced with a forged-steel crank. The 350-ci Olds engines produced from 1968 to 1972 were fitted with a nodular-iron crankshaft. Those 350s made from 1973 through 1975 could be either nodular or gray iron, and then gray iron material in all of the 1976 and later engines. All of the small-block 350 Oldsmobile cranks had a 3.385-inch stroke with 2.125-inch-diameter rod journals and 2.500-inch main journals, with the exception of the 350 diesel engines. These had a 3-inch main-journal diameter and were made of nodular iron.

The 330-ci crankshafts are easily recognized by their smooth surfaces, rounded counterweight noses, and wide parting lines on the forging. Use of this crankshaft requires a 330/400/425 flexplate/flywheel because the 1964–1967 small-block flange bolt pattern is different than the 1968-and-later Oldsmobile bolt pattern. Cast-iron 350-ci cranks are easily recognized by their somewhat rougher surface, squared-off edges on the counterweights, and narrow parting lines. The nodular-iron crankshafts are readily identified by a large "N" or "NA" designation cast into the number-1 counterweight.

These three versions are all dimensionally and functionally interchangeable. Although the steel crank is desirable for roughly 600- to 800-hp small-block engines, the nodular-iron crankshafts are very durable in the range of build that the gas 350 block will tolerate. The 350 Olds main bearing webs in the block will likely fail before your 350 nodular crank. The nodular-iron cranks support about 600 peak horsepower. The gray-iron cranks are well suited for stock and moderate performance builds up to about the 400-hp level.

Factory Big-Block Crank Identification and Application

The 1964–1967 "short-stroke" 400-ci engines were produced with

The thin parting lines on the ends of the throws indicate 350 nodular-iron crankshafts.

CRANKSHAFTS

Notice the undercuts in the ends of the rod and main journals on this 350 N crankshaft. At a quick glance, even with no micrometer, you can tell if the shafts have been ground undersize.

This part number, 388776, identifies a 330 Olds steel crankshaft.

The older 400 short-stroke and all 425 Olds cranks were steel and appeared very smooth (shown). You can verify that it is a 400/425 versus a steel 455 crank by the lack of a lightening hole in the side of the rod journal.

The 330 Olds crankshafts were all steel with the 3.385 stroke. They always have the wide parting lines at the ends of the rod journals and have a smooth finish compared to cast-iron crankshafts.

forged-steel cranks and are the same as their 425-ci brothers. Later-model (1968–1969) "long-stroke" 400-ci engines could have either cast nodular-iron or forged-steel crankshafts. Most of the big 455 Olds engines produced from 1968 to 1972 were equipped with a nodular-iron crankshaft, but a forged-steel unit can be found. There is wide speculation on exactly where these forged crankshafts were used, but ultimately, there seems to be no specific application where you can be sure to find one, and they're very difficult to find.

As with small-block cranks, steel big-block cranks have a smooth look, a wide parting line, and rounded crank-throw noses. The cast 455 cranks have narrow parting lines and squared crank-throw noses. The

The 400/425 needs the counterweights cut down about .300 inch (shown) to fit in a DX block. You only want to cut as much as you need to fit in the block to avoid having to add expensive Mallory metal.

OLDSMOBILE V-8 ENGINES: HOW TO BUILD MAX PERFORMANCE

Depending on the bobweight of the rotating assembly, you need to install Mallory slugs in the counterweights. Expect to pay about $25 to $30 per slug plus the cost of installation. A balance job can be pretty pricey.

The nodular cast crankshafts for 455s have a rather large "N" cast into the counterweight. In addition, they can have a small "CN" cast into the counterweights on later models. If you cannot find either, you have a low-performance, late-model crankshaft.

The 455 forged-steel crankshaft is the heaviest crankshaft; these weigh about 90 pounds.

455 steel crankshaft is extremely heavy. The weight possibly negates any material advantage there may be over a nodular-iron unit in applications less than 600 hp.

The 1973–1974 455 crankshafts could be either nodular iron or gray iron, and they were made exclusively of gray iron material until the end of the original 455 production run in 1977. As with the small-block crankshafts, the nodular-iron 455 cranks are identified by a large "N," "NA," or a small "CN" cast into the number-1 counterweight. You may notice that "CN" crankshafts have four lightening holes in the rod journals rather than two holes in the front and rear rod throw as on "N" cranks. Most of these are also machined for pilot bushing installation. The more of these I see, the more I think that they are the nicest of the Oldsmobile 455 cast crankshafts.

Unlike the small-block family, 425 and 455 cranks do not directly interchange. The 425-ci version has a 3.975-inch stroke with 2.50-inch-diameter rod journals, 3-inch-diameter main-bearing journals, and a flywheel/flexplate bolt pattern that matches the old 330 crankshafts. The 455 has a 4.250-inch stroke with 2.50-inch rod-journal diameter and 3-inch mains, and is drilled for the later flywheel bolt pattern that matches all the later small-block flanges.

This "CN" crankshaft is easily identifiable by the four lightening holes in the rod journals. They are the lightest, best-cast Oldsmobile crankshafts of all.

The 455 forged-steel crankshaft is very rare and often described as rather ugly.

CRANKSHAFTS

This 425 crankshaft was knife-edged on the CNC machine. Forget doing this operation by hand unless you have nothing but time.

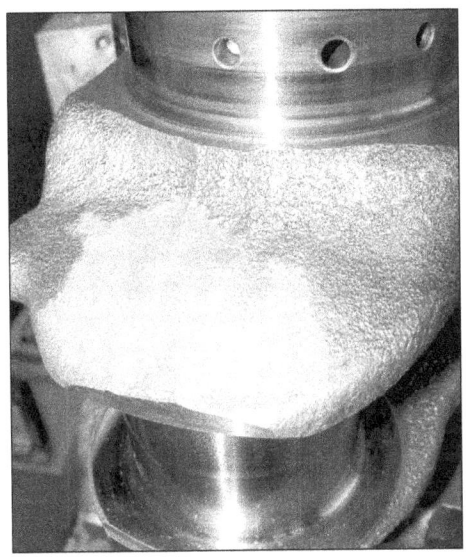

The wide parting line on the rod journal and lack of a lightening hole easily identifies a 400/425 crankshaft.

The easy way to identify a 455 forged-steel crankshaft is by the lightening hole in the rod journal.

Both the steel and nodular-iron crankshafts typically support more horsepower than the 455 blocks handle in ungirdled applications.

The biggest single performance improvement that can be made to the factory Oldsmobile crankshaft is to have the crank properly and professionally ground. This is the only machining investment necessary on a factory cast-iron crankshaft.

It is not necessary to cross-drill factory Oldsmobile crankshafts for increased oil flow; the main bearings are fully grooved and oil the connecting-rod journals 100 percent of the time. Upon grinding journals to final dimensions, it is not necessary to nitride treat nodular-iron crankshaft journals. Nodular cranks are very durable, and hold up just fine through the 600-hp level, as

Bryant Racing and Velasco Crankshafts make top-of-the-line billet crankshafts for Oldsmobiles. This 4.600-stroke model is made with premium material, center counterweights, hollow main journals, and many other features. The stiffness of the crankshaft reduces cap walk and main-bearing issues especially on the number-2 and -4 main bearings.

do the forged-steel cranks. Beyond these power levels, it's a coin toss as to which will fail first, the block or the crank. I am not saying nodular crankshafts absolutely fail at horsepower levels beyond 600; I have seen them live at higher outputs. I just have never seen a crankshaft break at the 600-hp level, and consider it a safe target for those choosing to use a factory nodular crankshaft.

Aftermarket Crankshafts

As of this writing, the only aftermarket production Oldsmobile crank-shaft produced is the big-block crank made by Eagle. It is characterized by Eagle as being a "cast-steel" crank. I have used some of these cast-steel crankshafts in some Pontiac engine builds making about 800 hp (with nitrous oxide) and they've never failed. I have found that the grinding job on these units is not necessarily flat, round, or sized properly, and required rework to be perfect. When purchasing these units, you should inspect them closely, and

CHAPTER 2

Crower has also manufactured a few Oldsmobile crankshafts. This model has big-block Chevrolet rod journals and a 4.250 stroke.

expect to grind them to suit your particular application.

Custom-crafted Oldsmobile crankshafts are available from Bryant Racing, Velasco, and Moldex, all of which are experienced in manufacturing premium-quality competition crankshafts for all big- and small-block applications. These crankshafts are expensive; manufacturing lead times range from 8 to 16 weeks, depending on the manufacturer's plant loading. For those who need them, they are worth the wait, and they represent the absolute peak of quality.

The price of these premium aftermarket crankshafts goes up as you add features. Expect to pay between $2,500 and $3,500 for a billet Oldsmobile crankshaft as of this writing. These more expensive billet crankshafts incorporate lightened, scalloped, and knife-edged counterweights. They feature hollow main journals, a center counterweight, drilled and lightened crankpins, a scalloped rear flange, and a surface-hardening treatment (such as nitriding).

The biggest advantages of using these billet units are less rotating weight and less crank flex. These two points are reasons why your high-performance Oldsmobile engine may live longer once equipped with one.

Bearing Clearance

If your goal is to rebuild a stock street cruiser that will never see more than 3,000 rpm and will use a

On most of my 750-hp or more powerful builds, I use Billet Bryant crankshafts that have a 4.600-inch stroke. You can make one with more stroke and get it to fit, but the 4.600 version fits well in the block without too much headache.

stock stall converter, there is no reason to read beyond this paragraph. Factory clearances and standard crank-grinding procedures are fine for your application.

However, maximum-performance engines require additional bearing clearance. You cannot check clearances at the time of assembly. By then it's too late. Proper clearances must be designed into the build and be part of the plan from the start.

You can't just take your crankshaft to a crank grinder and tell him to grind your crank 10/10 (.010 inch removed from the main-bearing journals and .010 inch removed from the rod journals). You will get your crankshaft back with standard crank journal diameters and should result in factory clearances with a standard bearing. Performance Olds engines require additional clearance. Your typical high-performance Oldsmobile engine cannot live with standard factory clearances.

As we know, all gasoline production Oldsmobile blocks are weak. Factory crankshafts, both iron and steel, flex when used in performance situations. As more torque is produced, both are stressed and the crank starts to bend and flex like a piece of linguini while the block is also flexing and moving. Therefore, allow enough bearing clearance so the flexing doesn't result in the engine clearancing itself because of the crank journal contacting the bearing. The higher the RPM, and the greater the weight of the reciprocating components, the more the connecting rods stretch and the sides of the bore close in. This requires more bearing clearance to compensate. If you stick to the factory .002-inch-clearance stuff, there is a good chance of trouble.

CRANKSHAFTS

When measuring bearing clearance, always measure vertical clearance. The horizontal clearance is always larger, depending on how much eccentricity is designed into the bearing.

The back-and-forth thrust clearance measurement, without the center main cap installed, should read the same as when the center main is torqued in place. If it is not the same, the cap is not in the proper location or the mating surface of the main cap is not square to the thrust surface.

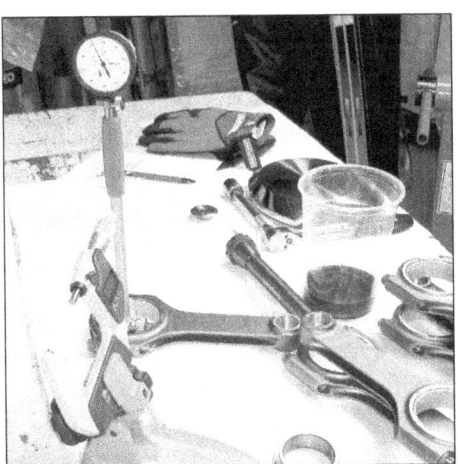

The only way to measure exact bearing clearance is to use micrometers and dial-bore gauges. Don't stress out over a few tenths here or there. If you have enough clearance, those few tenths won't mean anything.

If the clearances are too tight, and the bearing touches the crankshaft journal, the spinning engine parts grind against each other and machine themselves. If your bearing clearance is a little loose, there is no negative. I will not build a high-performance Oldsmobile engine with less than .0035 inch of bearing clearance on the rod journals and .0040 inch on the main journals. The more power the engine produces, the more the components flex,

To make sure you didn't install the incorrect undersize bearing, or if you simply do not have access to micrometers and dial bore gauges, use a feeler gauge to measure the vertical clearance. This has to be done with the bearings dry; oil takes up some clearance. Forget Plastigage.

and the more clearance is required. My personal 1,200-hp, 8,800-rpm, nitrous-enhanced Oldsmobile small-block engine has .0049-inch vertical clearance on its 2.500-inch main journals and .0043-inch clearance on its 1.888-inch (factory Honda-size) rod journals.

Experience has taught me that when a main bearing is tightened to specification (torqued) in the block, or a rod-bearing cap is torqued on a connecting rod, the bearing bore diameter will be pretty close to .0020 to .0025 inch over the nominal spec. For example, torque a big-block Oldsmobile rod bearing in a connecting rod, and it measures 2.5020 to 2.5025 inches for a standard-size bearing. Similarly, torque a big-block main bearing in a big-block housing bore and the inside diameter measures 3.0020 to 3.0025 inches on a standard-size bearing. The actual bearing clearance is the inside diameter dimension of the bearing in its housing, minus the dimension of the journal's outside diameter (OD). In general, the inside diameter of the bearing in the connecting rod and

CHAPTER 2

main journal is .002 inch over the nominal dimension. On undersized bearings (meaning .010-inch, or .020-inch, etc.) you simply subtract the undersize you are using from the nominal dimension.

As-manufactured or machining size errors can and do happen. Machinists sometimes make errors when sizing journals or cylinder bores, and there is a plus-or-minus size tolerance to the actual thickness of the manufactured bearing shells. Occasionally, mistakes are made in packaging or labeling manufactured parts. It never hurts to torque up a bearing in a rod or main journal and measure it yourself. The best way to achieve what you want is to torque up your bearings, measure with a dial-bore gauge, subtract the amount of clearance desired, and give that dimension to the crank grinder.

What should your bearing clearance be? See sidebar "Bearing Clearances" for my recommended bearing clearances. Keep in mind that non-rigid components require more main bearing clearance than more-rigid components. For example, an engine with a relatively heavy piston teamed with relatively soft factory connecting rods requires more rod bearing clearance than engines with lighter pistons and ultra strong connecting rod. You have to look at all your components to determine what clearances are best for your application. If you lack the experience to make these critical determinations, I must advise you to consult an expert who has this experience.

Rear Bearing Clearance and Number-4 Main Failure

If you have measured the bearing clearances in the main journals, you know that the rear main (also known as number-5 main) has an extra .0010- to .0015-inch bearing clearance if the crankshaft mains are all ground to the same dimension. The rear shells are, by design, thinner radially than the first four shells. The GM factory initiated this design and the aftermarket bearing companies simply copied them.

I don't know why the GM engineers gave that extra clearance to the rear main, but I can only guess that it is because of the additional width. I am absolutely convinced this additional clearance in the rear shells is the main reason for the notorious number-4 main bearing and number-4 main web failure. I have *never* seen a rear main wasted in an Oldsmobile engine, but I have seen *plenty* of number-4 main and main bearing failures.

If you think about what is going on here it makes perfect sense. If the rear main bearing clearance is .001 or .080 extra, and the rear of the crankshaft, which is attached to the flywheel, moves around as it starts to transfer power to the drivetrain, where do you think the load is transferred? You guessed it. It transfers the load to the next one in line, which is the number-4.

Chevrolet engines do not have additional clearance in the rear, and neither do Ford engines. In fact, most engines do not have that additional rear main clearance. The Oldsmobile is the only engine that has a notorious failure rate for number-4 main bearing shells and breaking blocks in the number-4 main webs.

You can easily fix this issue by simply machining the rear (number 5) main larger than the number-1 through -4 mains so that it takes the load. This is simple with undersize applications such as .010, .020, .030, etc. In crankshaft applications that have standard main journal sizes, the only way to help this situation is to purchase a main bearing set with .001 less clearance than you are working with and use the rear shell to tighten it up.

MAHLE Clevite manufactures a bearing set (PN MS 804 H-1) for big-block Oldsmobile applications that yields a .001 tighter clearance. In a typical standard-size main journal application, you can use the MS 804 H on the number-1 through -4 mains and use the rear shell from the MS 804 H-1 set to tighten the rear clearance by .001, which forces the rear journal to take the load off the number-4 main. You could also use the MS 804 HX bearings in numbers 1 through 4 to tighten the rear by .002 compared to the front four.

With all of these shell choices, you can set the main clearance to whatever size you want if you cannot machine it.

Crank Grinding

One of the most important machining operations you will do in your high-performance Oldsmobile engine build is the preparation and grinding of the crankshaft. Forget shopping around for the cheapest price for a crank grind! Always remember, you get what you pay for. Every machining operation takes time and care. Just because you stick the micrometer on the journal in one spot and its dimension is what you intended, the grind job may or may not be suitable. I have seen many improperly ground crank journals on re-grinds and, shockingly, on brand-new crankshafts. A properly ground crank journal should measure exactly the same

CRANKSHAFTS

Bearing Clearances

The information below represents the minimum amount of bearing clearance, and should keep you out of trouble. When checking your bearing clearances at the time of assembly, don't stress out if the actual measured clearance is more than anticipated. In the case of clearance, a little more is acceptable; any less is not.

200 to 400 hp with factory connecting rods	.0035-inch mains and .0035-inch rods
400 to 500 hp with factory connecting rods	.0038-inch mains and .0040-inch rods
500 to 750 hp with aftermarket steel or aluminum connecting rods	.0043-inch mains and .0040-inch rods
800+ hp with aftermarket steel or aluminum connecting rods	.0048-inch mains and .0043-inch rods

The chart below is a reasonably accurate guide for people who have no means of properly measuring their clearances prior to assembly. The housing bore dimensions and the main bearing cap material both slightly affect the bearing dimensions. My experience is that the dimensions in these charts are within a few ten thousandths of an inch, and that amount is nothing to worry about. For those who feel they need to have bearing clearances within .0001 inch, simply measure your components. This data is for all for standard-size bearings; for use with undersized bearings, simply subtract that undersize dimension (.010 inch, .020 inch, .030 inch, etc.)

Small-Block Olds

Mains

Main housing bore	2.6870 inches
Uncoated bearing	Clevite MS805P
Dimension of bearing torqued in main housing bore	2.5023 inches

Crankshaft Main Journal Dimension (inches)	Main Bearing Clearance (inch)
2.5000	.0023
2.4995	.0027
2.4990	.0033
2.4985	.0037
2.4980	.0043
2.4975	.0047
2.4970	.0053

Mains

Main housing bore	2.6870 inches
Polydyne coated bearing	Clevite MS805P
Dimension of bearing torqued in main housing bore	2.5010 inches

Crankshaft Main Journal Dimension (inches)	Main Bearing Clearance (inch)
2.5000	.0010
2.4995	.0015
2.4990	.0020
2.4985	.0025
2.4980	.0030
2.4975	.0035
2.4970	.0040
2.4965	.0045
2.4960	.0050

Connecting Rod

Rod housing bore	2.250 inches
Uncoated bearing	Clevite CB684P
Dimension of bearing torqued in rod housing bore	2.1273 inches

Crankshaft Main Journal Dimension (inches)	Main Bearing Clearance (inch)
2.1250	.0023
2.1245	.0028
2.1240	.0033
2.1235	.0038
2.1230	.0043
2.1225	.0048
2.1220	.0053

Connecting Rod

Rod housing bore	2.250 inches
Polydyne coated bearing	Clevite CB684P
Dimension of bearing torqued in main housing bore	2.1260 inches

Crankshaft Main Journal Dimension (inches)	Main Bearing Clearance (inch)
2.1250	.0010
2.1245	.0015
2.1240	.0020
2.1235	.0025
2.1230	.0030
2.1225	.0035
2.1220	.0040
2.1216	.0045
2.1210	.0050
2.1205	.0055

Bearing Clearances CONTINUED

Big-Block Olds

Mains
Main housing bore	3.1890 inches
Uncoated bearing	Clevite MS804P and H
Dimension of bearing torqued in main housing bore	3.0023 inches

Crankshaft Main Journal Dimension (inches)	Main Bearing Clearance (inch)
3.0000	.0023
2.9995	.0027
2.9990	.0033
2.9985	.0037
2.9980	.0043
2.9975	.0047
2.9970	.0053

Mains
Main housing bore	3.1890 inches
Polydyne coated bearing	Clevite MS804P and H
Dimension of bearing torqued in main housing bore	3.0010 inches

Crankshaft Main Journal Dimension (inches)	Main Bearing Clearance (inch)
3.0000	.0010
2.9995	.0015
2.9990	.0020
2.9985	.0025
2.9980	.0030
2.9975	.0035
2.9970	.0040
2.9965	.0045
2.9960	.0050

Connecting Rod
Rod housing bore	2.6250 inches
Uncoated bearing	Clevite CB542P and H
Dimension of bearing torqued in rod housing bore	2.5023 inches

Crankshaft Main Journal Dimension (inches)	Main Bearing Clearance (inch)
2.5000	.0023
2.4995	.0028
2.4990	.0033
2.4985	.0038
2.4980	.0043
2.4975	.0048
2.4970	.0053

Connecting rod
Rod housing bore	2.6250 inches
Polydyne coated bearing	Clevite CB542P and H
Dimension of bearing torqued in rod housing bore	2.5010 inches

Crankshaft Main Journal Dimension (inches)	Main Bearing Clearance (inch)
2.5000	.0010
2.4995	.0015
2.4990	.0020
2.4985	.0025
2.4980	.0030
2.4975	.0035
2.4970	.0040
2.4965	.0045
2.4960	.0050
2.4955	.0055

Small-Block Chevrolet

Connecting Rod (stroker applications)
Rod housing bore	2.2250 inches
Uncoated bearing	Clevite CB663 H
Dimension of bearing torqued in rod housing bore	2.1023 inches

Crankshaft Main Journal Dimension (inches)	Main Bearing Clearance (inch)
2.1000	.0023
2.0995	.0028
2.0990	.0033
2.0985	.0038
2.0980	.0043
2.0975	.0048
2.0970	.0053

Connecting Rod (stroker applications)
Rod housing bore	2.2250 inches
Polydyne coated bearing	Clevite CB663H
Dimension of bearing torqued in rod housing bore	2.1010 inches

CRANKSHAFTS

Crankshaft Main Journal Dimension (inches)	Main Bearing Clearance (inch)
2.1000	.0010
2.0995	.0015
2.0990	.0020
2.0985	.0025
2.0980	.0030
2.0975	.0035
2.0970	.0040
2.0965	.0045
2.0960	.0050
2.0955	.0055

Connecting Rod (stroker applications)

Rod housing bore	2.1250 inches
Uncoated bearing	Clevite CB745 H
Dimension of bearing torqued in rod housing bore	2.0023 inches

Crankshaft Main Journal Dimension (inches)	Main Bearing Clearance (inch)
2.0000	.0023
1.9995	.0028
1.9990	.0033
1.9985	.0038
1.9980	.0043
1.9975	.0048
1.9970	.0053

Connecting Rod (stroker applications)

Rod housing bore	2.1250 inches
Polydyne coated bearing	Clevite CB745H
Dimension of bearing torqued in rod housing bore	2.0010 inches

Crankshaft Main Journal Dimension (inches)	Main Bearing Clearance (inch)
2.0000	.0010
1.9995	.0015
1.9990	.0020
1.9985	.0025
1.9980	.0030
1.9975	.0035
1.9970	.0040
1.9965	.0045
1.9960	.0050
1.9955	.0055

Big-Block Chevrolet

Connecting Rod (stroker applications)

Rod housing bore	2.3250 inches
Uncoated bearing	Clevite CB743 H
Dimension of bearing torqued in rod housing bore	2.2023 inches

Crankshaft Main Journal Dimension (inches)	Main Bearing Clearance (inch)
2.2000	.0023
2.1995	.0028
2.1990	.0033
2.1985	.0038
2.1980	.0043
2.1975	.0048
2.1970	.0053

Connecting Rod (stroker applications)

Rod housing bore	2.3250 inches
Polydyne coated bearing	Clevite CB743H
Dimension of bearing torqued in rod housing bore	2.2010 inches

Crankshaft Main Journal Dimension (inches)	Main Bearing Clearance (inch)
2.2000	.0010
2.1995	.0015
2.1990	.0020
2.1985	.0025
2.1980	.0030
2.1975	.0035
2.1970	.0040
2.1965	.0045
2.1960	.0050
2.1955	.0055

everywhere on that particular journal. With improper or no dressing of the crankshaft grinder wheel, you may see taper or out-of-round (different measurements) from one side of the journal to the other. This means that clearance is tighter in some spots and the oil wedge is improper, lacking two perfectly flat surfaces.

The second area of concern is surface finish. You cannot have a crankshaft journal too flat or too smooth. A common procedure is to rough grind the journal and then superfinish it until it is smooth. You have to be very careful when superfinishing because the abrasive belt typically removes more material in the center of the journal and less on the ends.

Do yourself a favor; don't shop around for this operation. You get what you pay for. Find a good crank grinder who is easy to deal with and pay him for his time. Typically, if you have a conversation with the crank grinder and let him know that you are willing to pay for the extra time spent on a quality job, it is usually received very well. And he will be very happy to spend the extra time required to give you a high-quality grinding job. The extra expense is usually pennies when compared to the consequences of engine failure.

Stroking

One of the most popular Oldsmobile performance modifications is to increase the stroke of the crankshaft. This increased stroke not only increases the cubic inches of the engine, but has a few other advantages.

In general, an engine with increased stroke makes more torque at a lower-RPM range, which makes this modification ideal for high-performance street engines. More torque and horsepower in the lower-RPM ranges allows the use of tighter torque converters and low-numerical gears, which makes this modification a popular choice for high-performance street cars. I have not seen an engine yet that didn't like to be larger. An increased stroke makes more average horsepower and torque throughout the RPM range. I have never seen that to be a negative thing, whether it is a street engine or a race engine. Another advantage is that the rod-journal diameter is reduced, which allows the use of more popular (available and less-expensive) Chevrolet connecting rods, in addition to reduced friction and less weight.

This finished 3.750 destroked 425 crankshaft is knife-edged, balanced, and, with reduced-diameter counterweights, ready to be bolted into Greg Finnican's 394-ci DX Olds small-block.

This procedure is done to the crankshaft by changing the rod-journal diameter to that of a smaller-diameter engine (usually the common Chevrolet). By removing the material on the part of the rod journal closest to crankshaft centerline only, instead of removing the material all the way around, the stroke of the crankshaft is increased. The stroke is increased by the amount of material you remove from the bottom of the journal.

An example of a typical stroker Oldsmobile crank is a 455 big-block. The factory stroke is 4.250 inches, and the rod journal is 2.500 inches in diameter. If you want to increase stroke by .250, giving the crankshaft 4.500 inches of stroke, the rod journal is reduced by at least .250 inch. When stroking the 455 nodular-iron crankshafts to 4.500 stroke with the big-block Chevrolet 2.200 rod journal, they seem to have a problem with flexing at horsepower levels around 700, as I learned in the 2009 *Popular Hot Rodding [PHR]* Engine Masters Challenge. After two crankshafts wiped out the number-2 and number-4 main bearing on the dyno, it was pretty clear that the crank just wasn't going to handle it. I know for sure there is a problem with flex at the 700-hp level, but I have several successful builds at 600 hp.

Magnafluxing

There really isn't much you need to say about Magnafluxing, other than it is a relatively inexpensive procedure to look for any cracks on your crankshafts. If your crank shop has the proper equipment to do the job, just do it. It will detect a crack or defect in your crankshaft before you spend money machining it. Most

CRANKSHAFTS

MAHLE Clevite has released the performance H bearings for the big-block Oldsmobile. In contrast to the P bearings, they are a different color and are available in the X series for .001-inch extra clearance.

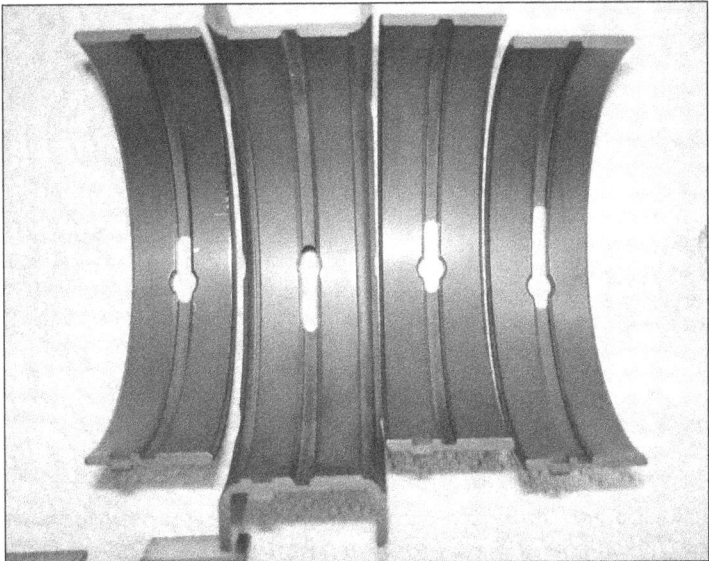

If you must modify your main bearings for increased oil flow, machine them like this. I have built numerous engines without modifying the holes at all and the bearings look great. I am not convinced that this modification is necessary.

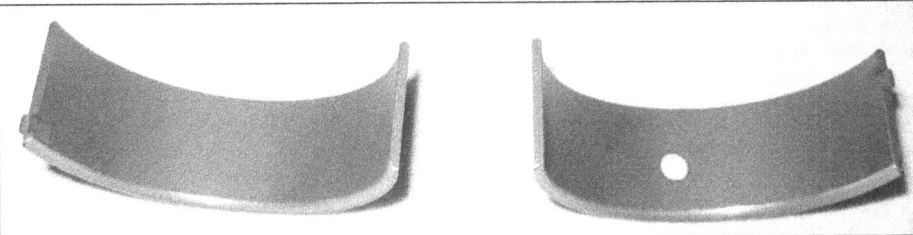

You can use rod bearings with dowel holes in the connecting rods with no dowel if you need to. These Polydyne-coated rod bearings were narrowed and chamfered due to interference with the radius on the rod journals. This interference is a common mistake people make when assembling their own engines. The way to see if the bearing edges are hitting the radius is to measure the rod journal width and subtract the big-end width of the two connecting rods on that journal. With that calculated number, the same size of feeler gauge should fit between the two connecting rods assembled on that journal. If it doesn't fit, chances are there is contact.

crank shops have the proper equipment to perform this operation. Make sure that they have a Magnafluxer designed for crankshafts. The entire crank sits in between two electrodes. When the machine is turned on, the crankshaft is magnetized. Powder (or liquid with powder in it) is applied, and cracks are very easy to see with the supplied black light. The hand-held magnafluxing units are not the best choice for this job. Look for a floor-mounted machine.

Engine Bearings

Manufacturers of crankshaft bearings include MAHLE Clevite, ACL, King, Vandervell, and Federal Mogul. In my 25 years of experience building engines, I have never had a single issue with Clevite main and rod bearings. I have had a few minor issues with some of the others, which is not to say that you should avoid them. But I simply don't mess with success, so Clevite remains my personal brand of choice.

The MS 804 H-1 main bearings are currently available but will likely be discontinued due to lack of sales. You may want to pick up a set while they are still around. The only reason you need the minus .001 clearance set is to tighten the rear main clearance on crankshaft applications with the standard journal diameter.

Oldsmobile V-8 Engines: How to Build Max Performance

CHAPTER 2

The MS805P bearing is the only small-block main bearing available through MAHLE Clevite. They are not meant for a 1,200-hp 8,800-rpm engine, but I have successfully run them for years and made many quarter-mile passes on a single set without so much as a scratch or rub. Even the Clevite engineers are amazed. A little extra bearing clearing can do wonders.

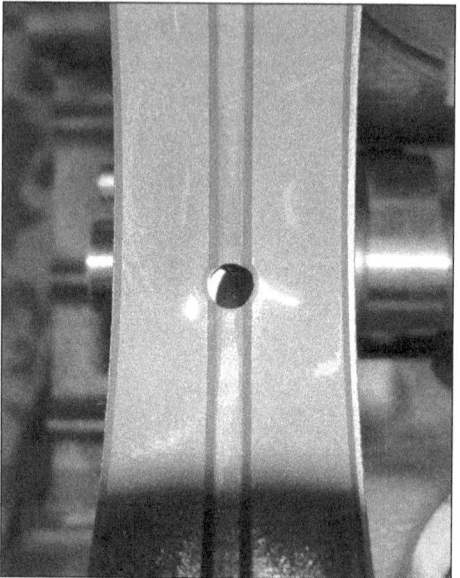

The front or number-1 main bearing always shows a slight misalignment between the hole in the bearing and the feed hole in the block. Even though it looks bad, I have on occasion forgotten to port the hole in the block so that there wasn't a restriction. However, I have never had an issue with the front bearing, with or without the modification. Do it if you remember, and if you forget, don't sweat it.

Until recently, the only available crankshaft bearings were the P-series Clevite bearings. The Tri Metal Clevite P-series bearings are indeed performance bearings and not to be confused with passenger-car bearings. Some say that the P bearings do not work in very high-horsepower applications, but I use the MS805P bearings in the mains of my 1,200-hp, 8,800-rpm Olds small-block with complete success. With proper clearance and journal-surface finish, these bearings do the job for 99 if not 100 percent of the Oldsmobile engines out there.

I have had the same set of Clevite MS805P-series main bearings in my engine from the 2004 all the way through the 2008 racing season. Remember, if everything has the proper clearance inside the engine, the crankshaft should never touch the bearing due to the oil film between them.

Oldsmobile experts throughout the years have recommended enlarging the main-bearing oil holes in a variety of ways, including drilling the oil-feed hole larger and/or slotting it for more oil flow. Years ago I did these modifications and in recent years have stopped. I have not seen a difference in the way the bearings wear, whether I modify them or not. I do not modify anything if it doesn't have an issue.

Recently, MAHLE Clevite introduced the H-series main and rod bearings for the big-block Oldsmobile engines. The main difference between the H-series and the P-series bearings is the amount of eccentricity. The P-series bearings have the greatest amount of eccentricity, and the H-series bearings have a medium amount of eccentricity. Eccentricity means that the bearing-bore diameter measures wider horizontally, or between the parting lines, than the vertical, which is where you measure to set clearance. You may actually have more room for error with the P-series bearings on stock Olds connecting-rod performance applications where the connecting rods are soft and tend to suck in the sides at higher RPM, even though most builders select the H-series bearings in most performance applications.

Anti-Friction Coatings

A number of anti-friction coatings can be applied to your engine bearings of choice. Bearings can also be purchased with the coating already applied. These bearing coatings are not all the same. Some of the more popular companies that offer this service are Polymer Dynamics (better known as Polydyne), Calico, MAHLE Clevite, and Swain Technologies. My company, BTR Performance, uses Swain Tech coatings exclusively on all of its engines. We have run many

CRANKSHAFTS

Performance Engine Bearings

Small-Block Performance Main Bearing Sets

Manufacturer	Part Number
MAHLE/Clevite	MS805

Big-Block Performance Main Bearing Sets

Manufacturer	Part Number
MAHLE/Clevite	MS804P MS804H MS804HX
Federal Mogul	108M

Small-Block Performance Rod Bearing Sets

Manufacturer	Part Number
MAHLE/Clevite	CB684

Big-Block Performance Rod Bearing Sets

Manufacturer	Part Number
MAHLE/Clevite	CB542P CB542HN
	CB542HNX

Clevite Oversizes

Big-Block

Part Number	Size
804P	STD
804P	.010
804P	.020
804P	.030
MS804H	STD
MS804H	−.001
MS804H	.010
MS804H	.020
CB542HN	STD
CB542HN	−.001
CB542HN	.010
CB542HN	.020
CB542HXN	+.001
542P	STD
542P	.010
542P	.020
542P	.030
542P	.040

Small-Block Main

Part Number	Size
MS805P	STD
805P	.010
805P	.020
805P	.030

Small-Block Rod

Part Number	Size
CB684P	STD
684P	.010
684P	.020
684P	.030
684P	.040

---

engines (including our own) that, after constant abuse, don't show as much as a scratch on them.

The main thing to consider when using coated bearings is the film thickness. I have found that different companies' coatings have different film thicknesses. The amount of coating thickness absolutely does affect bearing clearance. From these different companies, I have measured as little as .0003 to as much as .0007 inch on each shell. This film thickness can affect bearing clearance by closing it by as much as .0015 inch. When using coated bearings, the crankshaft journals have to be sized accordingly. The Swain Tech–coated bearings used in my shop have consistently measured .0003- to .0004-inch film thickness per shell, which closes journal clearance by about .001 inch. As discussed earlier, torquing a standard-size big-block Olds bearing in a connecting rod generally measures 2.5020 inches on the vertical inside diameter. When torquing a Swain Tech–coated rod bearing in a similar fashion, it usually measures about 2.501.

Crankshaft Balancing

There is no performance advantage to proper balancing, just reliability. A few years ago, before we had our own Hines crankshaft balancer at BTR, we had farmed out a balancing job and they did not do the job properly, if at all. The job was off by about 350 grams, which is huge! This 750-hp Olds engine beat the hell out of the bearings in just a few dyno pulls. Interestingly enough, once the crankshaft was balanced properly, it didn't shake anymore but produced the exact amount of horsepower. I would have never guessed that one!

When balancing your assembly, you weight match the reciprocating and rotating components, calculate what is known as the "bobweight," and then use a crankshaft balancing machine to balance the crankshaft to those components.

There are basically two ways of balancing your crankshaft. The first is commonly known as an "internal balance," where the balancing operation is performed on the crankshaft's counterweights, and anything outside of the engine (such as the harmonic balancer and the flywheel or flexplate) has no added counterweight(s). The second way of crankshaft balancing is known as an "external balance," in which the harmonic balancer and/or the flywheel or flexplate has an additional counterweight added to achieve balance. The latter is more common on Oldsmobile engines.

In the internally balanced procedure, the flywheel/flexplate and harmonic balancer is not installed on

All of our crankshafts are balanced on a Hines balancer. The measurements are calculated on the left and right stanchions. The most important part of the operation is that the end-to-end measurements are within 1 gram.

When you cut the counterweights considerably and knife-edge them, as on this PHR *Engine Masters Challenge* engine crankshaft, be prepared to spend all day on the Hines balancer and take out a home equity loan for all the Mallory. This crankshaft needed six slugs.

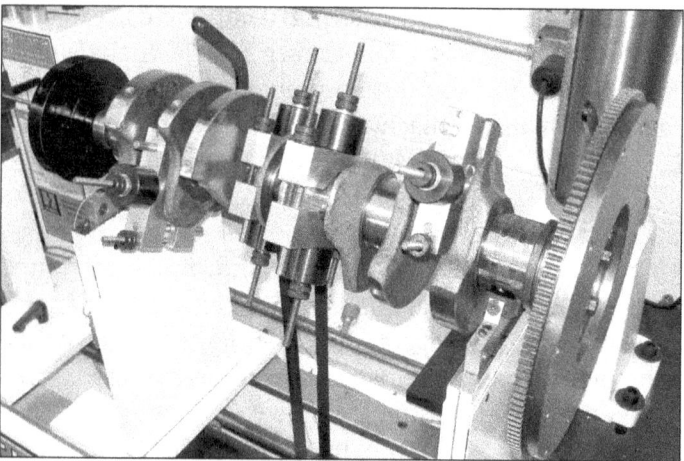

When you are balancing a crankshaft externally, the flywheel/flexplate and harmonic balancer must be installed. Be sure that the shop that balances your crankshaft does all of the correction on the crankshaft only. No alterations are allowed on the balancer or flywheel/flexplate. Internally balanced crankshafts are not balanced with these items.

the crankshaft when it is spun on the balancing machine. In the externally balanced crankshaft procedure, the flywheel/flexplate and harmonic balancer must be installed on the crankshaft during the balancing process.

It is best to balance your assembly internally, but is generally unacceptable on heavier assemblies due to the amount of heavy metal (Mallory) required to do the job. Comparatively lighter-weight assemblies, like 400-gram pistons and aluminum connecting rods, can be internally balanced very easily. The heavier the pistons and connecting rods are, the heavier the counterweights need to be to compensate. Most stock-type piston/steel connecting rod combinations typically require external balancing. The internally balanced crankshaft is one of those "nice to have" benefits, but is nothing to stress out over.

The most important thing you need to know about having your assembly balanced externally is to specify to the balance shop that the harmonic balancer and the flywheel/flexplate remain unaltered. The crankshaft balancing process takes less time by altering the counterweights attached to those external components, and some take this shortcut. The negative effect of this is that the flywheel and balancer are unique to that assembly once they have been modified. Should one of these now-unique items fail and need replacing, you are in trouble. If those

CRANKSHAFTS

To cut the counterweights on a crankshaft, you need a very robust lathe. The intermittent cut tends to rip the cross slide right off on a light-duty lathe.

items remain unaltered from their as-manufactured form (and weight), you can generally replace that item with a new one of the same brand and the balancing is unaffected.

Harmonic Balancers

Factory and most aftermarket harmonic balancers are of the elastomer type and in general consist of three parts: an inner hub that fits over the crankshaft snout and is keyed in position; an outer ring; and a rubber elastomer between them, bonding the two pieces together.

Factory Oldsmobile harmonic balancers are good for stock engines that average speeds of 1,000 to 3,000 rpm. That is what they were designed for. If you plan to spin higher RPM levels in your high-performance Oldsmobile engine, then you need to upgrade your harmonic balancer to deal with it. Many times over the years I have seen the outer ring on the factory Oldsmobile harmonic balancers rotate out of position. Once this happens, your top-dead-center (TDC) timing mark is no longer in the original spot. Ignition timing set while using this reference mark is no longer accurate, and performance inevitably suffers while tuning headaches set in. In addition to the outer ring rotating, I have also seen the outer ring loosen up and work itself right off the inner hub, causing enough of a vibration to make you think your high-performance world is coming to an end.

Safety rules dictate that any car that runs faster than a 10.99-second elapsed time in the quarter-mile must have an SFI-approved harmonic balancer. This SFI mandate basically means that if the unit fails, it will not be catastrophic. It is not a measure of quality, but rather an assurance of safety.

There are many choices in aftermarket harmonic balancers for the

This 400/425 factory harmonic balancer looks different than the one on 1968 and later engines.

This counterweight from the old 400/425 balancer is different than a 1968 and later harmonic balancer. Although they fit any Oldsmobile crankshaft, they do not interchange unless the assembly is balanced with the unit.

The ATI harmonic balancer for an Oldsmobile engine needs an aftermarket timing pointer, which is available through BTR. You must clearance the bottom of the water pump so it doesn't hit. This is a nice thing to know before the pump is bolted on with silicone sealer.

ATI balancers are available in counterweighted and neutral versions. They are also available in several different-weight outer rings and elastomers, depending on the crankshaft stroke and RPM of the engine. Did you ever wonder why crankshafts crack, flex, or the engine has vibration but has been balanced? You can't just stick any old thing on the end of the crankshaft snout.

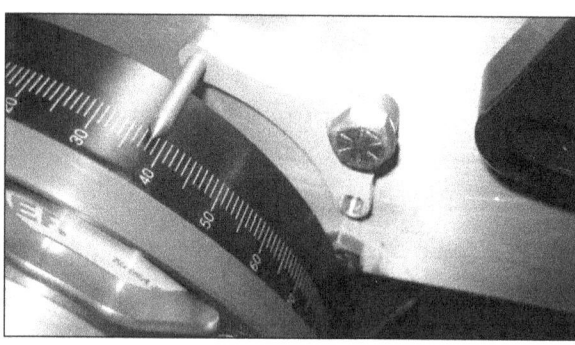

The diameter of the ATI balancer is too large to work with stock timing pointers. One like this from BTR is required for these balancers.

Oldsmobile engine, including Pro Race, Professional Products, BHJ Products, Innovators West, PRW, Fluidampr, TCI, and ATI.

Some of these aftermarket elastomer-type balancers have the same issues as the factory balancers. The outer ring can, on occasion, rotate on these aftermarket balancers, but cannot walk off the hub (due to the design, which gives it its SFI approval). The only elastomer balancer that cannot fail in any way is the unit manufactured by ATI Performance. The difference between this SFI elastomer unit and the others is that the outer ring is allowed to rotate

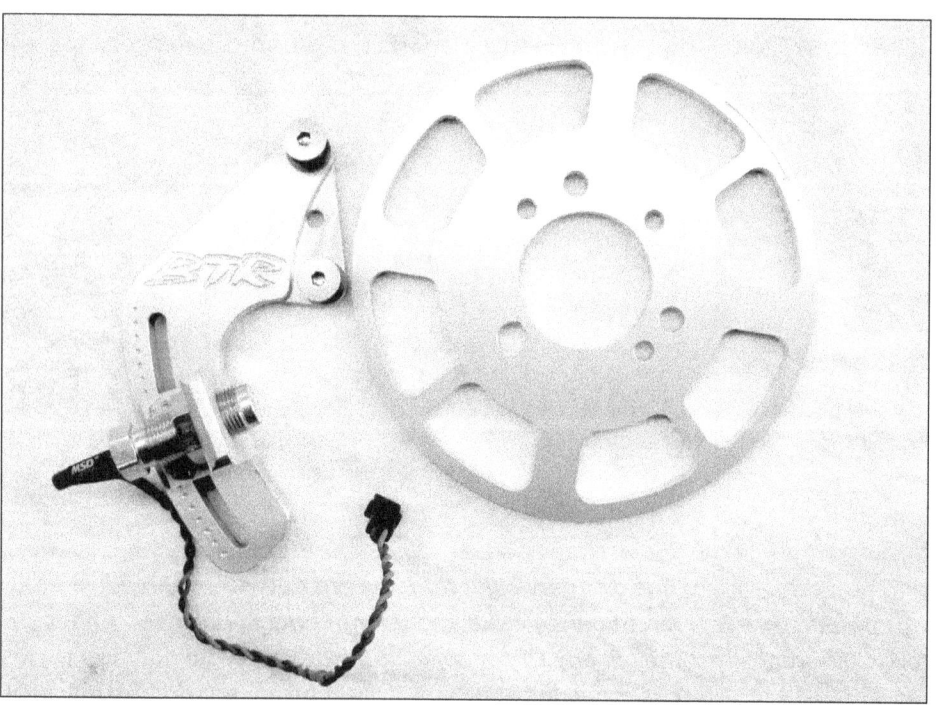

The BTR Performance crank trigger kit fits stock four-hole harmonic balancers and ATI three-hole harmonic balancers. Crank triggers give an Olds engine the most accurate ignition timing due to the large diameter and space between each magnet, compared to the pickup inside the distributor (which is about 1 inch in diameter) and has very little space between the magnets.

CRANKSHAFTS

The Fluidampr is a relatively heavy balancer. I have used a few of these, but do not have a great deal of experience with them.

I have used one Innovators West harmonic damper on Dave Laurer's 427 small-block nitrous-powered Olds and can say it has never had or caused a problem. It also has a crank-trigger wheel built in, which is kind of a nice feature. This design has some sort of a wet-clutch mechanism inside, is rebuildable, and is SFI approved.

If you have an ATI damper you have to purchase a three-hole pulley or re-drill yours to the three-hole pattern. You can use the ATI hub as a fixture by locating the hub in the center hole of your crankshaft pulley. Then, using a 5/16-inch spot punch to locate the three spots, you must drill it to a 3/8-inch diameter.

The PRW balancer has a bolt-on counterweight and can also be used in internal balance applications.

The Pro Race balancer is SFI approved. However, I have seen a few on which the outer ring spun.

without failure. The fully degreed outer shell is fixed to the inner hub and cannot change or rotate. It is the most reliable and most popular unit in all the high-performance engines in racing. The only issue with the Oldsmobile ATI balancer is that the pulley bolt pattern is a three-hole big-block Chevrolet pattern instead of a four-hole Oldsmobile pattern and must be redrilled. Other than that, it retains all the Oldsmobile dimensions that allow the use of factory Oldsmobile crankshaft pulleys.

Regarding the above-mentioned aftermarket harmonic balancers, the Innovators West, TCI Rattler, and the Fluidampr harmonic balancers are not elastomer-type designs and are each uniquely engineered. I do not

The Pro Race balancer uses a bolt-on counterweight so that it may be used in multiple applications.

This harmonic balancer is the factory unit for W-31 350 engines. They are extremely rare and sell for big dollars if you can find one.

I am not really sure why Olds engineers spec'd a different balancer on the W-31. The only thing I can think of is that they expected the user to elevate the RPM of the engine more so than others. This balancer has quite a bit more mass.

Rear Main Seal Chart

	Victor	FelPro
Small-Block	JV748	N/A
Big-Block	JV618	QBS40032

have any personal experience with these and cannot comment on their quality or reliability.

Rear Main Bearing Seals

All Oldsmobile V-8s came from the factory with rope-style rear main bearing seals. Today, it is best to use a neoprene rear main seal. They are available for big-block and small-block Olds engines. They are available through several sources, including Fel-Pro and Victor. The big-block Olds rear seal is sold as an Oldsmobile part, but is actually a 460 Ford rear-main-bearing seal that has been repackaged. These seals can sometimes be very tight. The rear-seal-journal diameter where the "lip" portion of the seal touches is a larger diameter on the big-block Oldsmobile compared to the 460 Ford. I have assembled many big-block Oldsmobile short-blocks with these seals

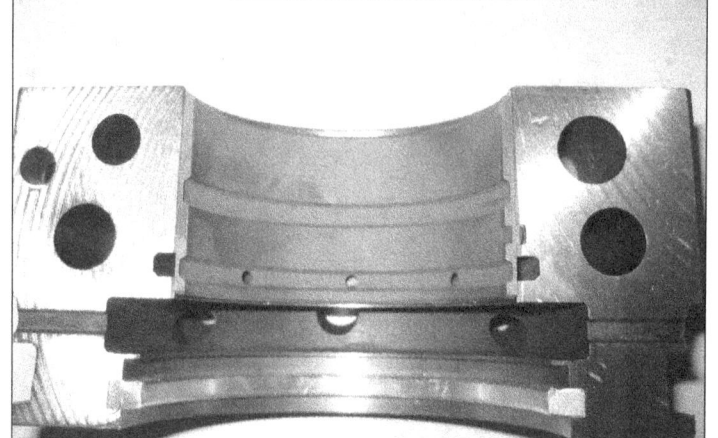

On small-block applications, we convert the rear of the block to use a big-block Chevrolet rear main seal by boring the factory rear seal area and making an insert to accept it. This seal has less drag and seals better.

This rear main seal adapter is designed to convert a D or DX Oldsmobile diesel 3-inch main seal area to a small-block Oldsmobile seal when you install a small-block gas Olds crankshaft.

and some seem to have the proper drag. Others drag excessively and wear out as you turn the crankshaft to install the pistons.

There are a couple of solutions to get the proper fit. One method is to machine the sealing-surface dimension on the crankshaft to that of a 460 Ford. I prefer the second method, which is to use a razor knife to trim the back side of the seal down to the metal reinforcement inside the seal. The amount of material removed is slight and reduces the drag to a point where the seal does not wear prematurely and still does not leak.

CHAPTER 3

CAMSHAFTS AND VALVETRAIN

The limited performance capabilities of the factory Oldsmobile V-8 valvetrain design require a step up for serious performance. A wide range of upgrades is available, but which one best suits your particular application? Teaming the best-possible camshaft choice with the proper valvetrain equipment is key, and this chapter holds all the answers.

Rocker Arms

The basic motion of the rocker arms hides the pressures and conditions they must survive in. The aggressive opening and closing ramps of today's camshafts require high valvespring pressures. Choosing the best-possible rocker arms requires some research.

Stock Rocker Arms

Factory Olds rocker arms are generally good for about .500-inch maximum lift camshafts and applications that do not exceed about 350 pounds of open spring pressure. In the late 1980s, I raced a 1970 442 W30 in the NHRA's Stock Eliminator class, when stock rocker arms were mandatory equipment. I made hundreds of passes with a very aggressive hydraulic camshaft and did not have one rocker-arm or trunnion failure. In a limited-budget application, the stock rocker arms work just fine and perform reasonably well for mild-performance applications.

One trick that was done on my Stock Eliminator's 455-ci engine with the stock rocker arms and stock length valves was to shim up the pedestal and lengthen the pushrod accordingly until I achieved the maximum valve lift specified for the camshaft. I bolted the stands in the stock location, and the lift at the valve was up to .025 inch less than advertised. I added about .125 inch of shim between the cylinder head and the rocker-arm stand. The only way to determine the correct amount

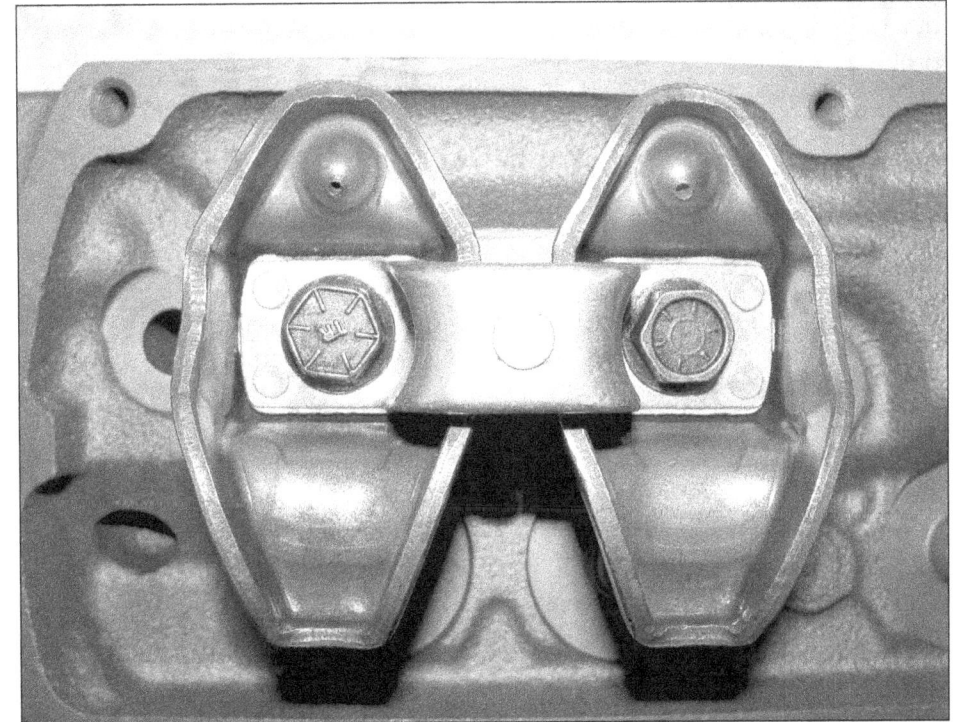
Aluminum trunnions work fine for mild applications with less than 350 pounds of open-spring pressure.

CHAPTER 3

This stock rocker-arm setup is from a 1965 425 engine, and came off some "A" heads. The rocker arms are equipped with 3/8-inch screw-in studs and individual rocker pivots. These rocker arms are not adjustable, as the their pivot bottoms out against the shoulder on the stud.

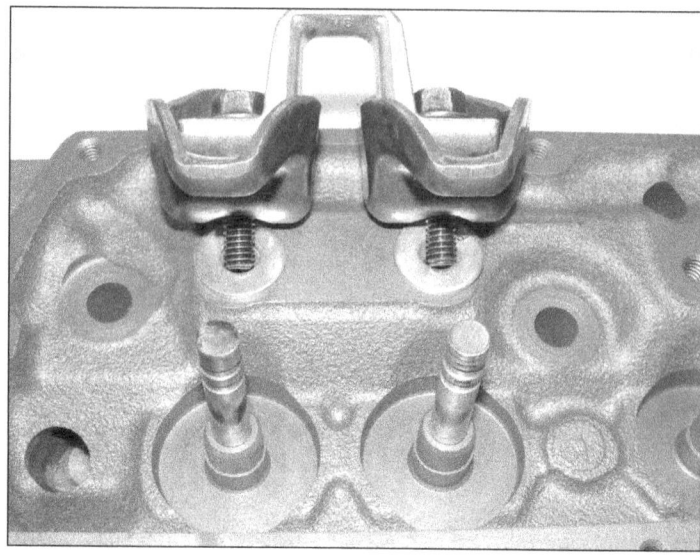

Shimming the stands often corrects geometry issues that are causing loss of valve lift. Make sure you install equal-thickness shims.

of shim required is to use a checking spring, adjustable pushrod, and dial indicator. You have to keep adding shims and lengthening the pushrod until maximum lift is achieved. This loss of lift was not due to the rocker-arm ratio not being 1.6:1, but rather to a rocker-arm geometry problem.

If you need to modify your stock rocker arm or trunnion for your performance application, then you may be better off with a set of adjustable aftermarket roller rocker arms.

Stud-Mounted Roller Rocker

Oldsmobile enthusiasts have a variety of choices of stud-mounted roller rocker arms with a variety of ratios. The most popular Oldsmobile roller rockers are made by Comp Cams and Harland Sharp.

For mild-performance applications or as a great stock part replacement, the PN 1442-16 Comp Cams Magnum roller-tip rocker is a great choice. These rocker arms have a stock 1.6:1 ratio, a roller tip to decrease friction on the valvestem and use a ball and socket like a stock-type Chevrolet rocker arm. This type of rocker arm gives you the adjustability to set lash when using a mechanical (solid, non-hydraulic) flat-tappet camshaft, or exact preload for a hydraulic cam-

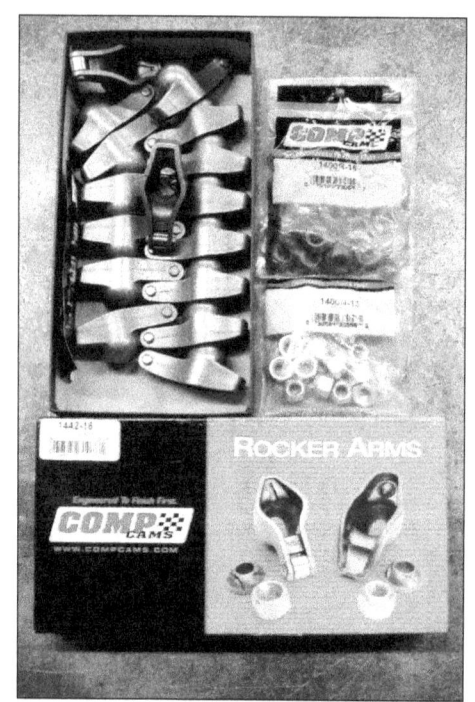

The Comp Cams Magnum roller-tip rocker set is very popular for inexpensive street applications.

shaft; whereas, the stock rocker arms require an adjustable pushrod to do so. These rockers are economically priced, and with the Comp Cams Magnum screw-in studs and guide plates, they bolt right into the factory

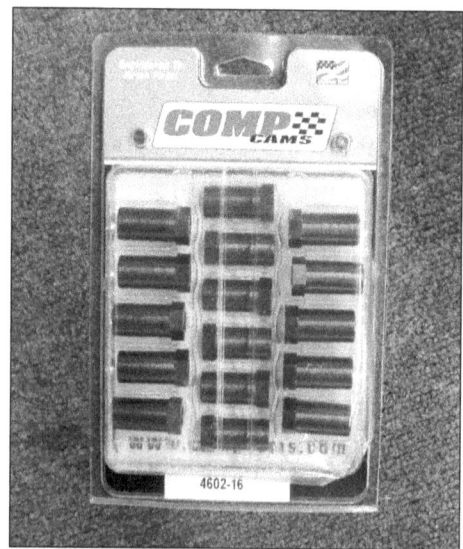

When purchasing Comp Cams Magnum roller rockers, it is a good idea to get the poly lock set (PN 4602). The rocker arms come with standard lock nuts that can move, causing the rocker arms to come out of adjustment.

40 OLDSMOBILE V-8 ENGINES: HOW TO BUILD MAX PERFORMANCE

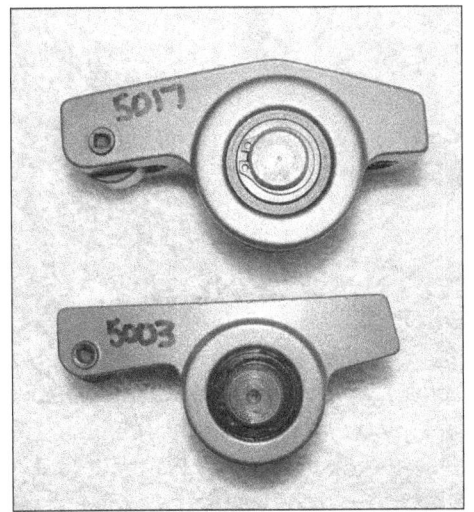

Sometimes referred to as the Bulldog rocker, Harland Sharpe part numbers 5016 and 5017 are the best-fitting stud-mounted roller rocker arm for any Olds head. The angle of the pushrod cup in the Oldsmobile Harland Sharpe 5003 is essentially a Ford-designed rocker, but works well on an Olds in lower-lift applications.

The Crane Gold rocker arm has an incorrect pushrod cup angle, as do most aftermarket Oldsmobile stud-mounted roller rocker arms.

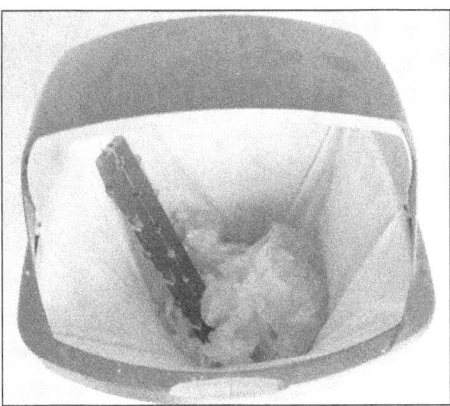

Many stud girdles cause more valvetrain issues than they fix. They never seem to line up with all eight studs and almost always cause some sort of bind. This old stud girdle for a Batten head is where it should be, in the trash.

cylinder heads with no modifications required. Although these are a great stock replacement for a mild performance application, they are limited by the valvespring pressure because the 5/16-18 mounting thread is the weak link here. I suggest that you limit the open pressure to about 300 pounds.

The next level of performance with increased spring pressures and RPM requires a full-roller rocker. Many different brands and styles are available. I have found that the only stud-mounted roller rocker arms specifically designed for the shallow-valve-angle Oldsmobile engine is the Harland Sharp 1.6:1 ratio (PN 5016) and the 1.7:1 ratio (PN 5017) aluminum roller rocker arm. Notice the shape of the back (pushrod) side of the rocker arm on the PN 5017 as compared to the PN 5003 Harland Sharp or, even worse, the Crane Gold rocker arms. The body on the PN 5016/PN 5017 arms is shaped in such a manner that when the rocker-arm geometry is properly configured, the pushrod remains fully surrounded by the pushrod cup in the back side of the rocker, and you do not run out of rocker-arm travel at high lift.

This is a common occurrence with other rockers, which are typically Ford rocker arms with an Oldsmobile part number. One of these two rocker-arm part numbers is the best stud-mounted rocker arm for Oldsmobile applications.

Harland Sharp also manufactures a lower cost PN 5001- and PN 5003-series rocker arms, and they are great choices for milder applications requiring a full roller rocker. Unfortunately, these generally do not have enough slot length for adequate travel if used with valve lifts higher than about .540 inch when the rocker-arm geometry is set properly.

Stud Girdles

I have yet to see an Oldsmobile stud girdle that fit each and every rocker stud properly without inducing unwanted stress by cocking studs in any direction other than vertical. This is because the holes or radii in the girdle did not match the stud locations in the cylinder heads. In my professional opinion, throw them in the garbage, or sell them on eBay to someone who thinks they stabilize the valvetrain. If you are running stud-mounted rockers in your Olds engine, you are better off without stud girdles.

Shaft Rocker Arms

Shaft-mounted rocker systems are the ultimate in valvetrain stability, reliability, and performance. It is a common belief that when you run some sort of mechanical cam (whether it is a flat-tappet or a solid roller) you have to frequently adjust valve lash. This isn't the case with shaft-mounted rocker assemblies. They are very stable by design and, once bolted down and adjusted, nothing moves.

Another advantage: they are not rocker-ratio limited. Power is gained by increasing the rocker ratio on the intake side. You cannot open the valve too fast when seeking maximum

CHAPTER 3

Notice the angles of the pushrods to match up with the offset shaft rockers so that intake ports can be widened. Although it looks kind of funky, I have had numerous engines with pushrod angles like this (and even more extreme) turn very high RPM with no issues.

Shaft rocker systems, such as this one manufactured by T&D Machine, are very rigid and can be purchased in just about any fulcrum length, offset, and rocker ratio as high as 2.2:1.

The one-piece, steel rocker-arm support bar bolts to all of the rocker stud holes in the cylinder head, which keeps the valvetrain from flexing and doing things it shouldn't be doing at high RPM. When you set the lash on this type of setup, it does not move. The only reason to check the lash is to make sure you don't have an issue with a lifter or a valve.

The Isky Racing Cams adjustable guide plates work in all applications. They are available for 5/16 and 3/8 pushrods and come in handy when pushrod-to-pushrod hole clearance is very tight and requires placing the pushrod in an exact location. It is best to tighten it slightly and tap with a small hammer and punch until you have everything where you want it, then torque in place. It is best to TIG-weld it together, once in place.

power. With stud-mounted rockers, you can only bring the pushrod cup so close to the centerline of the rocker arm for a ratio increase because of the stud and slot positioning. With shaft-mounted setups, you can achieve these higher ratios with ease, and without any extra cost.

The largest advantage you have in purchasing a set of shaft-mounted rocker arms is the ability to offset the pushrod away from the intake port. This allows you to maximize the cross-sectional area at the pushrod pinch point in the intake port, which is generally the smallest area and greatest restriction of an Oldsmobile cylinder head. There is considerable horsepower to be gained there.

Several companies deal in custom shaft assemblies for Oldsmobile

Notice the little springy thingy? This allowed me to make the semi-finals at an NMCA race. It allowed the pushrod to go up and down, holding the lifter in place without opening the intake valve and nitrous oxide going into the crank case because I had burned a hole in a piston in the prior round. It stayed together at 8,800 rpm and did the job.

The roller tip contacts the valve at zero lift. It is not in the center, but it's not a problem.

At full valve lift, the contact point on the valve is exactly in the same spot. This is perfect rocker-arm geometry and pushrod length. This situation achieves maximum valve lift.

engines. These companies include Harland Sharp, T&D Machine, and Jesel. These custom assemblies are generally around $1,300, which is pricey. However, it is always worth the investment for the person who is looking for best-possible valvetrain performance and reliability.

If you add the cost of the components for a comparable stud-based rocker assembly (rocker arms, top-quality rocker studs, adjustable pushrod guide plates, and a stud girdle) the additional cost is not that much more. The durability and reliability justify it, and the potential to rework the intake port for increased flow seals the deal. If you really want to go big, shaft-based rocker arms are the way to do it.

Proper Rocker-Arm Geometry

Improper rocker-arm geometry basically has two negative effects. When the tip of the rocker arm sweeps in an incorrect arc in relationship to the valve, the rocker arm's motion pushes the valve fore or aft while moving. This adds force

The pushrod is in the trunnion side of the pushrod cup at zero lift.

At full lift, the pushrod is at the other side of the pushrod cup, but is fully contacting the entire pushrod cup in the rocker body. This style and shape of rocker body allows this to take place.

The backside of this rocker arm body is not shaped properly for an Oldsmobile cylinder head and is less than desirable, but it works.

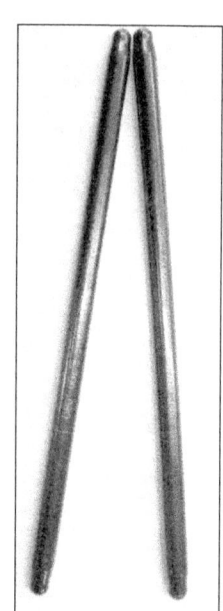

Many companies use one-piece pushrods. They are great for all but the most serious applications. I have never had an issue with the Comp Cams brand and I have sold many. Avoid using Manley pushrods similar to these. I have found that the ball end is not concentric with the pushrod body. I have noticed that the body wobbles quite a bit when rotated between the rocker and lifter.

to the valve in a direction other than straight down.

This incorrect motion reduces valve lift and wears out valveguides. The height of the body of the rocker changes this sweeping motion of the arm. Whether a stud-type or a rigid-stand-type rocker arm, the rocker body must be raised or lowered until the sweep is correct. The goal when searching for proper rocker arm geometry is to note where the roller tip is at zero lift regardless of where the roller tip is sitting on that valve. That roller tip should end up in exactly the same spot at maximum valve lift. This proper motion pushes the valve straight down instead of fore or aft while opening the valve. Forget trying to make the roller tip sit in the middle of the valvestem. The rocker arm's fulcrum length determines where the roller tip sits on the valve; that distance is rarely exactly what is needed.

The fulcrum length is the distance from the center of the rocker arm fulcrum or pivot point to the center of the roller tip and cannot be changed because it is manufactured into the rocker arm. If that roller tip travels on one side of center or the other, it's okay as long as the roller tip does not get too close to the edge, or roll off the edge of the valvestem. If that is the case, you need a rocker arm with the correct fulcrum length. When your rocker-arm geometry is set properly, proper pushrod length can be determined.

Pushrods

When selecting pushrods for your high-performance Oldsmobile engine, you cannot choose one that is too thick or too stiff, for valvetrain stability and reliability. The norm for Oldsmobile applications is a 3/8-inch-diameter pushrod, due to the layout of the cylinder head. There just isn't much room for a larger-diameter part. Pushrods in Oldsmobile engines are comparatively long, because of the physical height of the block. With that in mind, these long pushrods wiggle and flex like a piece of linguini under moderate spring loads and RPM levels, unless they are made with a heavier wall thickness and diameter. Forget lightweight pushrods. The common one-piece 3/8-inch-diameter, .080-inch thick-wall "high-tech" pushrods from Comp Cams work well in flat-tappet Olds applications with limited valvespring pressure.

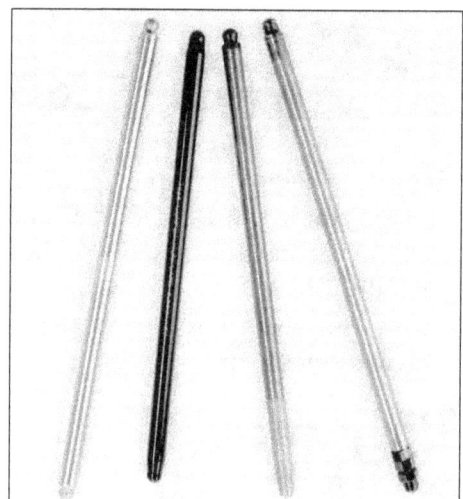

Adjustable pushrods are acceptable for light-duty applications. When you have a serious performance application, you cannot have a pushrod that is too rigid. Don't worry about the weight; it is not an issue. A pushrod that flexes is.

Enthusiasts or engine builders trying to extract every last ounce of reliability, power, and RPM should purchase a heavier pushrod with an even greater wall thickness. For these maximum-performance applications, I use a 3/8-inch-diameter Trend .135-inch-wall one-piece, or a Manton 3/8 .140-inch thick-wall. If you can fit it, the 7/16-diameter, maximum wall thickness pushrod from Manton Racing Products is the best option. Whenever you get a certain diameter pushrod for your maximum-performance application you always get the thickest wall tubing available. These companies have many wall thicknesses, heat treatments, and pushrod end designs; they can also make a custom set in any length.

Determining Proper Pushrod Length

Before you try to determine pushrod length in your high-performance Oldsmobile engine, you must first understand proper rocker-arm geometry.

The method of determining pushrod length is different between a stud rocker application and a stock rocker/shaft-mounted setup. In that stock or shaft-mounted application, the height of the rocker stand is fixed and the rocker-arm geometry is set properly regardless of pushrod length. Once that geometry is set properly, the pushrod simply fills in the void between the rocker-arm pushrod cup and the lifter cup with valve lash or hydraulic lifter preload set.

The method for determining pushrod length for a stud rocker application is a little more complicated. In those applications, the length of the pushrod raises and lowers the body of the rocker arm, changing the geometry in which the rocker sweeps across the valve. To determine pushrod length in these stud rocker applications, you must use an adjustable pushrod, set at a given length that you think may be correct. First set your valve lash, tighten your rocker-arm locking nut, cycle the camshaft, and then watch the way the rocker arm travels throughout the range.

If the contact point of the roller tip travels away from stud centerline as it reaches maximum lift, your pushrod is too short. If your contact point travels toward stud centerline from zero lift to maximum lift, your pushrod is too long. If the contact point at zero lift and full valve lift is the same contact point on the valvestem, then your pushrod length is correct, maximum valve lift is achieved, and proper rocker-arm geometry is set.

In hydraulic-lifter applications, this procedure has to be performed with lightweight checking springs instead of regular valvesprings so that the lifter plunger does not collapse during the lift cycle. In this hydraulic-lifter application, you need to add .050 inch or so to the pushrod length to allow for the recommended .050-inch lifter preload in the hydraulic lifter.

Rollmaster timing chain sets are good quality. Unfortunately, I have seen more than one of these sets that had the timing marks or dots a tooth off when the cam was degreed in properly. This is normal in the Oldsmobile world. Always degree in your camshaft!

Timing Chains

I have used many brands and styles of timing-chain sets over the years and have never had one fail. I have found them all to be reliable and they simply work. I do, however, recommend billet-steel gear chain sets in mechanical-roller camshaft applications with heavy springs. Rollmaster, Cloyes, and ProGear manufacture billet-steel chain sets. The Cloyes and Rollmaster chains have adjustability in the lower gear for advancing and retarding the camshaft timing in relation to the crankshaft. The Pro-Gear billet set is adjustable in the top gear by using multiple dowel holes, which is a nice feature. Unfortunately, all of the dowel holes are incorrectly marked and are called out in camshaft degrees, which are double the crankshaft degrees. This mistake renders all but two of the holes useless.

After contacting ProGear about the problem to no avail, I decided to manufacture my own. Oldsmobile

CHAPTER 3

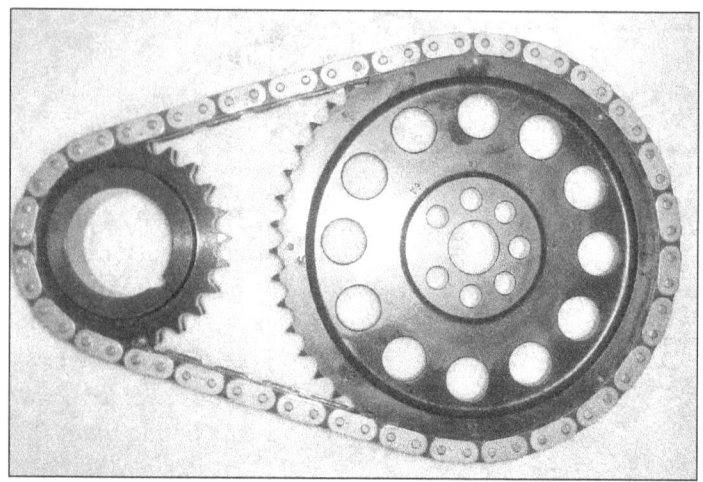

The ProGear timing chain is a nice set; too bad it machines the dowel holes in the wrong spot. We can only hope that ProGear fixes this issue.

My BTR multi-hole chain set is available with a billet-steel gear set, and the inexpensive cast-iron gears. If I want it done right, I have to do it myself!

performance chain sets with an indexable upper gear are now available through BTR in billet-steel sets and a quality cast-iron set, which is less expensive and performs well in 99 percent of performance Oldsmobile applications. The multiple-hole feature on the upper gear is very handy and makes degreeing a camshaft much less time consuming.

I am not a big fan of the Cloyes Hex-A-Just chain set; there is a possibility of that upper cam gear moving from its original position.

Another decent timing chain set is the Rollmaster. It is the lightest of the billet-steel chain sets. Olds Performance Products is a supplier of Rollmaster chain sets for Oldsmobiles and measures each set for proper center-to-center distance. They have a variety of under sizes for the customer who wants a properly sized timing chain with no slop or slack once installed.

Roller-Bearing Cam Bolt and Camshaft Walk

Olds Performance Products and BTR manufacture a rather slick cam-gear bolt that utilizes a roller bearing to ride against the timing cover in order to eliminate cam walk.

Flat-tappet engines do not necessarily require the elimination of

endplay in the camshaft because of the counter-clockwise rotation of the distributor gear and the taper on the camshaft lobes. These features drive the camshaft rearward and push the camshaft thrust surface against

Numerous camshaft bolt designs are available through multiple Oldsmobile vendors to control thrust on your Oldsmobile camshaft. They all work well. This design is sold through BTR Performance.

Machining the cam bolt and using a roller bearing to eliminate cam walk is always a plus. You can purchase these and machine them yourself or, in a pinch, you can put your factory cam bolt in a drill and radius the head on a bench grinder, polish it, and shim it .005 inch from the timing cover. Although the latter may seem to be kind of a backyard mod, it only wears a very slight amount between the bolt head and the timing cover and works for anyone on a budget.

the block. Setting the camshaft thrust to a minimum with a roller cam bolt for a flat-tappet engine is not a bad thing; it is just not as critical as when you have a roller lifter–equipped camshaft. If you upgrade to roller lifters (either hydraulic or solid), limiting the camshaft's fore and aft motion within the block is an absolute must.

To set this endplay on your Oldsmobile engine, you must not have any load on the thrust surface, and keep camshaft endplay to a minimum of .002 inch and a maximum of about .010 inch. You can set that endplay using a button designed for this purpose, which is mounted on the front of the camshaft. Its endplay dimension is checked with a straightedge across the timing cover surface, but ultimately you should install the timing cover with no sealer; bolt that cover tight; and check that endplay by sticking a screwdriver inside the lifter bore and witnessing how much that camshaft moves, if at all, forward and aft in the tunnel. The timing cover is rarely flat, and once bolted on the front of the engine, your endplay is different than you originally witnessed.

Camshafts and Camshaft Selection

Selecting the best-possible camshaft for your high-performance Oldsmobile engine is a mixture of art and science and based on many factors. The weight of your car, its intended purpose, your other choices for engine components, the type of transmission you plan to run, the rear axle's gear ratio, and more figure into designing the best-possible cam for your particular engine. This is not a task to be taken lightly and is best left to the experts with the experience to make the right decisions.

I don't feel that all aspects of camshafts can be discussed in one chapter. You could write a book on that subject alone (others have); I can only highlight the basics. I see too many people selecting something out of a catalog or, worse yet, polling Internet websites for opinions and help. Plenty of successful Oldsmobile racers and engine builders have a good handle on this subject and the experience to offer sound advice. I suggest you buy a camshaft from one of these experienced experts who work exclusively with high-performance Olds engines. Typically there is very little or no additional cost to purchase through these Oldsmobile experienced companies versus purchasing directly through the camshaft manufacturers, so why not take advantage of their experience? Even with the best-possible intentions, someone without Oldsmobile engine experience simply cannot give you the best advice.

The first decision is whether to use a flat-tappet or roller-type lifter design, and cost is usually what determines that choice. I always recommend the use of rollers. With the elimination of zinc in today's engine oils, flat-tappet cam-and-lifter sets have less of a chance of surviving, especially during the break-in procedure. Also, with that break-in procedure being more critical, it requires the use of additives, special oils, and reduction of valvespring pressures during that process. Even after you have taken all of these precautions, there is still a chance of flat-tappet failure. Who wants to deal with that? Just select a roller cam, which not only outperforms the others, but there are no break-in concerns to worry about. Just fire up your brand-new engine, let it idle, and

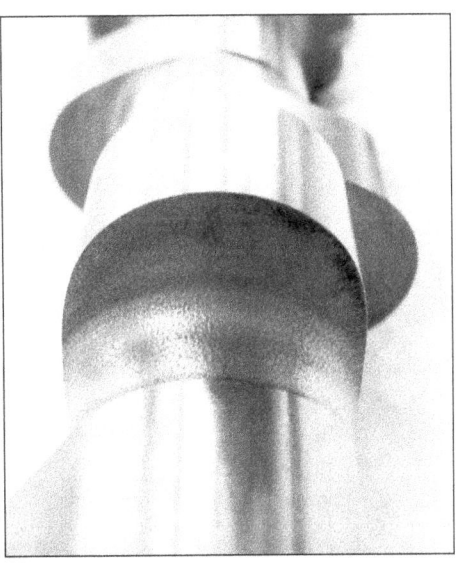

This mechanical-roller lobe is pretty aggressive as far as opening the valve, keeping it open, and closing it quickly in order to produce cylinder pressure. A roller-camshaft lobe is much more aggressive than a flat-tappet camshaft.

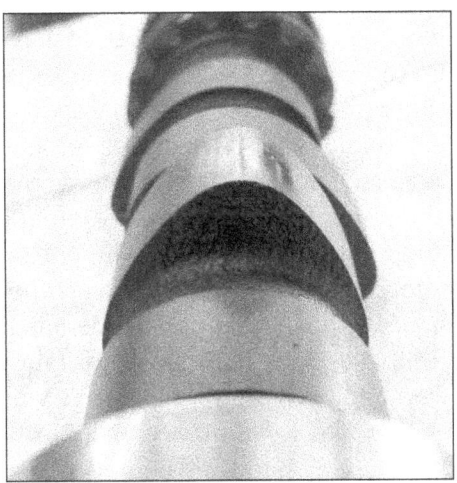

This flat-tappet Oldsmobile camshaft is made of cast iron that has a surface hardening called Parkerizing. Although the surface is extremely hard, the material underneath is very soft and doesn't withstand extreme spring pressures. It's easy to understand why a roller camshaft outperforms a flat-tappet.

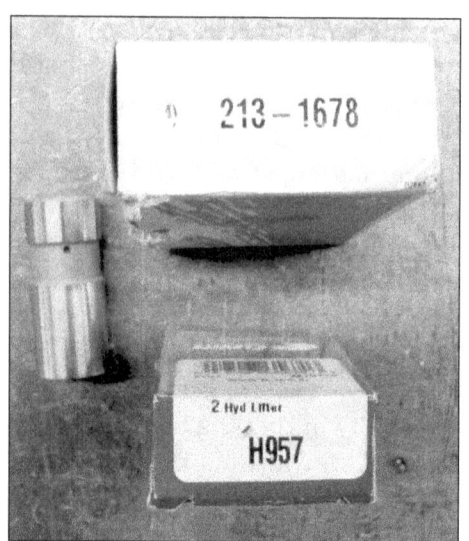

Aftermarket NOS .921 hydraulic lifters are available for a large-lifter Oldsmobile block. The MAHLE Clevite lifters are below; the Perfect Circle lifters are above.

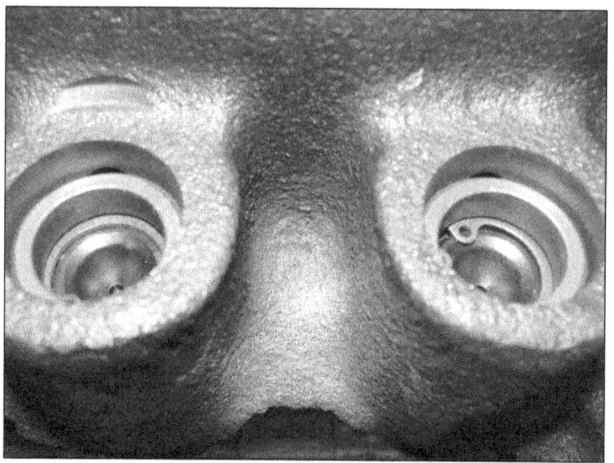

When using a flat-tappet camshaft, always make sure that the base circle is large enough so that the oil hole is covered. You don't want to cause 16 tiny oil leaks and low oil pressure. You won't have to deal with this on any roller cams and lifters.

If your flat-tappet camshaft has too small of a base circle and your lifters are too short (top), you can purchase taller lifters that have a button added to the top (bottom). However, I have used them in the past and the buttons usually come out after some run time.

This is a good example of the proper wear pattern on a flat-tappet camshaft.

enjoy. Problem solved. Yes, it costs more, and it's worth it.

Hydraulic flat-tappet camshafts are good for the average high-performance street engine spinning less than 5,500 rpm. Most hydraulic camshafts, whether flat-tappet or roller cam, become unstable between 6,000 and 6,500, depending on lobe aggressiveness, valvetrain weight, and spring pressure. Oldsmobile engines that rev under 6,000 rpm are rarely a problem with basic components. When your engine is designed to make power in an RPM range above 6,000, lightweight retainers and proper valvesprings are a necessity. If you build an engine to rev higher than 6,500 rpm, it requires a non-hydraulic (called "solid" or "mechanical") camshaft.

I consider the solid flat-tappet lifter upgrade the next level in performance in your high-performance Oldsmobile. It outperforms the hydraulic flat-tappet camshaft any day of the week. The main reason

On the left is a Chevrolet solid lifter and on the right is an Oldsmobile lifter. Notice the difference in the oil band. Both are Comp Cams products.

CAMSHAFTS AND VALVETRAIN

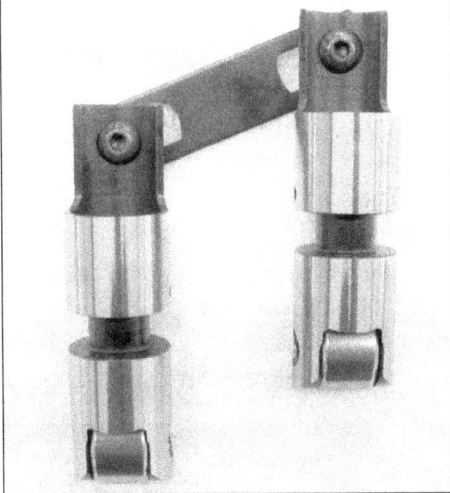

Comp Cams is one of the few companies that produces hydraulic roller lifters for an Oldsmobile. I have had examples on which the internals stuck and required replacement. Keep in mind that any hydraulic lifter has some of the tightest tolerances of any engine part. Still, it is the best oil filter in the engine and any sort of debris can make the plunger stick.

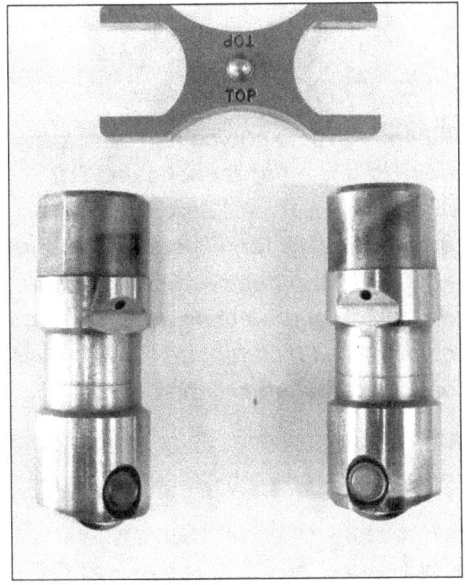

These .921-diameter factory-produced roller-hydraulic lifters are from an Oldsmobile diesel engine. I have not tried them in a performance application, but they should work okay in applications of 6,000 rpm and lower.

For whatever reason, people have given the Comp Cams solid-roller lifters a bad rap on Oldsmobile Internet forums. If you use proper spring pressures and everything in the valvetrain is in order, you don't have failures. I use them and have never had one fail in any of my engines.

people steer away from these for street applications is the valvetrain noise (when compared to hydraulics) and they think they have to adjust lash all the time. That statement is only partially true. Valvetrain noise is minimal with tight-lash solids and proper rocker arm geometry. As far as adjusting lash all the time? With the valvetrain set up properly and polylocks tightened properly, the lash adjustment doesn't move. If it does, something is wearing.

The next level in performance is a camshaft equipped with hydraulic roller lifters. As long as the maximum RPM is below about 6,500 rpm, they outperform the solid-lifter cam-shafts because of lobe aggressiveness. With beehive valvesprings, increased spring pressures, and titanium valvespring retainers, these hydraulic roller cam engines can see almost 7,000 rpm without going into valve float. This should accommodate all but maximum-effort Oldsmobile performance engines.

The ultimate in Oldsmobile performance is to use a mechanical roller lifter and its matching camshaft. These camshafts basically open and close the valves very quickly and hold those valves higher throughout the duration the valves are open. This allows more air and fuel to be ingested. When you compare a roller-cam lobe to a flat-tappet lobe, it is easy to see that the valve opens much quicker on the roller-cam lobe.

Remember, the valves still need to open and close at the right times for the engine to perform properly. With a more aggressive lobe, more valvespring pressure is required to keep the lifter following the lobe. However, mechanical roller cams may not be the best choice for street driving. Although it may be all right for heading to the local cruise night once a week, it is probably not the best choice for an engine that is driven constantly and does not get any maintenance.

The little needle bearings in the roller lifters can only take so much abuse with the higher spring pressure required for aggressive roller-cam lobes. Fortunately, the latest solid-roller lifters are better than ever; increased oiling has resulted in longer life spans for these bearings. Even the improved performance of modern synthetic engine oils has contributed to longer life for solid-roller lifters. But, it's still a good idea to have them checked annually.

If there's a period of time your car is off the road every year (like winter, or racing's off-season) it's a good idea to send the roller lifters back to the manufacturer for rebuilding. This is an inexpensive process and cheap insurance for your engine. Plus, you get to keep the steep lift and duration numbers and the high spring pressures to make really big power.

39- versus 45-Degree Camshafts

Over the years I have helped numerous Oldsmobile enthusiasts figure out whether they or their engine builder made a mistake and installed a camshaft with an incorrect bank angle. Sometimes the engine assembler cannot identify whether the camshaft and engine block is a match. Perhaps the manufacturer of the camshaft made a mistake and ground it incorrectly or packaged it erroneously.

You may *think* that you are installing the correct camshaft in your engine. The cam card shows that the camshaft has a 45-degree bank angle, and the camshaft is engraved or stamped "45 degrees." The block is 45-degree bank angle, but you just cannot get this engine running properly as a result of someone's mistake with one of the components.

The problem is easily prevented when you assemble the engine. When degreeing in the camshaft, simply set all of the events off the number-1 cylinder as you always do. When you finish, check the number-6 cylinder and you should achieve the same results, plus or minus a degree or two. If the numbers are off by a lot, you have a compatibility issue. If you don't have a degree wheel, you can simply check camshaft lift at any common point, such as TDC, and the two cylinders should match.

You can even do this with the engine in the car. Simply remove the valvecovers and then remove the rockers on the number-1 and number-6 cylinders. Use a dial indicator to measure pushrod lift at TDC

When I have no choice and absolutely have to use a flat-tappet camshaft in an engine, I use Comp Cams' break-in oil. Other oils are on the market, but Comp has designed its oil to do the job of protecting its flat-tappet camshafts. I recommend it regardless of your camshaft brand.

Flat-Tappet Camshaft Break-In Procedure

Breaking in a flat-tappet camshaft is relatively straightforward. Pretty much everyone knows to start up the engine and run it for 20 minutes at 1,800 to 2,000 rpm. However, the attention to detail is what will get you through it. Here are a few tips that will help your chances of success:

- Make sure that the lobe has some offset to the rear of the lifter bore when assembling the engine.
- When assembling the engine, make sure that the lifters rotate *very* easily in the lifter bores because any binding can cause the lifters not to rotate, which then leads to instant destruction.
- When coating the lifters with thick assembly lube, do not coat the sides. Use oil on the sides so that the lifter can spin easily and quickly upon fire-up.
- When assembling cylinder heads, make sure that the inner valvesprings are left out. Install the inner springs only after the break-in period is complete.
- Make sure that you prime the oil pump; then set your static timing properly and precisely so that the engine fires up instantly.
- Do not rotate the engine to TDC, point the rotor to the number-1 cylinder on the distributor cap, and install the distributor. Do not run the engine at TDC. Set the harmonic balancer at or slightly above the number at which you plan to run the engine, such as at 36 degrees. Now point the rotor to #1 on the distributor cap so that the engine fires right up and your ignition is close and the engine runs well on initial fire-up.
- Be sure that you set the idle screw up from stock and have the timing light hooked up and ready to go so that when the engine fires you can quickly set the timing and engine speed properly.
- Use a break-in oil such as Comp Cams break-in oil. I suggest that you avoid adding other oils and additives.

on the number-1 cylinder; any harmonic balancer has a TDC mark. Then, simply mount the dial indicator on the number-6 cylinder in the same fashion and rotate the engine until the pushrod lift number is the same. At that point, you should be at TDC if the block and camshaft are compatible. If that mark is off by a considerable amount, you have a problem.

Camshaft Specifications

The three basic cam specifications that everyone looks at are valve lift, duration at .050 inch of lift, and lobe separation.

Valve Lift

For performance applications, you almost cannot have too much valve lift on the intake lobe in your engine when searching for maximum horsepower. When looking at two camshaft lobes of the same duration at .050 inch of lift, the lobe with the greater lift is more aggressive, opens the valve faster, and makes more horsepower. On the exhaust side of the engine, an aggressive camshaft lobe is not necessarily the way to go. Be conservative on the lift/aggressiveness when selecting your exhaust lobes. Slow, lazy exhaust lobes, in general, make more torque.

Duration

The largest factor for determining intake duration is the amount of mechanical compression the engine has. Cylinder pressure is the key to performance, and the position on the intake stroke where the intake valve closes determines that. The intake-closing event is the most critical of all of the events in the camshaft cycle. The more intake duration you have, the later the intake valve closes, thus reducing cylinder pressure. The sooner the intake valve closes, the more the cylinder pressure rises. The balance of compression, swept volume (engine size), and the intake-closing event directly affect cylinder pressure, which has a large effect on performance.

The largest factor for determining exhaust duration is crankshaft stroke and the operating engine RPM. It is not cylinder-head exhaust-port flow as most think. The exhaust opening point is the second most critical event in the camshaft cycle. An exhaust duration that is too large for the application reduces torque considerably. This occurs when an exhaust valve opens too early in the power cycle, relieving the cylinder of the valuable combustion/cylinder pressure that is pushing the piston down, thus rotating the crankshaft.

Lobe Separation

Lobe separation by itself actually means nothing. It is simply the measurement of the angle between the centerline of the intake and exhaust lobe for one cylinder. Altering the lobe separation on a camshaft simply changes the opening and closing events on that camshaft; in addition, it changes valve overlap. For example, if you have two camshafts, one with 114 degrees of lobe separation and another with 106 degrees of lobe separation, the normal thinking is that the 106-degree lobe-separation camshaft makes more low-end torque, and that is generally true.

The reason this occurs is that when both camshafts are installed with no advance or retard, the camshaft with the smaller lobe separation closes the intake valve sooner. This raises cylinder pressure, and opens the exhaust valve later, which raises low-RPM torque. Both of these camshaft cycle events shift the power range lower, thus boosting low-end torque. You need to pay attention to the opening and closing events, not the lobe separation. Keep in mind that all of these opening and closing events must be designed for the application and are relative to the position of the piston (cam timing).

Cranking Compression

A cranking compression test is an excellent way to determine if your camshaft is matched to your compression and engine-design combination. A good range to be in for maximum racing performance with good high-octane fuel is 210 to 230 psi.

For street performance with pump gas, you should be a little on the conservative side, in the 185- to 200-psi range. This cylinder pressure is determined by mechanical compression ratio, the exact time that the intake valve closes as the piston is traveling up the bore on the compression stroke, and swept volume. If your engine, regardless of the compression ratio, cranks under about 180 psi, chances are good that the camshaft selected for your combination is too large, or is installed incorrectly.

Lifters

I always use roller camshafts in my Oldsmobile engines, whether it is a stock rebuild or any other high-performance engine. Negatives associated with using flat-tappet camshafts include lobe-lifter failure and lack of valvetrain control due to lack of spring pressure. It is simply not worth saving a few bucks to have future issues.

Flat-Tappet Lifters

Flat-tappet lifters are made of heat-treated cast iron. The bottoms of the lifters are not actually flat, but have a radius of about 30 inches ground onto the bottom camshaft's mating surface. It is best to use flat-tappet lifters from the camshaft manufacturer to have the best chance of a successful cam and lifter life. This is because it usually specifies hardness and the foot radius on them to be compatible.

One problem that enthusiasts of high-performance Oldsmobiles need to be aware of with flat-tappet lifters is the relationship between the lifter bore oil-feed hole and the lifter body. On some higher-lift camshafts, in order for the camshaft lobe to physically fit in the block, the size of the lobe cannot be any larger than the OD of the smallest journal diameter. The more lobe lift, and the smaller the base circle on the lobe, the lower the lifter body sits in the lifter bore. Sometimes, in this situation, the tops of the lifter bodies rest below the oil-feed holes drilled in the block's lifter bores; this creates a severe reduction in valuable oil pressure.

I have made some custom buttons, which I secured into the lifter body with Loctite, to cover that hole and seal the uncovered lifter feed hole in the block, but they tend to come loose and rattle around after a short time. This is another good reason to run a roller camshaft and lifters; this situation does not occur with the taller-body roller lifters available.

Factory Hydraulic Roller Lifters

The only time that I used a factory hydraulic roller lifter was in the Turbo S 71 engine build that can be viewed on YouTube. To my knowledge, there have been no issues with that engine to date. I consider it acceptable in limited RPM applications with .921 lifter bores to use the factory components. The only thing that scares me about that factory setup is the sheet-metal tray that holds the lifter locators or "dogbones" in place. Catastrophes happen when a valvetrain is out of control. Sometimes the engine isn't operating at the RPM level for which it was designed or an incorrect valvetrain design (such as linguini pushrods) is used. As long as the valvetrain is in control, all of these parts usually just do their thing properly.

Aftermarket Hydraulic Roller Lifters

Through the years I have exclusively used the Comp Cams PN 857-16 hydraulic roller lifters in my builds. According to Internet forums, there have been issues with sticking plungers, and I must admit I have had a few of those problems. Unfortunately, the hydraulic lifter is, by design, the best oil filter in the engine due to extremely tight tolerances. Even though the engine builder may spend a great deal of time cleaning a block prior to assembly, I cannot say that it is possible to ever get a 40-year-old cast-iron block with numerous passages 100 percent clean.

With that said, I don't feel that you can completely blame the lifter if it sticks. With all of the complaints that Comp Cams received, its Oldsmobile/Pontiac lifter was redesigned in 2013. At this time, I have used many of the new-style lifters and have not had one single issue.

Solid Roller Lifters

A few different companies manufacture solid roller lifters for Oldsmobile engines. Two styles that I have used are the Crane Cams .842-diameter (PN 28570-16) and Comp Cams .842-diameter (PN 849-16) roller lifters. In my personal engines that have spun as high as 9,000 rpm, I have found that they are reliable and that they oil the valvetrain properly due to proper band and oil hole placement.

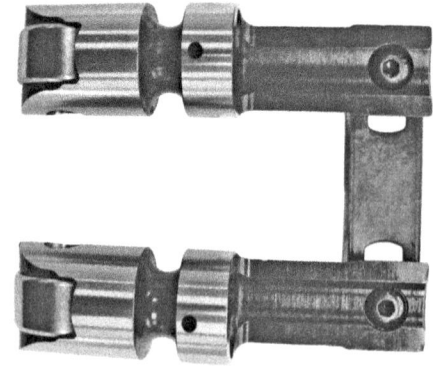

The 892C Comp Cams .904-diameter roller lifters are the best choice for solid-roller applications if you are installing bronze bushings in your Oldsmobile block. The larger wheel diameter on the bushings and more needle bearings make them stronger. To use these lifters in your Oldsmobile engine, machine a band in the OD of the bushing and relocate the oil feed hole.

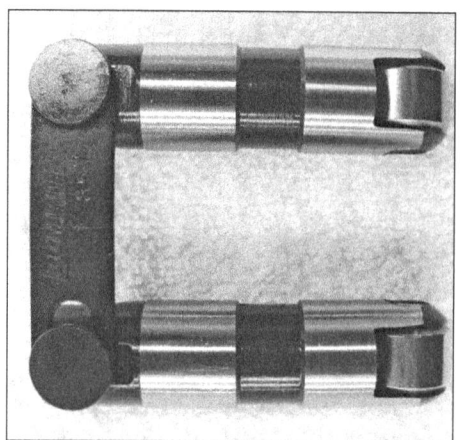

The newly designed Comp Cams 857 hydraulic roller lifter has performed trouble-free for every engine I have built since they became available in 2012.

The proper placement of the band is extremely important. If it is placed incorrectly, the valvetrain is either over-oiled or gets no oil at all. Oil restrictors do not correct an over-oiling issue because of an incorrect band–to–lifter bore oil hole relationship.

I have heard of some other engine builders having oiling problems with other brands, but I have no experience with other brands.

The safe bet for your build is to simply use the above-mentioned lifters. I have also used the Comp Cams .904-diameter in bronze-bushed applications (PN 892 C1). With these, you simply need to make sure that the oil feed hole in the bronze bushing is positioned in the oil band or in the recessed feature in the roller lifter during its up and down travel.

The advantage to using the .904 lifter is that the roller wheel diameter increases to .800 OD while the .842 lifters have the smaller .750 OD wheel diameter. You may be tempted to use an offset pushrod cup in the lifter that has a right offset, such as a Comp Cams PN 892 R1. Or you can use the PN 892 L1 that has a left-offset cup to straighten the pushrod angle or get that pushrod away from the intake port.

I cannot tell you why, but I did this on one of my engines in the Starfire and broke the tie-bar in two lifters. I quit trying to figure out why they broke and went back to centered pushrod cup lifters without any failure. I can only guess that it had something to do with the 42-degree lifter bore angle in the block. It is very costly to have a roller lifter break in an engine during a run so if you want to figure it out, knock yourself out. I am using centered lifters from now on in Oldsmobile applications.

The Comp Cams beehive spring (on the left) with a lightweight titanium retainer was used on the 2008 Engine Masters Challenge engine. The 977-16 Comp Cams dual valvespring (on the right) fits an Edelbrock Performer RPM cylinder head without modifications. It uses the supplied Edelbrock steel spring retainer, and has the proper spring pressure for a hydraulic roller camshaft.

Valvesprings, Retainers and Locks

Selecting the right valvesprings for your application is just like selecting your camshaft. It is best to work with the Oldsmobile expert who sells the camshaft to you; he or she has a great deal of experience in this matter and can help you get the right parts for your application. A few basic rules are involved with selecting your valvesprings.

First, you only need as much valvespring pressure as is required to keep the lifter against the cam lobe at peak (redline) RPM.

It is best to install valvesprings with an ID locator (left) or an OD locator (right). The less they wiggle and move around, the better the valvetrain control and longevity.

Here is a comparison of brand-new valvespring shims (left) and valvespring shims that have been through severe valve float (right). If your valvespring shims look like this, you need more pressure or lighter components.

CHAPTER 3

With beehive springs, titanium retainers, and a stable valvetrain, this 455 engine revved to 7,200 rpm and remained stable without valve float. This is the ultimate setup for hydraulic roller and flat-tappet applications.

The top-of-the-line, lightweight titanium retainer and titanium lock is referred to as a Super 7. I am not really sure why they are called that; the taper is actually 8 degrees. Others are referred to by their actual taper measurement, such as 10-degrees, 7-degrees.

Second, the higher RPM the engine turns, the higher the valvespring pressure that is required. More RPM requires more spring pressure to control it.

Finally, valvesprings should be located properly in the retainer and cylinder head. They should not wiggle and walk around. You should use a valvespring retainer that fits the spring without slop. Use a locating spring cup underneath the valve-spring, or a spring that fits the machined seat surface in the cylinder head with a minimum amount of clearance.

Proper valvesprings should be selected so that the full valve lift pushes the spring to .050 to .100 inch before the spring binds and cannot compress any farther (called "coil bind"). This is especially critical in higher-RPM applications.

When you don't have enough valvespring pressure, or have too much valvetrain weight for the maximum RPM your engine turns, valve float occurs. This is a situation where the pressure of the spring is insufficient, and the valves remain open farther and/or longer than they should. When experiencing valve float, the engine generally makes a noise similar to an ignition-controlled RPM limiter. This valve float situation stops the engine from revving any higher. It can allow valves to hit pistons, beat valve faces and valveseats, and, even worse, allow the valve locks to come loose and drop a valve into the cylinder. Nothing good happens as a result of valve float; avoid it at all costs.

In general, high-performance flat-tappet lifters are valvespring limited. This means you can only run so much valvespring pressure to control the valve because the extreme pressure

A digital valvespring tester is a must for every serious shop. Longacre manufactures this one. Some valvesprings lose tension if you bring them to coil bind a few times before installing. Very good-quality springs are not affected.

These are specially made back-grooved cam bearings by Durabond. They allow more oil to be forced into the highest loaded part, which is the bottom side. They should be installed so that the oil hole is in the 3-o'clock position as you face the front of the engine.

from the springs causes premature excessive wear on the cam lobes and lifter faces. These flat-tappet camshafts in general use valvesprings with about 110 to 130 pounds for installed-height seat pressure and about 300 to 340 pounds at full valve lift without wearing out lobes. I have used valvespring pressures on flat-tappet camshafts up to 180 pounds at the installed height on the seat and 500 pounds open pressure on conventional cast-iron camshafts and lifters, but this requires special attention to detail.

Dual valvespring designs are the preferred type to use in most average flat-tappet applications because they simplify the camshaft break-in process. You can simply remove the inner spring to reduce the pressure during that period. If conservative flat-tappet valvespring pressures are not enough for your application, it's time for a roller lifter and camshaft combination.

Hydraulic roller camshafts are much more aggressive than their flat-tappet counterparts, thus requiring more valvespring pressure, lighter-weight retainers, and lighter valves depending on how much RPM the engine combination sees. Beehive-design valvesprings are perfect for these applications. They have low mass and a very small, lightweight retainer. Valvespring pressures in these hydraulic roller Oldsmobile applications can be 140 to 180 pounds at the recommended installed height on the seat and 370 to 450 pounds at full valve lift, depending on the maximum RPM level the engine is to see.

Solid-roller camshaft and lifter kits are the most aggressive and power-producing design you can use in your high-performance Oldsmobile, and they require the highest valvespring pressures to keep the lifters following the lobes. Lobe aggressiveness, valvetrain weight, and maximum RPM typically dictate how much spring pressure is ultimately required. Roller-cam spring pressures in some of the best-performing Olds engines out there fall into the range of 250 to 300 pounds on the seat and 650 to 800 pounds at maximum lift. In these high-spring-pressure roller-cam applications, you can run much less spring pressure on the exhaust side to reduce stress on the lifters. There is no reason to run more valvespring pressure than necessary. In my maximum-effort builds, I purchase the intake and exhaust springs separately.

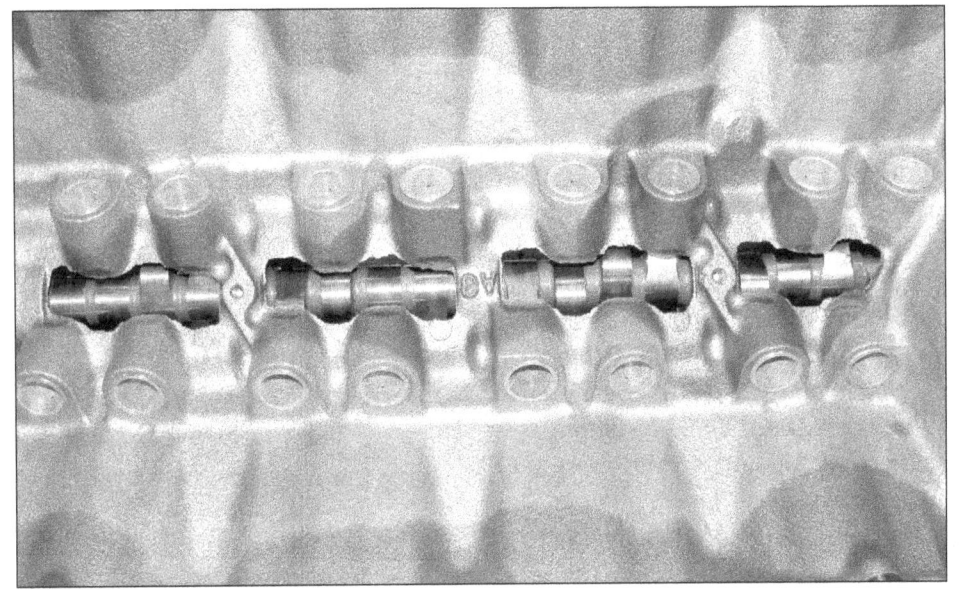

If you have chosen back-grooved cam bearings for your high-performance Olds project, make sure that the two 1/4-20 holes that hold down the factory camshaft cover are plugged, or have the bolts installed. Otherwise, the oil band in the backside of the number-2 and -4 cam bearings is exposed to these holes, sprays oil, and causes oil pressure loss.

CHAPTER 4

CONNECTING RODS

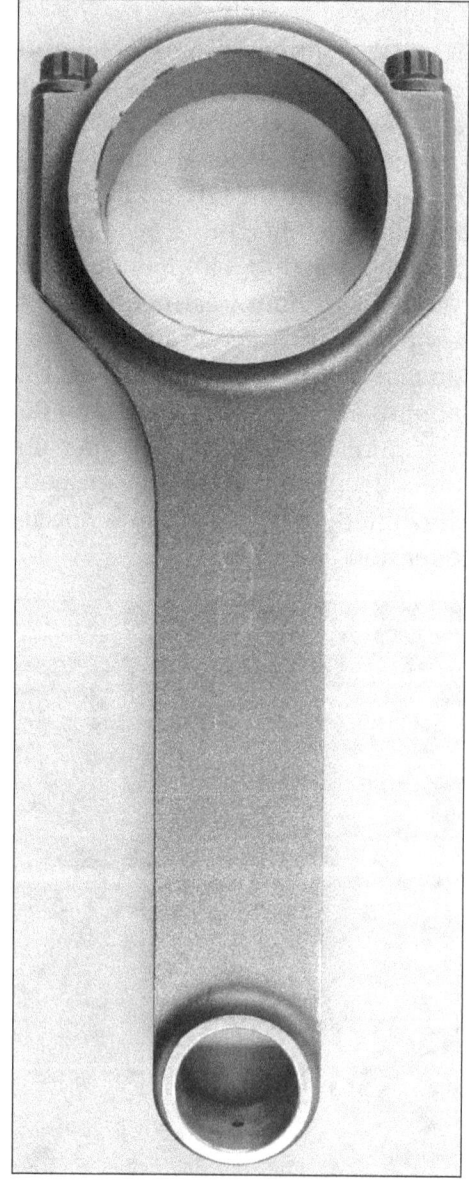

The Eagle CRS 7.100-inch rods are a good choice for 4.500-stroke 496 engines. These big-block Chevrolet connecting rods need to be modified to fit the Olds engine by cutting one side of the big end. It's not as easy as you may think; there is no good way to hold them and they are made of extremely hard material.

It's unfortunate that Olds enthusiasts were never given a truly great factory connecting rod. How can you make the best of the situation? A wide range of connecting rods are available that are up to the task of living long-term in a powerful Olds V-8, and this chapter details the best way to determine what's right for you.

Factory Connecting Rods

All of the factory Oldsmobile connecting rods are forged steel. The construction is relatively similar between all of the forgings. There are basically four styles. All of the small-block factory connecting rods are 6.000 inches long and use a 2.250-inch-diameter housing bore. The big end width measures .937 inch and shares a small-end bore diameter of .978 inch to allow the factory .980-inch small-end bore to be held in place by interference fit. The late-model Oldsmobile diesel engines share all of these features with the exception of its pin diameter set at 1.094 inches.

Two lengths of big-block connecting rods were manufactured. Early 400 "short-stroke" engines and 425-ci models used 7.000-inch connecting rods, while all others used 6.735-inch-long rods. These big-block connecting rods, other than the length, shared a big-end housing bore of 2.625 inches and a big-end width of .937 inch, while each piston-pin bore measures .978 inch for an interference fit, just like the small-block engines.

The factory connecting rods are one of the weakest links in an Oldsmobile engine. The main reason for this is the fact that they are dead soft. In high-performance use, when cylinder pressures and RPM are elevated, they move around dimensionally, which ultimately causes failure. Years ago, when I used to run them in my own engines making about 550 to 600 hp, I re-sized the big end perfectly round and to proper dimension during freshening. Every time the engine came apart and was inspected, the big

CONNECTING RODS

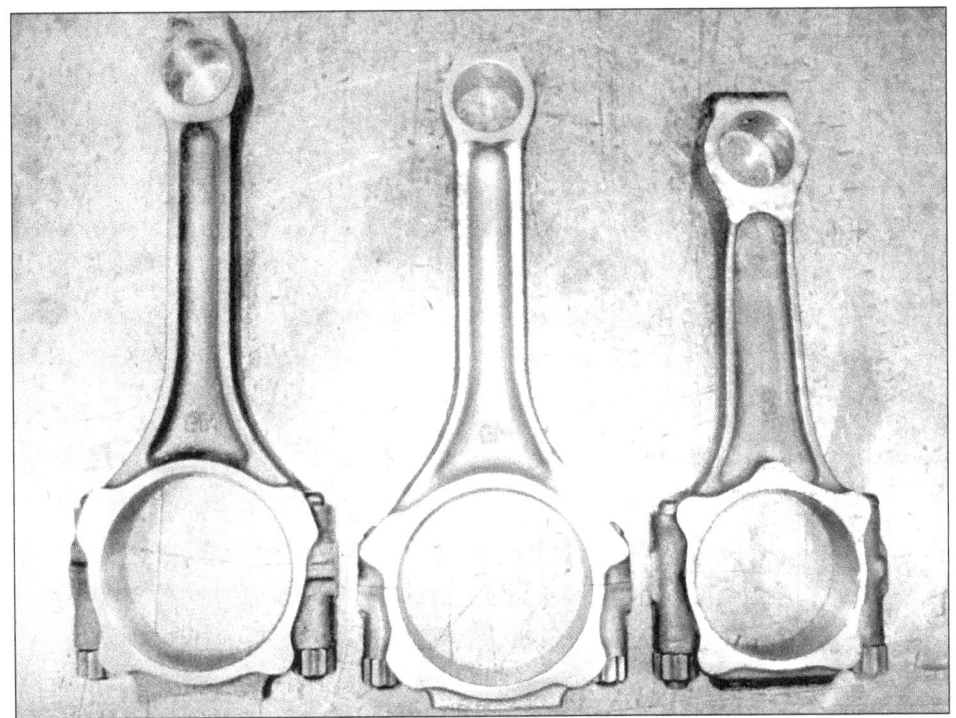

From left to right are: 7-inch 400/425 connecting rod, 455 connecting rod, 350 diesel connecting rod. It simply isn't worth putting money into any of these; they are heavy and as soft as rubber. Stock rods are acceptable for stock rebuild applications if RPM, compression, and horsepower remain low.

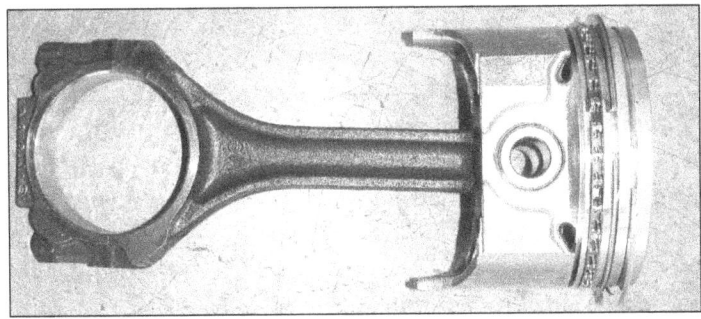

This pressed-pin application works well, but removing the pin from the rod in a press usually distorts the piston. If you want to reuse the piston you have to be very careful when separating it. When installing piston pins, you don't actually press them. You heat the small end of the rod to 350 to 400 degrees F and slide it right in. How do you know when it reaches the proper temperature? Oil starts to burn around 350 degrees. Wipe a little on and wait for the smoke.

end was always out of round and out of tolerance. It seemed as though as soon as I fired up the engine, the big ends went out of round.

I came to the conclusion that they were just too soft to hold their shape in high-performance use. Don't be misled by the fact they are forged steel. They are not a strong piece. The factory connecting rods are good for mild-performance engines up to about 400 hp and less than 5,500 rpm.

Factory Connecting-Rod Modifications

The best modification you can do to a factory connecting rod for high-performance use is to chuck it in the scrap bin for recycling! I have done all of the expert recommended factory connecting rod modifications such as polishing beams, upgrading bolts, shot peening, lightening, and notching the big ends for alleged oil-flow increases. All of these modifications do nothing to increase strength and do not do anything to make this soft connecting rod better than a factory unmodified rod.

I have also tried heat treating factory connecting rods. What happens in this case is, if there are any stresses in the metal due to them being recycled or used, they "move around" on a molecular level during the heat-treating process and come out of the oven unusable. The biggest reason they are unusable is that the big-end housing bore distorts and the connecting-rod bolts, after being pressed back in, are not parallel anymore due to the big end spreading and not fitting into the lower cap.

Don't waste your time and hard-earned money playing with this stuff; I have already figured it out for you. In the case of replacing the connecting rod bolts on these factory rods with stronger ones, it is not necessary. I have never seen a connecting-rod bolt break. If you have ever seen what looks like a rod bolt failure, chances are something else caused it.

If you insist on replacing the bolts to an aftermarket high-strength set, measure the bolt holes with pin gauges or some other accurate form of measurement to determine the amount of press fit. There are bolts out there that are incorrect for the rod, but are sold as Oldsmobile connecting-rod bolts. I have found these bolts to be too large for the hole in the rod. Pressing these in distorts the rod and causes failure.

Aftermarket Steel Connecting Rods

Truly high-quality connecting rods have never been more available or affordable than they are now. The relatively wide selection means there are plenty of choices at all budget levels. Let's investigate the aftermarket and see what's best for you.

Big-Block Applications

There are a few choices in steel connecting rods. The most popular in stock big-block rod journal diameter connecting-rod applications are the H-beam models available through Eagle, M&J Proformance, and Dick Miller Racing. The "Chinese" H-beam connecting rods are pretty strong pieces. They Rockwell test very hard, which keeps them dimensionally stable. They stay round, unlike the weak factory pieces. I have used H-beam rods in many Oldsmobile builds and high-horsepower Chevrolet, Ford, and Pontiac builds with great success. Using these H-beam rods is a no-brainer for all but the most serious high-performance Oldsmobile applications. I have used many of the 6.735-inch-long Eagle rods and have not found any defects.

The 7.000-inch-long Oldsmobile H-beam connecting rod has recently become available. As of this writing, I have not used any of them, but they are currently available through M&J Proformance and Dick Miller Racing. All of these Oldsmobile H-beam connecting rods come with bronze bushings installed in the small end for use with pistons with .980-inch-diameter floating pins. These factory Oldsmobile replacement H-beam connecting rods are not available without bushings for press-fit applications as of

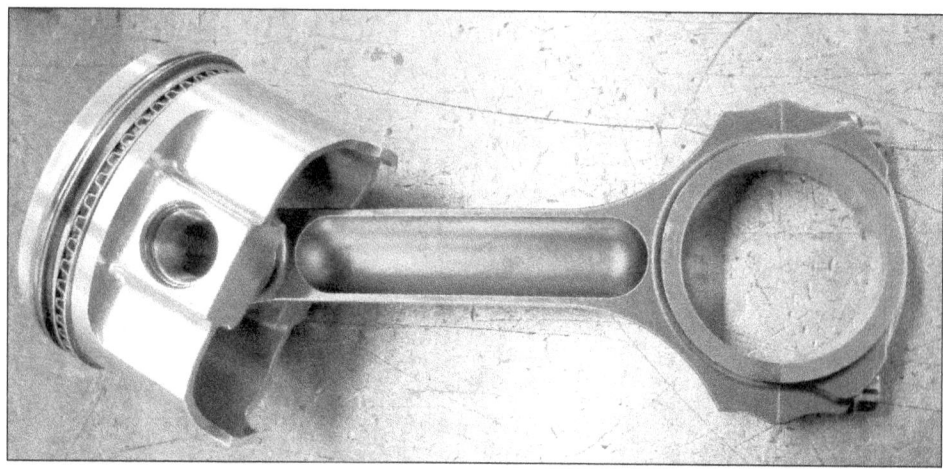

Oliver made 6.735-inch-long rods for an Oldsmobile with a 2.200 big-block Chevrolet rod journal.

Eagle's CRS 6.735 H-beam rod is one of the best deals out there! It is a stable connecting rod due to the material and hardness. With a rod like this available, it doesn't pay to mess with stock rods. But they are not always available when you need them.

this writing, so your piston choice needs floating-pin provisions.

Small-Block Steel Connecting Rods

As of this writing, no aftermarket steel replacement is available for small-block Oldsmobile connecting rods. The easiest way to handle this situation is to grind your small-block Oldsmobile crankshaft to Chevrolet 2.100 dimensions by asking the crank grinder for a .025-under grind job on the rod-journal diameter. The machinist must also side-grind the rod journal for the desired rod side clearance because most of the aftermarket Chevrolet connecting rods are .940-inch wide. This allows the use of a variety of aftermarket 6.000-inch Chevrolet connecting rods. Plenty of choices are available. The only modification that has to be done to the connecting rod is that the small end has to be bored for the stock (.980) Oldsmobile pin diameter.

There is usually enough material in these rods for this modification. You have to inspect them to make the final determination. I have made these modifications with Scat

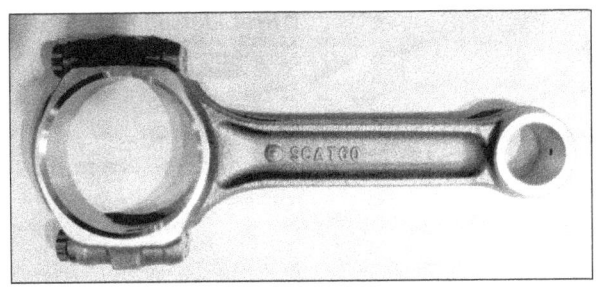

I have used a Scat 6-inch I-beam rod in budget-stroker 350s. By offset-grinding the stock Olds 330 or 350 crankshaft to a small-block Chevrolet 2-inch rod journal, you can have a 3.500-stroke 378-ci engine. The big ends of the small-block Chevrolet rods are slightly wider than Olds rods, so you need to widen the rod journals on the crankshaft when grinding, or narrow the big ends slightly. Make sure you check for interference between the small end of the rod and the pin bosses in the piston; the beam is offset on a Chevrolet and straight on all Oldsmobile engines.

H-beam and I-beam connecting rods by either re-bushing them for floating .980-diameter pins and boring and honing to .978 or utilizing an interference fit to hold the pin in as in stock-type applications. If you choose a custom piston in your small-block Oldsmobile build, also choose a .927 pin size and you won't have to modify the connecting rod at all.

In stroker applications with reduced rod-journal diameters, there are many choices of quality aftermarket steel Chevrolet connecting rods. It is common and inexpensive to use aftermarket big-block Chevrolet connecting rods for big-block Oldsmobile stroker applications and aftermarket small-block Chevrolet connecting rods for small-block Oldsmobile stroker applications.

When using small-block Chevrolet connecting rods in Oldsmobile applications, always check for interference between the sides of the small end of the connecting rod and the sides of the pin bosses on the underside of the piston. This situation is due to the fact that Chevrolet connecting rods have an offset beam and Oldsmobile connecting rods have a centered beam.

Most often you have clearance between the small end and the pin boss, but sometimes you don't. If this occurs, some material has to be removed from one side of the pin boss of the piston. It is best to check this clearance by installing number-1 and number-2 pistons and rods during a mock-up assembly of the short-block. Inspecting these two first, before installing all of the pistons to the rods, may save you some hassle by finding out about an interference problem before all are mounted and the whole short-block is together.

The popularity of Chevrolet LS series engines in recent years means that more connecting rod options are available for your small-block Oldsmobile project. The LS series connecting rods have a centered beam as do the Oldsmobile engines, and therefore these can be used in the Olds small-block.

Aluminum Connecting Rods

I am a big fan of aluminum connecting rods. In many engine builds at BTR we use GRP aluminum connecting rods. I use them for the same reason I use other specific manufacturers' products; they are the utmost in quality and I have never had an issue with them. I use them exclusively in all race applications due to the light weight, which helps the engine accelerate quicker and reduces elapsed times. We also use these custom connecting rods because they allow us to design the piston properly for best performance and fill in the distance between the crankshaft journal and the piston. Finally, they allow engine builders to have the exact rod side clearance and pin diameter.

I also use GRP connecting rods with great success in many street-driven engines. Although this is not common practice with most builders, I have found that it works rather well. In my own engine, I use a very light GRP connecting rod and I am always pushing the limits. After two seasons of abuse, or about 200 runs, I replace them, but they appear to be perfect. With that stated, I refuse to believe that you could hurt one in a lower-RPM application with a slightly heavier-duty model. When connecting rods fail, whether steel or aluminum, the failure is almost always due to the bearing grabbing the journal for some reason, not the connecting rod failing.

GRP utilizes very strong 7075 T6 material in its standard aluminum rods. GPR has an upgraded material that it refers to as its "Pro Material." This upgraded material's main advantage is that, at elevated temperatures, the yield strength remains as good as the 7075 at higher temperatures, which is acceptable for moderate street use. I don't know if I would use them in an engine that was driving from New York to California, but for the average high-performance street car that drives to the local cruise in or the local race track, I wouldn't be afraid to use them. I've done it.

CHAPTER 4

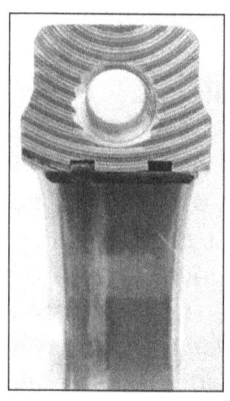

The serrations in the GRP connecting rods locate the cap to the connecting rod exactly where they were when manufactured. Any high-end aluminum rod has this feature.

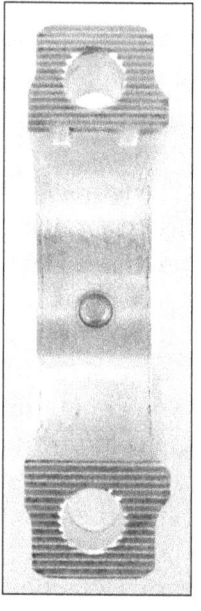

Some lesser-quality aluminum rods have serrations that allow the cap to move fore and aft before torquing the bolts. When you torque the connecting rods, you must insert the maximum-thickness feeler gauges between the two rods to set the cap in the proper location while torquing the bolts.

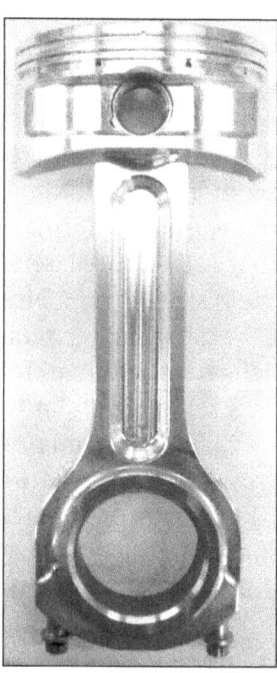

This rather long 7.350-inch rod for a 496 pump-gas build lasts a long time, due to the RPM that these engines turn.

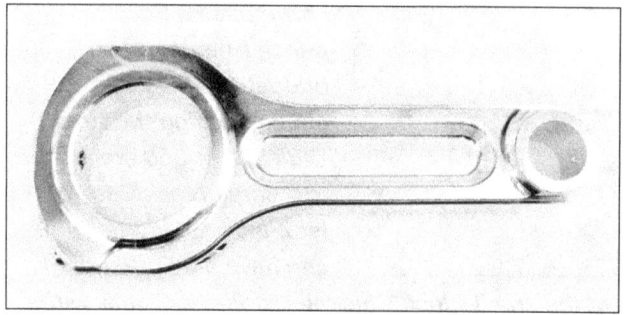

GRP billet-aluminum connecting rods are very strong. GRP makes so many different variations that there is sure to be a rod for your application. Lightweight connecting rods certainly help make an Oldsmobile reliable.

If you plan on contacting GRP or any aluminum connecting rod manufacturer to ask if this is acceptable, I wouldn't bother. Chances are they will not tell you that they are acceptable for street use because no one wants possible liability. All that I can tell you is that I have used the GRP aluminum connecting rods on a number of street engines with 100-percent success. I do not have experience with other manufacturers' aluminum connecting rods and cannot comment on them.

Connecting-Rod Side Clearance

Connecting-rod side clearance is one of the most important aspects of building a successful short-block. This, like bearing clearances, is something that you cannot change after the fact. It has to be designed into the build. Some may argue that it doesn't mean anything, but it is very important.

The typical Oldsmobile crankshaft journal width is 1.880 to 1.885 inches. The typical stock Oldsmobile connecting rod big end width is .935 to .937. A typical rod side-clearance measurement on a stock Oldsmobile engine is anywhere from .008 to .0013 inch. Your typical builder opens up this clearance to allow more oil to pass and allegedly cool the bearing. But the bearing is already plenty cool if it isn't rubbing and creating heat. Proper bearing clearance and journal surface finish take care of that issue.

On all of my builds, I try to keep the connecting rod side clearance at .008 to .012 inch on steel-rod engines and .014 to .018 inch on aluminum-rod engines. By keeping your rod side clearances to a minimum, the amount of oil sprayed on the cylinder walls is reduced, and it is easier to maintain hot oil pressure. A common problem with excessive connecting-rod side clearance is when the engine warms up, the oil pressure is drastically reduced.

When grinding your stroker Oldsmobile crankshaft using Chevrolet connecting rods, be sure to specify journal width after measuring the big-end width of the rods you are using. Your typical aftermarket, small-block Chevrolet connecting rod measures .940 inch and your typical big-block Chevrolet connecting rod measures .990 inch. With that in mind, you can design your connecting-rod side clearance into your build by machining the crankshaft or connecting rods to suit. The crankshaft grinder can typically take the journal width from 1.885 to 1.900 inch without too much trouble, but they generally don't go from 1.885 to 2.000 inch due to time spent and the fact that side grinding is slightly dangerous. In this case you have to narrow the big-end width of the connecting rods.

Rod-to-Stroke Ratio

The rod-to-stroke (rod/stroke) ratio is defined as the ratio between the length of the connecting rod and the length of the crankshaft stroke. This is calculated by dividing the connecting-rod length by the stroke of the crankshaft.

The effects of a longer connecting rod in an engine, in contrast to the shorter, is that in the engine with the larger rod-to-stroke ratio, the piston dwells in the vicinity of TDC for a longer period of time and moves away more slowly. The effect is just the opposite at BDC. The piston accelerates away from BDC faster. The shorter rod-to-stroke-ratio engine has exactly the opposite effects.

The effect of rod-to-stroke ratio has occasionally been a highly debated subject. The common opinion out there is that the longer connecting rod is always better. This opinion appears to have come from the legacy of the late Smokey Yunick. Years ago, there was a technical article in National Dragster by David Reher from Reher and Morrison Racing Engines. In that article, he basically claimed that, through testing, rod-to-stroke ratio doesn't mean anything.

I think that the rod/stroke ratio does have an effect on how the engine performs. For an engine that maintains very high RPM with a narrow usable-RPM range, that combination may like a larger rod/stroke ratio. But as far as Oldsmobile engines are concerned, it is generally a lower-RPM engine that uses a wide-RPM range; a lower rod/stroke ratio may be of benefit.

In 2002, I had built a small-block Olds 337-ci nitrous engine with a rod/stroke ratio of 2.0:1, which was con-

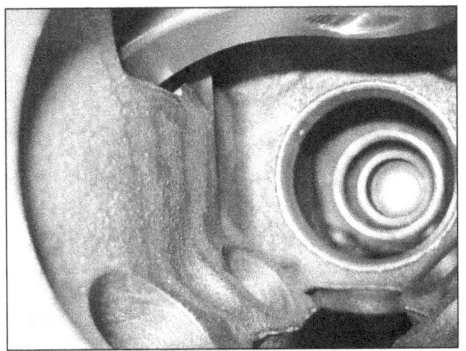

Aluminum rods sometimes require some clearancing at the bottoms of the cylinder bores. Install number-1 and -2 individually and look through the cam tunnel. Don't wait to check until everything is together. I've built engines with a 4.700 stroke and have not had a connecting rod hit the cam lobe yet; but don't take my word for it, take a look!

sidered exceptionally high, especially for a nitrous engine. The nitrous experts told me it would not work due to the major amount of dwell time around TDC. What I learned from this particular engine is that the camshaft requirements were quite unconventional because of this unusual rod-to-stroke ratio, and the ignition timing was later than normal. With these changes to this engine, it did eventually go fast and function properly. What I learned with this combination is that the rod/stroke ratio affected camshaft selection.

Oldsmobile engines had rod/stroke ratios from 1.58 to 1.77:1. These factory rod/stroke ratios are right in line with other General Motors engines of this era.

For the purpose of building a high-performance Oldsmobile engine, only the basics on this subject need to be covered. My thought is that the lower-RPM, pump-gas Oldsmobile engines benefit from rod-to-stroke ratios in the neighbor-

Rod/Stroke Ratios

Oldsmobile
455	1.58
400/425	1.75
350/403	1.77

Big-Block Chevrolet
454	1.53
396/427	1.63

Small-Block Chevrolet
400	1.50
350	1.63
327	1.75
302	1.90

Make sure you number the rods with something like an electric engraver and not a punch and hammer so you don't risk damaging the rods. If you don't do that first and then mix up the caps, it is not easy to figure out which cap goes to which body.

hood of 1.5 to 1.6:1. But this spec should not be the criteria for selecting your components for your engine combination. When designing your Oldsmobile engine project, the piston compression distance/design and crankshaft stroke are the most important part of the design. The least important aspect considered in the design should be your rod/stroke ratio, but you shouldn't ignore it.

CHAPTER 5

PISTONS, RINGS AND PINS

For many Oldsmobile enthusiasts, pistons are definitely one of the most misunderstood engine components. Just because a piston fits in the cylinder and the rings fit in the groove does not mean that the engine seals up and makes power. Essentially, a piston's function is to allow the rings to do the job of sealing up the cylinders.

The ring grooves need to be machined absolutely smooth, flat, and parallel to the piston pin. The piston skirt must have a properly designed shape for the application. The piston skirt's function is to hold the piston square in the bore with the least amount of friction and to prevent that piston from rocking inside the bore. Excessive piston rock in the bore inhibits ring seal. The rings seal best when held squarely against the bore. Over the years, piston manufacturers have tweaked the piston design here and there to accomplish these tasks in the overall goal of sealing these piston rings better.

Factory Cast Pistons

There really isn't much to discuss about factory Oldsmobile pistons. The pistons on the Oldsmobile engine, whether big-block or small-block, high-performance or smog engine, were made of cast aluminum. This cast-aluminum design was simply the way pistons were manufactured at the time. It is a relatively inexpensive process. In performance use, they often fail in a variety of ways. I have seen and experienced failure in the ring land area due to detonation. The ring lands broke apart and turned into a bunch of small chunks that further broke apart and got sent through the cylinder.

Another common failure is the pin boss cracking and failing, causing the piston pin to come right out of the pin bore, and ensuing catastrophic failure. We certainly have learned something since cast-aluminum

Most factory replacement pistons have an offset pin bore. This reduces side loading on the bore by changing the rod angle near bottom dead center.

PISTONS, RINGS AND PINS

The old L-3078 TRW piston has a 12-cc dish. I ran this piston in my NHRA Stock Eliminator for quite a while because it had the smallest dish of all the legal pistons. Eventually, the piston came apart and destroyed the engine. That's what you get for racing with a cast piston.

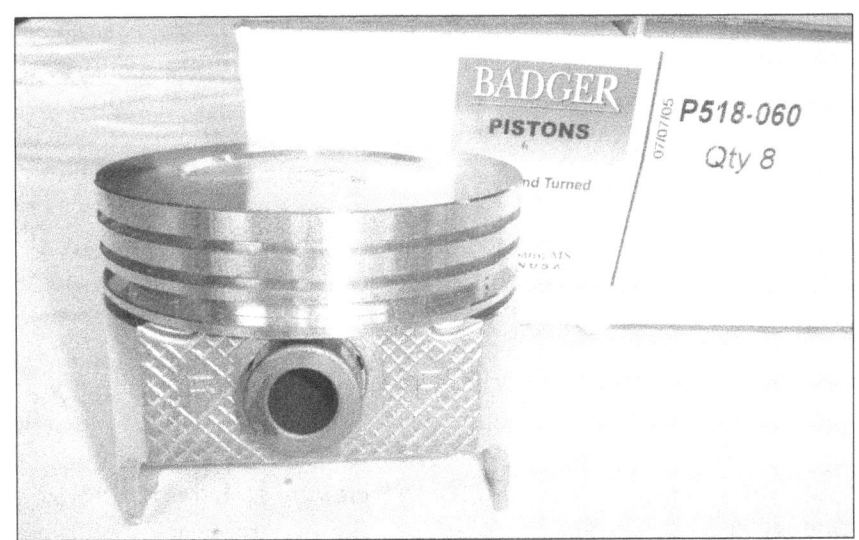

Badger Pistons makes many cast factory replacement pistons.

When your engine "pings" from preignition, it knocks the ring lands right out of a cast piston. I do not want to run a cast piston in any engine.

Big, wide, high-tension factory-type piston rings are very hard on the cylinder walls. With all that tension, no wonder there is always a ridge when you pull an engine apart. Wide rings are a thing of the past.

This piston needs to be installed with the arrow pointing to the front of the engine. That means the piston has an offset pin bore and you must install it on the connecting rod the correct way.

OLDSMOBILE V-8 ENGINES: HOW TO BUILD MAX PERFORMANCE

pistons were first designed. Knowing and understanding engines like we do today, I wouldn't even use a cast-aluminum piston in a stock rebuild or in any engine that I cared about.

Aftermarket Forged Pistons

A variety of aftermarket forged pistons are available for Oldsmobile engines. The cost typically goes up with quality. There are essentially two types of forged piston. The typical street-type, and some custom-forged pistons, are made of 4032 high-silicon aluminum, while most other custom pistons are made of 2618 aluminum alloy.

Typical TRW, Probe, Keith Black, SRP, etc., pistons are made from 4032 high-silicon alloy. This alloy is used for street-type engines because the expansion rates are lower than traditional 2618 forgings. And they have a higher silica content, which is supposed to have better scuff resistance. The thought here is that your engine has less piston noise on start up due to the piston operating with less clearance than traditional forgings. But one drawback with these pistons is that the material is very hard (more brittle) than the 2618 stuff. Remember that silica is basically sand; you know, the stuff they make glass with. If these pistons have too much clearance, they beat the hell out of the bores, and fracture or break, much like cast/hypereutectic pistons. You better get that clearance right with this stuff.

Any piston is typically designed for a specific bore size. As an example, the popular TRW 2323F forged 455 .030-over piston is designed for a 4.155 bore, but sticks and galls in the bore at that dimension. My years of experience on that model typically dictate a 4.157- or .002-inch over nominal bore to run without galling. I am not a big fan of this style of piston, but they are generally inexpensive and popular with consumers.

Off-the-Shelf Pistons

A few off-the-shelf piston options are available for Oldsmobile engines, including those manufactured by MAHLE, Icon, AutoTech, SRP, Probe, Sealed Power, and CP Pistons. I use CP Pistons in my Oldsmobile engines because their quality and service are exceptional.

This is an old TRW forged 425 piston. It has smoother surfaces than cast-aluminum replacements.

The top of this Keith Black forged flat-top has some pretty deep valve notches.

This Keith Black flat-top piston for the 455 is set up for floating pins. They are kind of rough and need some deburring before they can be used.

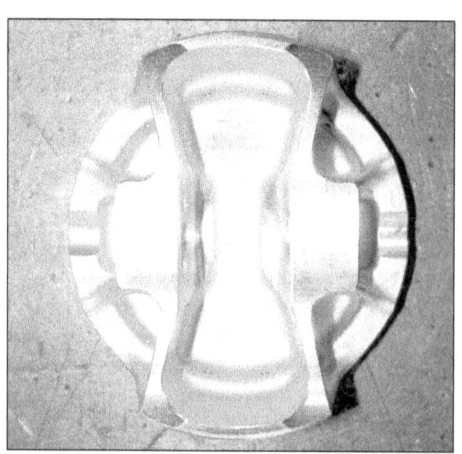

The X-forged (or strut-type) piston is very light and strong. It also uses a narrow pin for another weight advantage.

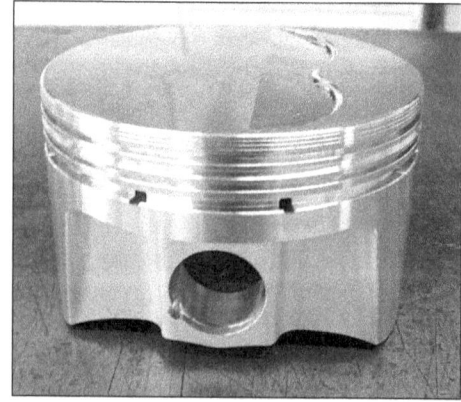

The CP Bullet piston is now available for long- and short-stroke 400 engines. Both piston designs require the Eagle 6.735 long connecting rod because of the floating pin.

In about 2009, CP developed the Bullet Series, and I was asked to help design some for the Oldsmobile engines. I essentially copied the most popular custom orders that I had been placing throughout the years. These designs include the 455 flat-top, 455 10.5:1 dished, stock 350 flat-top, stroker 350, long-stroke and short-stroke 400 engines, and my most popular Oldsmobile engine build, the 496 stroker pump-gas engine.

These Bullet Series pistons have the benefits of high-quality custom pistons at an affordable price. These kits include lightweight forgings, lightweight pins, and low-tension metric rings.

Custom Pistons

I am a big fan of custom pistons. Using them in your Oldsmobile build allows you to take advantage of getting exactly what you want for compression, piston rings, and other design features that seal the engine better (eliminating nasty smoke coming out of your breathers) and promote longevity. There are a variety of custom piston manufacturers. I have used every manufacturer's pistons at one time or another on my own builds or a customer's engine. Almost every engine build at BTR uses pistons from CP Pistons in Irvine, California. You cannot buy anything that is too good for an engine, especially a piston, and I think CP's are the best. The engineers at CP are top notch and have always helped design the lightest, strongest piston for the application.

Constant feedback from top engine builders/dealers constantly improves the performance of these products. As previously stated, the key to a piston's performance is for

The rings have been moved down on this particular X-forging because the owner plans to run pump-gas and nitrous oxide. This style of piston handles a lot of power.

that piston to move up and down squarely in the bore, with a minimal amount of friction. When a piston is properly designed for the application, the cylinder bore has a minimum amount of wear over time. No ridges in your bores with the good stuff! Ironically, when the piston is designed properly for the application, the skirt clearance on these 2618 forgings is as tight or tighter than most of the low-expansion 4032 alloy pistons.

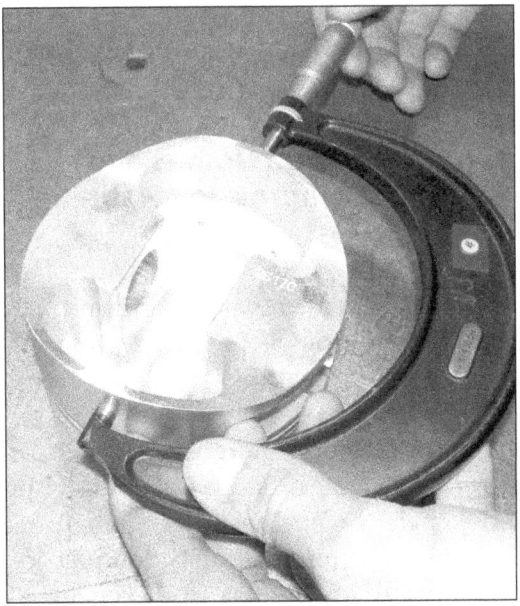

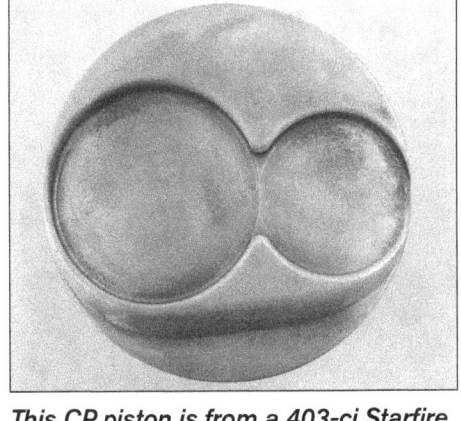

This CP piston is from a 403-ci Starfire engine. Even with the dome, the volume is 8 cc. Cylinder heads with a flat valve angle (such as on an Oldsmobile) require plunge-cut valve pocket. Every thousandth of an inch of valve-relief depth counts for compression.

It's all about the skirt shape. One of the key aspects that CP is noted for is the accuracy of the ring grooves and the skirts. The way this is achieved is that the pistons are rough machined, and then the most critical operations (such as on the ring grooves and skirts) are performed last because things move around during the machining process. The skirts are sized so accurately that the proper

CP custom pistons are manufactured accurately enough that if you want to hone the bores to a particular size, you can then order the piston in that size. You don't want to use a micrometer to measure the skirt and set clearance as with some other pistons. First, the skirt is not straight or round, and chances are you cannot measure the exact spot accurately. Second, the skirt clearance is set for you, so don't reinvent the wheel and change it from the designed clearance. I have followed this method with 100-percent success.

CHAPTER 5

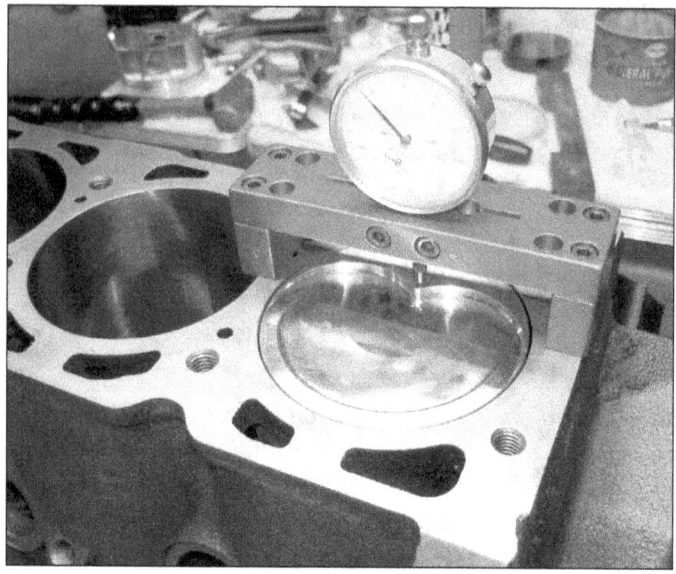

The deck height can be checked with this tool. If you do your homework when building an engine, your deck height is designed into the build by subtracting the block deck height from the piston compression height, the rod length, and half of the crankshaft stroke.

The tiny holes in the piston are referred to as vertical gas ports. They help seal the top ring by loading the backside of the ring with combustion pressure. I design them into any custom piston where I am trying to squeeze out every ounce of power.

way to set the skirt clearance is to hone the cylinders to a final dimension and order the piston to that bore size.

I have ordered pistons for bore sizes to the one-half thousandth. Forget measuring the piston and honing to size. The skirt is not perfectly round and not straight from top to bottom by design; the average guy will just screw it up. Do yourself a favor if you purchase these quality pistons; follow the manufacturer's recommended bore size and finish hone to that. I order pistons all the time for a certain bore size and finish hone the engine block long before the pistons ever arrive.

Piston Domes and Compression Ratio

Most Oldsmobile enthusiasts use dished or flat-top pistons. The selection of pistons with those features is relatively straightforward. When you get into domes, the piston is much more complicated. In race engines that are naturally aspirated, or engines that use nitrous oxide, I put as much compression into the engine as I can get. In my maximum-effort builds, 15:1 to 16:1 compression is the norm.

If you are willing to spend money on race fuel, then why not buy the proper fuel and make the compression ratio as high as you can, assuming that you have designed the bottom end accordingly? The more torque, the more horsepower, period. It is easier to achieve higher compression ratios in larger-cubic-inch engines, and much more difficult to achieve higher compression ratios in smaller-cubic-inch engines. It is relatively easy to achieve 12:1 to 14:1 compression in big-block engines with a dome that clears the combustion chamber and has valve pocket depth for ample piston-to-valve clearance.

In general, on a 500-ci Oldsmobile big-block, you can achieve 15:1 compression with a flat-top piston with 3 cc of valve relief, and a 55-cc combustion chamber. The same flat-top-piston design with the same combustion chamber at 350-ci has about 11.5:1 compression. In this case you cannot build a dome that would fit in the chamber that would allow you to achieve 15:1 compression, no matter how tight that dome fits in the combustion chamber. It's all about swept volume. Oldsmobile engines have a relatively small, flat combustion chamber due to the shallow 6-degree valve angle, which makes designing a dome much easier than on other engines.

For the average do-it-yourselfer who wants to purchase a domed Oldsmobile piston for his or her project, my advice is to work with a custom piston dealer who has experience in high-performance Oldsmobile engines.

When designing a dome for an Oldsmobile engine, you have to take many aspects into consideration.

PISTONS, RINGS AND PINS

I just love the quality of the CPs! Aren't they handsome?

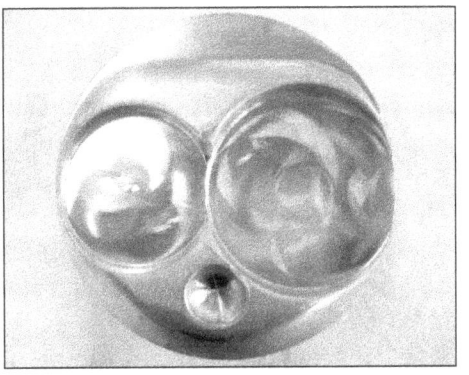
This piston has the maximum dome for a Rocket Racing/Wenzler head.

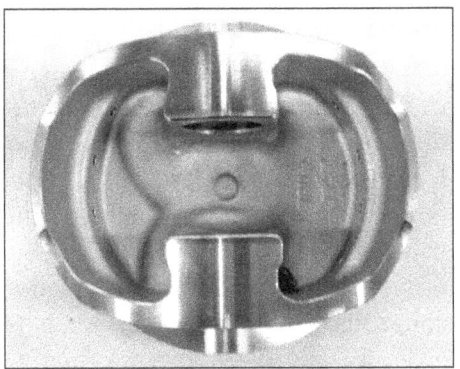
Notice the discoloration caused by heat due to a lean condition.

This piston top ring land is curled up due to too much fuel or too rich a tune-up on a nitrous engine. This always occurs on the intake side.

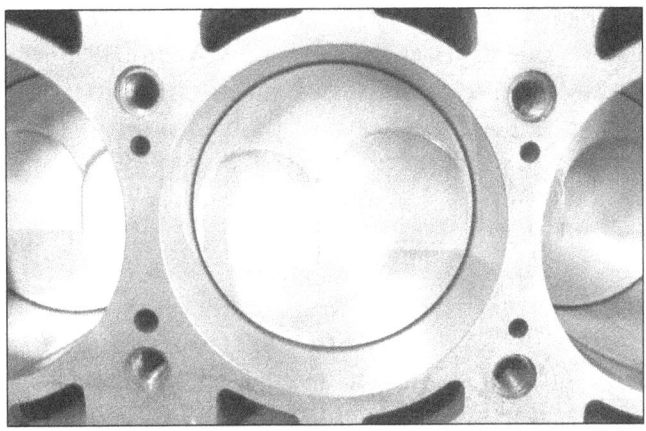
When designing custom pistons, it is always best to have your valve pockets as shallow as possible for the best flame travel.

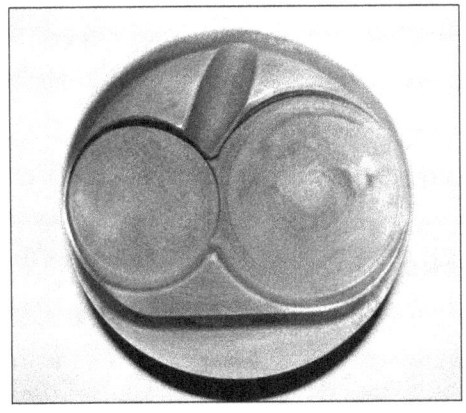
This maximum-dome small-block Olds piston has a "fire slot." This is for clearancing the spark plug and to direct the flame toward the exhaust side of the combustion chamber.

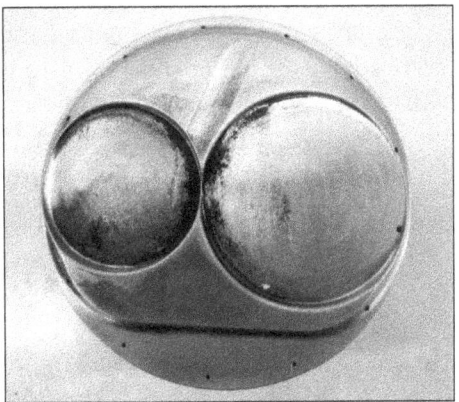
This piston has vertical gas ports that load the backside of the ring for pressure loading the top piston ring. I have used them in street applications with no ill effect.

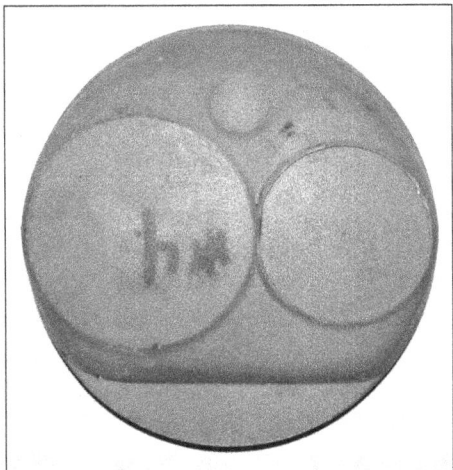
This 2001 mold was made of the cast-iron Batten combustion chamber for my 337-ci NMCA EZ Street engine. I had sent it and my "blob" dome pistons to RebCo Machine in Kansas City for machining an exact duplicate. It was difficult to get compression on this little engine and the dome needed to fit like a glove.

These items include valve-head diameter, valve location in relation to the center of the cylinder, valve pocket depth, and the exact shape of the combustion chamber.

Regarding valve-head diameters, the cutter used to clear and/or plunge valve-pocket depth is generally .100 inch greater in diameter, leaving .050-inch clearance around the valves. The shallow 6-degree valve angle of the Oldsmobile engine usually requires plunge cuts into the dome, which leave no extra room for valve-to-piston clearance without considerably reducing dome size and compression.

At BTR, we have developed a computer program that allows us to enter all the pertinent information like stroke, rod length, camshaft specifications, deck height, etc., so we can simulate where the valve is in relation to the deck of the piston at certain crankshaft degree points. Then, we can mathematically determine valve-to-piston clearance. This allows us to design a piston that has a minimum amount of valve-to-piston clearance, and therefore more dome displacement.

As far as dome design is concerned, you will never achieve the maximum dome unless the combustion chambers are CNC machined and the reverse shape is machined into the piston dome. A number of dome designs may be close to fitting. But through experience I can tell you that achieving a high compression ratio is not as simple as it may seem.

When a high-compression dome is designed, spark-plug clearance is usually an issue. I have machined fire slots (a trough, machined to clear the dome around the spark plug) for clearance and provided a path for the initial combustion charge, directing that charge to the center of the dome. I have also provided spark plug clearance with a plunge only in order to have as much dome displacement as possible. I cannot say that I have seen a difference here. But if I had dome to spare, I use the fire slot because it makes sense, but not if I was fighting for every bit of compression.

Piston Rings

Piston rings are obviously an important part of your engine build. Not everyone realizes how much. Three piston rings are used in a ring stack. The rings used in factory Oldsmobile engines were what I refer to as the 5/64-5/64-3/16 ring pack. These dimensions refer to the vertical height of the ring. This ring pack is the most common size used in the muscle-car era. These ring sets have a great deal of friction and cause a great deal of heat and frictional horsepower loss. I have found that most overheating problems with street cars are not cooling system issues. Friction in the rings is the largest culprit. If you must use an inferior piston design with wide-stock-type ring grooves, a custom ring set can be designed to reduce some of the friction associated with this stock-type design and purchased through Total Seal Inc.

Today's new cars (foreign and domestic) use higher-quality pistons with thinner, reduced-radial-tension piston rings for the purpose of reducing friction and increasing horsepower and gas mileage. Why wouldn't you do this in your high-performance Oldsmobile engine? Did you ever wonder why an old muscle-car-era engine would wear out at 80,000 to 100,000 miles? When you disassemble these engines you see a ridge at the top of the cylinders where the top ring didn't touch. Today's engines go well beyond 100,000 miles without wearing out. Why? They use thin, lower-tension piston rings.

A common belief is that a vacuum pump is required for these thin, reduced-tension rings. I have not found that to be the case. I have used ring packs in engines that are very low tension with no signs of chamber oiling, such as with circle-track engines that were not allowed to have vacuum pumps. The secret is high-quality pistons, proper bore clearance, and round cylinders. Remember: Lighter-tension rings conform better to cylinder wall distortion and offer better "point pressure" with their narrower contact surfaces.

The top ring is called the compression ring and serves the function of keeping the hot gases on the top side of the piston. The top piston ring

Notice the ring spacers in the stock 5/64-inch ring grooves. This little trick allows the use of thin, low-tension, modern rings for applications such as stock and NHRA Stock Eliminator where you are trying to eliminate friction to reduce heat and increase gas mileage for street applications.

It's always a good idea to check the radial depth of your piston rings by installing the ring as shown. Several radial-thickness rings are available and you wouldn't want to find out there were incorrect rings in your pistons. The engine will lock up on the dyno for sure!

Oil Ring Rails

Some piston designs require an oil ring support rail. I have used them in many highly stressed applications and they simply do the job. They are a little tricky to install and remove, but the photos below show an easy way to do this.

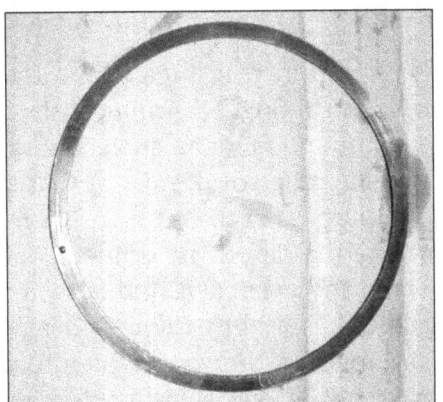

1 This is an oil ring support rail. It is used when the compression height is short enough that the piston-pin bore is in the oil ring.

2 The oil ring support rails are a little tricky to install without scratching the piston.

3 The rail flexes quite a bit before it becomes permanently out of shape.

4 When the ring is partially installed, use a smooth tool to secure it in the groove.

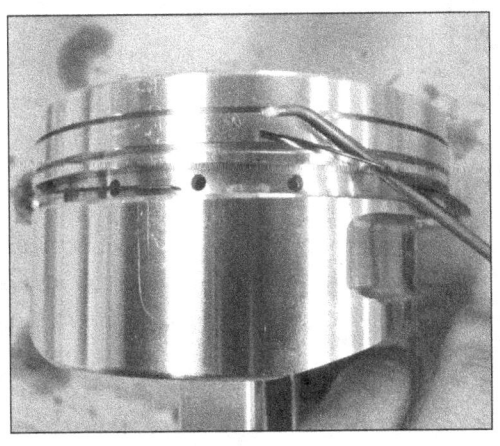

5 Carefully guide the end of the support rail into the groove. Be careful; these have a lot of tension and can get away from you.

6 Make sure the dimple is down, or away from the oil ring, and is in the open space above the piston pin. Also, make sure that the radial thickness of the support rail is correct and does not stick out past the land on the piston.

seals only partially with ring tension. The rest of the job is done with the positive pressure on the top side of the ring, pushing it down against the bottom of the top ring groove. With the two flat surfaces sealing against each other, the pressure behind the ring pushes the ring against the cylinder wall.

The most common type of top ring is a moly-faced ring. These rings work for 98 percent of stock and high-performance naturally aspirated applications. They are typically made of a ductile iron and have a groove machined in the face where the moly is inlaid. They work great in these applications, but, in high-stress applications where power adders are introduced (such as nitrous oxide, turbochargers, or blowers), the moly can flake off and destroy ring seal. A variety of top rings are available that withstand the added stress and heat.

These high-stress compression rings can be made in a variety of different configurations, but the best ones I have used have no coatings or anything to flake off or separate from the piston ring. I normally use a Hellfire top ring (made by MAHLE), which is a steel ring. The guys at CP and Total Seal usually have a good handle on which rings are available for the bore size you are using and can select the right one for your application.

The second ring is not a compression ring; it's an oil "wiper" ring. Many different styles are available. At a quick glance, the edge appears square, but has a taper to scrape oil off the cylinder wall. The second ring on a piston contributes significantly to engine performance. There are a few different styles of second rings. The most common is referred to as a "reverse torsional twist second ring." It has been the industry standard for many years, but offers only a limited performance advantage. These common second rings typically have quite a bit of radial tension, which causes frictional horsepower loss and heat and can allow back-pressure buildup from combustion gases leaking past the top ring, especially if the second ring cap is insufficient. If this pressure is not controlled, it can cause the top ring to float (commonly referred to as "ring flutter"), breaking the combustion seal, and reducing power.

A better version of the second ring has been rediscovered and is referred to as the Napier, or tapered hook groove (THG) ring made by Dana, MAHLE Clevite, etc. These rings provide better oil control than a traditional taper-face ring by using an undercut in the face of the ring, which allows it to collect oil better as it wipes the cylinder wall during the down stroke of the piston. Most important, the second ring acts as a check valve to relieve excessive combustion pressure buildup under the top ring, thus stabilizing it and reducing the possibility of compression gases being trapped between the top and second ring (remember "flutter"). This is why, today, we use more "end gap" clearance on the second ring than on the top ring, and why we never use gapless second rings. Since THG rings do a better job by design, not tension, they also have a reduced radial tension, which reduces heat and frictional horsepower losses.

The third ring is referred to as the oil-control ring. This ring consists of two thin oil rails and an expander to provide different degrees of tension. The purpose of the oil ring rails is to scrape the oil off the cylinder walls, while the expander's job is to force those rails against the cylinder wall and to direct the scraped oil into the passages in the third ring groove. This groove typically has holes or slots that send that oil to the bottom side of the piston so it can return to the crankcase.

Gapless Rings

Gapless rings are available through Total Seal, Inc., which was the originator of that design. I have never used them in my engines and have not felt the need. Total Seal has used them in the second groove and, recently, in the top groove. I never use a gapless ring in a second groove because, in order for the top ring to function properly, pressure cannot

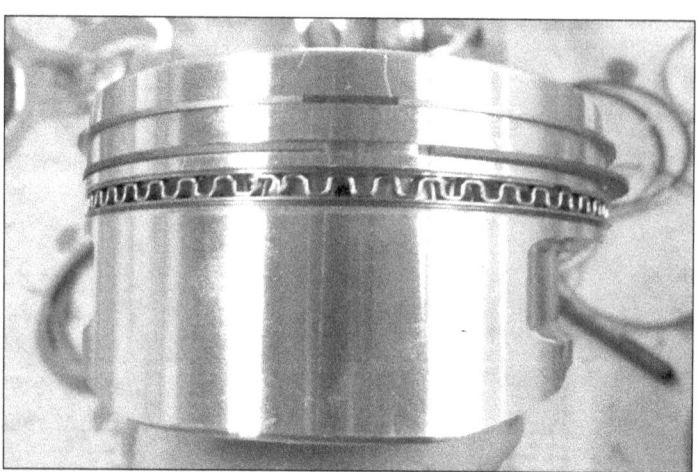

When your rings are installed, you don't need to worry about misaligning the top and second ring before you install the piston in the bore. It doesn't make any difference; they spin in the bores anyway.

be trapped between the top and second ring. I personally have not tested them for use in the top groove as a compression ring, but I do know of some well-known NHRA Pro Stock engine builders who use them as a compression ring with great success. The choice is yours.

Piston Clearances

The clearances that I regard as important are piston-skirt-to-bore clearance, pin-to-pin bore clearance, and ring-land-to-ring vertical clearance.

Piston-skirt clearances, whether forged, cast, or custom, are all different and are determined by skirt shape, piston material, and design. A common misconception is that forged pistons need a great deal of extra clearance. I have seen a variety of different manufacturers' forged pistons have skirt clearance as little as .004 inch and as great as .010 inch. The point is: You cannot treat them all the same simply because they are forged. The piston manufacturer and the engine builder's experience ultimately determine clearance.

On any of the CP pistons that I use, whether they are custom or off-the-shelf design (such as the Bullet Series), I hone the block to the diameter for which the piston is designed. The exception is, perhaps, a marine application where more skirt clearance is required.

I run more pin-bore and bearing clearances than the average engine builder. If the clearance is too tight, there could be a potential problem. If it is a little on the loose side, there seems to be no ill effect. Tight pin clearances can result in piston noise and cylinder/skirt scuffing in cold startups. Tight pin clearances in high-horsepower applications can result in ripping the pin bosses right out of the bottom of the piston due to pin flex. If the pin flexes due to extreme stress, and there is no room for flex, then can you guess what happens?

I recommend .0015-inch clearance at an absolute minimum in any stock or street application. With a thin-wall pin or in very-high-horsepower applications, I run .0022-inch clearance and have run as much as .0030-inch. In engines with that much clearance, the pin bores still had the same hone crosshatch that I witnessed during original assembly. Is it possible that there was a cushion of oil between the pin and the pin bore?

Piston Pins

In street and mild high-performance applications, you can pretty much use the pins that come with the pistons. These generic piston pins are typically made of 4340 chrome-moly steel and are more than adequate for most low-RPM Oldsmobile engines that make 600 or less horsepower. One trick for the TRW piston guy is to use a stock-type big-block Chevrolet (.990-inch diameter) pin in place of the standard (.980-inch diameter) Oldsmobile pin. You have to pin-fit the pistons and rods to the larger .990 dimension, but it can save about 40 grams in pin weight.

In higher-horsepower applications (above 600 hp), I don't feel a piston pin is an area to skimp on. It is relatively inexpensive to buy a quality piston pin. These higher-quality

Oil Ring Tension

There are a variety of oil ring tensions available, and these are usually referred to by the amount of drag they produce, measured in the pounds of force it takes to move a piston equipped with them in an appropriate-sized cylinder. This can be measured with some sort of fish weighing scale found at your local sporting goods store. The force measurement is the average weight while the scale is pulling the piston up the bore with the oil-control ring installed on the piston. When you purchase a (non-performance) stock ring set, the oil ring tension is very high (in excess of 22 pounds of force). You don't want this for any application, especially a performance application. There are generally four oil-control ring tensions available:

Tension	Pounds	Application
High	35+	Found in low-priced stock sets
Standard	20+	Found in performance sets
Low	15+	Special order
Ultra-low	3+	Special order

I have used ultra-low tension in race applications (without a vacuum pump) with success. What you get away with all depends on attention to detail, such as piston quality, cylinder wall roundness, and finish. Which oil ring do you use? You or your engine builder must make that choice depending on your application.

Piston Part Numbers

Manufacturer	Application	Part Number	Material	Oversize
KB (Icon)	260	KB1634	Silv-O-Lite Cast	Std, 0.020
	307	KB1636	Silv-O-Lite Cast	Std, 0.020
	350	KB1633	Silv-O-Lite Cast	Std, 0.030, 0.040, 0.060
	403	KB405	Hypereutectic Cast	Std, 0.025, 0.040
	403	KB1635	Silv-O-Lite Cast	Std, 0.020, 0.030. 0.040, 0.060
	455	KB886	Forged 2618	Std, 0.030, 0.040, 0.060
	455	KB887	Forged 2618	Std, 0.030, 0.040, 0.060
	455	KB132	Hypereutectic Cast	Std, 0.020, 0.030, 0.040, 0.060
	455	KB277	Hypereutectic Cast	Std, 0.030, 0.040, 0.060
	455	KB1631	Silv-O-Lite Cast	Std, 0.020, 0.030. 0.040, 0.060
	455	KB1630	Silv-O-Lite Cast	Std, 0.020, 0.030. 0.040, 0.060
TRW / Speed Pro	307	H801	Cast	Std, 0.030, 0.040, 0.060
	350	L2321F	Forged	Std, 0.030
	350	L2320F	Forged	Std, 0.020, 0.030
	400	L2346F	Forged	Std., 0.040
	403	L2451F	Forged	Std, 0.030
	403	L3067F	Forged	Std, 0.030
	455	L2390F	Forged	Std, 0.030
	455	L2323F	Forged	Std, 0.030, 0.040, 0.060
Federal Mogul/Sterling	260	Z449	Cast	Std., 0.030, 0.040
	307	Z472P	Cast	Std, 0.020, 0.030, 0.040, 0.060
	307	ZH801CP	Hypereutectic Cast	Std, 0.020, 0.030, 0.040, 0.060
	350	Z332AP	Cast	Std, 0.020, 0.030, 0.040, 0.060
	403	Z466P	Cast	Std, 0.020, 0.030, 0.040, 0.060
	455	ZW344	Cast	Std, 0.020, 0.030, 0.040, 0.060
	455	ZW369	Cast	Std, 0.030, 0.040, 0.060
SRP	455	208803	Forged	0.060
	455	206072	Forged	0.030
Venolia	260	3037F	Cast	Std, 0.030
	307	5842	Forged	Std, 0.030
	350	5830	Forged	Specify
	350	5840	Forged	Specify
	350	350-240	Forged	Std, 0.030
	403	403 V	Forged	Std, 0.030
	455	5850	Forged	Specify
	455	5860	Forged	Specify
	455	5861	Forged	Std, 0.030
		Custom Line Also		
Wiseco	455	PT053	Forged	Std, 0.030, 0.040, 0.060 0.0625 0.0625 0.1875
Zollner	307	9371	Cast	Std, 0.040, 0.060
	350	9374	Cast	Std, 0.040, 0.060
	455	9419	Cast	Std, 0.040, 0.060 0.078 0.078 0.1875
Badger	403	B411	Cast	Std, 0.030, 0.060
	455	P511	Cast	Std, 0.030, 0.060 0.078 0.078 0.1875

PISTONS, RINGS AND PINS

Dish (cc)	Weight (grams)	Top Groove (inch)	Second Groove (inch)	Oil Groove (inch)
11.7		0.078	0.078	0.1875
10.3		0.078	0.078	0.1875
24.1		0.078	0.078	0.1875
6.0	674	0.078	0.078	0.1875
19.6		0.078	0.078	0.1875
14.4	557	0.0625	0.0625	0.1875
25.0	583	0.0625	0.0625	0.1875
30.0	600	0.078	0.078	0.1875
15.0	635	0.078	0.078	0.1875
13.3		0.078	0.078	0.1875
36.3		0.078	0.078	0.1875
14.4		0.078	0.078	0.1875
5.8		0.078	0.078	0.1875
0.0	655	0.078	0.078	0.1875
1.0		0.078	0.078	0.1875
	673	0.078	0.078	0.1875
	673	0.078	0.078	0.1875
23.4	672	0.078	0.078	0.1875
18.0	684	0.078	0.078	0.1875
11.8		0.078	0.078	0.1875
11.6	538	0.078	0.078	0.1875
14.4		0.078	0.078	0.1875
23.6		0.078	0.078	0.1875
20.4	673	0.078	0.078	0.1875
39.4		0.078	0.078	0.1875
13.3		0.078	0.078	0.1875
5.0	574	0.0625	0.0625	0.1875
5.0	574	0.0625	0.0625	0.1875
11.8	464	0.078	0.078	0.1875
10.3	538	0.078	0.078	0.1875
0.0		Specify	Specify	Specify
Custom Specify		Specify	Specify	Specify
23.6	480	0.078	0.078	0.1875
20.4	673	0.078	0.078	0.1875
0.0		Specify	Specify	Specify
Custom Specify		Specify	Specify	Specify
13.3		0.078	0.078	0.1875
		0.078	0.078	0.1875
		0.078	0.078	0.1875
20.4	673	0.078	0.078	0.1875

OLDSMOBILE V-8 ENGINES: HOW TO BUILD MAX PERFORMANCE

Piston Part Numbers CONTINUED

Manufacturer	Application	Part Number	Material	Oversize
Arias	403	16100100	Forged	Std, 0.030, 0.040
	455	1610200	Forged	Std, 0.030, 0.060
	Custom Line Also			
Ross	260	104399	Forged	Std, 0.030
	307	74229	Forged	Std, 0.030
	350	75100	Forged	Std, 0.030
	350	78690	Forged	Std, 0.030
	455	38720	Forged	Std, 0.030
	455	54176	Forged	Std, 0.030
	Custom Line Also			
JE	307	154251	Forged	Std, 0.030
	Custom Line Also			
CP Bullet Series	350	B07000-008	Forged Flat Top	4.065 bore
	350 stroker (375)	B07010-068	Forged	4.125 bore x 3.5 stroke 6.000 rod
	455	B07020	Forged	0.030/0.060
	455		Forged Flat Top	0.030/0.060
	455 stroker (496)	B07030	Forged	4.185 bore

Precision Products Performance superfinished wrist pins are top of the line. The surface finish is very smooth, the material is appropriate, and the sizes are always right on the money. This product comes in many sizes and weights and you are sure to find a pin for your application. I had a wrist-pin failure once and it isn't pretty. This is not a place to save money.

This lightweight .090-inch-thick wrist pin is from an engine with only a few dyno pulls. The pin was out of round and it surely would have failed eventually. You want to have lightweight components, but a .090-inch straight-wall pin is not one of them.

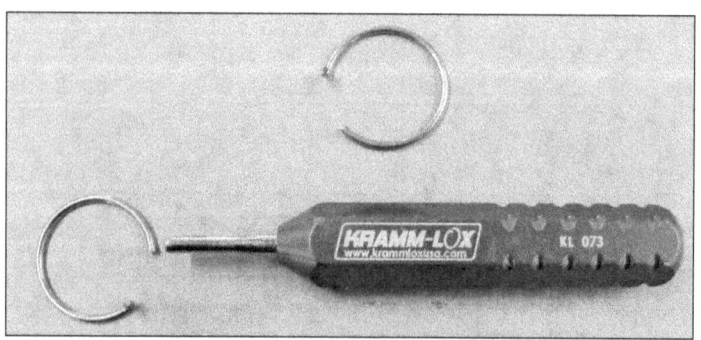

If you hate Spiroloxes, the new Kramm Lox makes life a little easier. These wire locks have a little "tail" of the end of the lock. The tool allows you to install the locks into the grooves inside the piston's pin bores. You must use piston pins and matching grooves designed for the Kramm Lox. You cannot use these new locks in Spirolox-designed pistons and pins.

Dish (cc)	Weight (grams)	Top Groove (inch)	Second Groove (inch)	Oil Groove (inch)
3.0	608	0.078	0.078	0.1875
1.5	563	0.078	0.078	0.1875
11.8	464	0.078	0.078	0.1875
10.3	538	0.078	0.078	0.1875
23.6	480	0.078	0.078	0.1875
3.0	629	0.078	0.078	0.1875
18.0	574	0.078	0.078	0.1875
23.4	650	0.078	0.078	0.1875
10.3	538	0.078	0.078	0.1875
1.4	N/A	1.5	1.5	3 mm
1.4	N/A	1.5	1.5	3 mm
12	N/A	1.5	1.5	3 mm
1.4	N/A	1.5	1.5	3 mm
18.0	N/A	1.5	1.5	3 mm

piston pins are usually made of 9310 steel, which is one of the toughest steels on the planet. A very good set of piston pins generally costs around $200. The better material allows the pins to be lighter due to design and thinner walls.

On most of my Oldsmobile builds using custom pistons, I use .927-inch-diameter pins. They are more than adequate in strength, are lighter in weight, and give more room for the piston designer to place the ring grooves in the best locations without the oil ring groove getting into the pin bore.

Coatings

I have never found a use for piston coatings. I typically use a well-designed, good-quality piston that doesn't tear up cylinder walls. If, after run time, the piston skirts are not wearing the cylinder walls, then what is a coating going to do? If there is no wear, there cannot be much friction. As far as thermal coatings on the piston tops, I have not seen a need for it, either.

When reading spark plugs, especially in nitrous applications, a tuning aid is used to look for little shiny balls of aluminum that usually collect on the porcelain in the spark plug. These shiny aluminum balls are from the tops of the pistons and are due to detonation. This tells you how close you are to having optimum timing or having too much timing. You do not see that with thermal-coated piston tops. One-half degree of ignition timing on a nitrous engine is all it may take to cross the line, detonate, and blow right through that coating without warning.

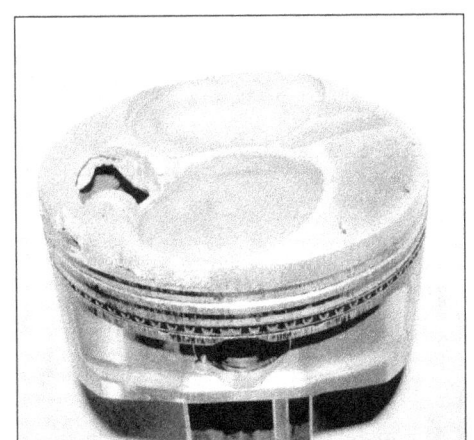

Can you say "lean"? When a piston burns like this, it doesn't take a rocket scientist to figure it out.

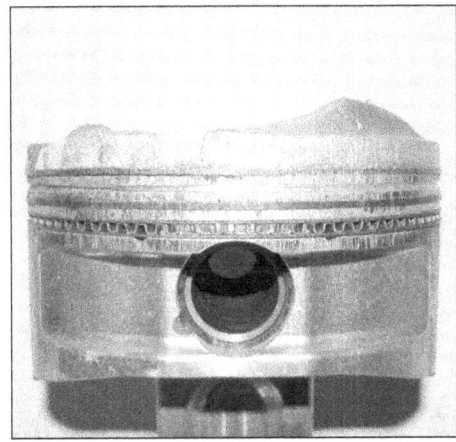

When a piston starts burning at the exhaust valve pocket, and burns down that side, it's lean!

Ring Gaps

Piston ring end gaps are not as critical as some may think. The minimum gaps are the most critical; piston ring butting destroys a ring and wears a cylinder very quickly. Each piston ring (top, second, and oil-control rings) needs to have an end gap different from one another to function properly because each ring serves a different purpose and is affected by heat differently.

Top-ring end gaps are usually set at a minimum to control blow-by or leakage past the ring. Ideally, you want the gap to be nearly closed at the maximum temperature that occurs. However, I have not really seen excessive blow-by or horsepower loss due to ring gaps that are well above the minimum recommended. This is another area (like bearing clearance) where it fails if it is too tight, but there is no major issue with your engine if it is too loose.

Second-ring gap should be larger than the compression-ring gap above it. The controlled leakage of the second ring allows the compression ring to lie flat against the ring land and seal. I believe tight second gaps are what cause the old term "ring flutter." When gapping your second rings, simply gap the ring about 30 percent larger than the top gap. If you make a mistake and it is larger than that, don't worry about it. Just use it. In 2005, when I had set the NSCA Limited Street record at 7.90 seconds at 175 mph, I was testing larger second-ring gaps that were .060 inch. With a gap that large, I expected combustion oiling but never saw it and set the record on the first pass off the trailer.

The oil-control rings should always have some gap. What I mean by that is: If the oil-control rings are designed for the bore size you are using, the roundness of the ring conforms to the cylinder wall and the gap is meaningless. In the event you have a cylinder that has a smaller diameter than the oil-control ring is designed for, you should make sure that there is a minimum of .010-inch rail end gap. This is difficult to check because the rails are very thin and flimsy. You have to install one rail in the cylinder and press that rail against the cylinder wall firmly and inspect it. In the event there is less than .010 inch, you probably have the wrong ring for that bore size.

What is the proper ring gap in a high-performance Oldsmobile engine? You can gap your rings tighter in an engine that has been honed with a torque plate and is perfectly round. If that isn't the case, you better loosen it up a bit. The gaps on engines with power adders (superchargers/nitrous oxide) have to be opened up farther. The more boost/nitrous horsepower increase, the more top-ring gap is required. Increased gaps are safer and have no risk of the ring butting due to unexpected heat introduced into the engine. The second rings are to be set 30 percent larger than the top-ring gap.

I recommend the following for setting the absolute minimum top-ring end gaps for torque-plate-honed round cylinders.

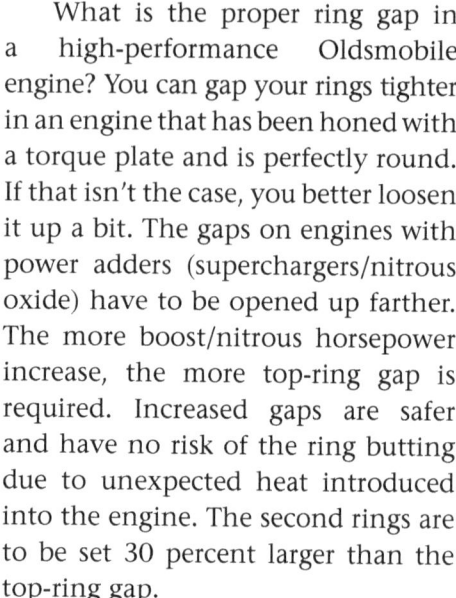

Top Ring Gap	
Bore Size (inches)	Naturally Aspirated (minimum)
3.875	.011
4.000	.012
4.057	.013
4.087	.014
4.125	.015
4.155	.017
4.185	.018
4.250	.022
4.320	.024
4.350	.025

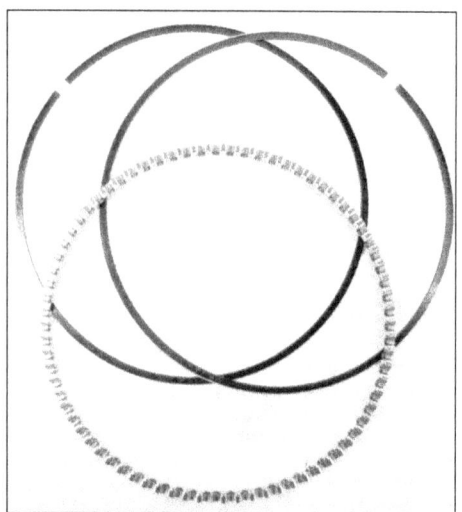

These are Hastings-type oil rings. This style of expander has an unlimited amount of drag choices available through Total Seal.

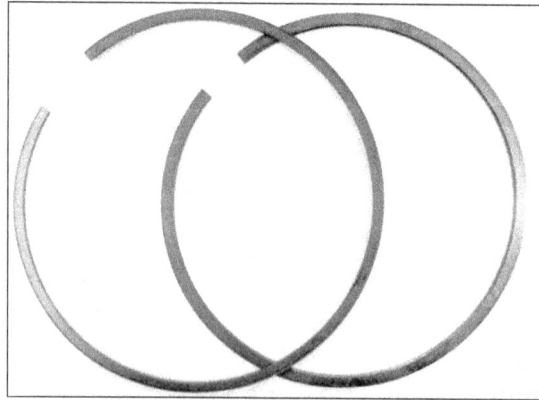

There are so many types of rings available today, that it doesn't pay to purchase a generic set. Get the best ring for your application.

PISTONS, RINGS AND PINS

Installing Spirolox

The circular clips commonly used in forged pistons to retain a full-floating piston pin can be tricky to install and/or remove. They're commonly called Spirolox pistons and the frustration and fingertip wounds they can cause are legendary among professional engine builders. Amateurs may find the task of installing or removing them impossible. It's not, of course, if you know the proper technique. The photos show how I do it.

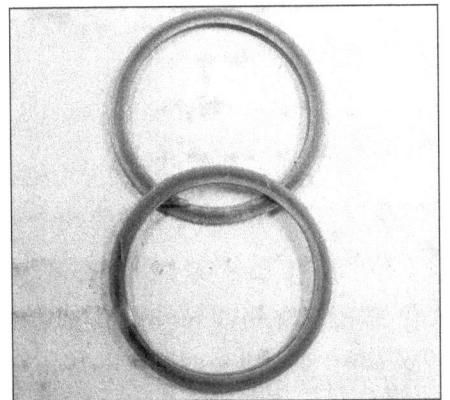

1 Always count the Spiroloxes before you assemble an engine. You don't want to install the last piston and find you have locks left over. If you don't count them first, you will have to pull everything apart to out find if you left one out by mistake, or if the piston company gave you the gift of an extra one.

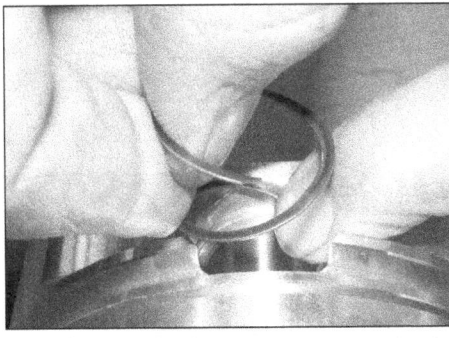

2 Installing a Spirolox is not that difficult.

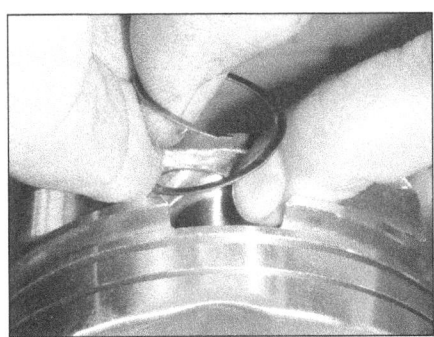

3 You just need a firm grip. It can stretch and spring back.

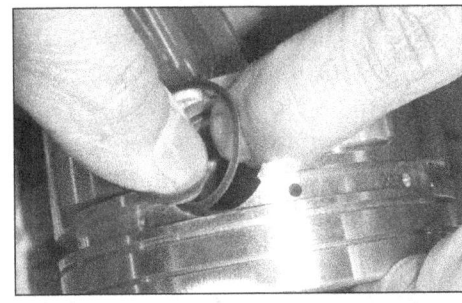

4 You may have bloody fingers after your first couple of tries.

5 Once it's past the halfway point, you are nearly home free!

6 You just keep walking the ring around the piston.

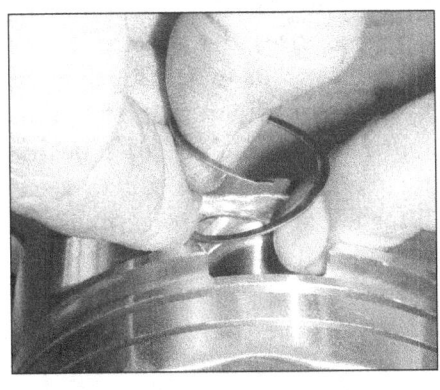

7 Make sure you leave the tail past the removal notches. If you don't, it will be difficult to remove.

8 CP pistons include lock-removal notches. Some cheaper pistons don't have them. If they are a machining option, you will want them. Trust me!

OLDSMOBILE V-8 ENGINES: HOW TO BUILD MAX PERFORMANCE

CHAPTER 6

OILING SYSTEM

For years, Oldsmobile engines have been noted for having a problematic oiling system that needs a number of modifications to make these engines survive in high-performance applications. Although the factory oiling system could be designed better, I have not found it to be a problem. Over the years, I have performed all of the well-known oiling-system modifications, including using oil restrictors, shimming oil pumps, polishing or painting intake valleys, porting oil passages, drilling main-bearing feed holes larger, etc. Also, over the years, I have eliminated these practices one by one; none of these modifications did a darn thing other than waste my time. An old saying goes, "If it ain't broke, don't fix it." It holds true here. My 1,200-hp 8,800-rpm 403-ci small-block has made an awful lot of successful quarter-mile passes without any of the above-listed modifications. The secret to the Oldsmobile oiling system is to leave it alone.

Oiling-System Flow Path

Pressurized engine oil from the oil pump first travels through the main cap and goes through the passage that leads to the outside portion of the oil filter. It then passes through the outside portion of the oil-filter media, is filtered, and travels up through the center of the oil filter, through the screw-in portion of the oil-filter adapter. From there, the oil pressurizes the driver-side main oil gallery. This main oil gallery runs from the rear main to the front main journal, feeds the five main bearings, the five cam bearings, and driver-side lifter bank. At the front main journal, the oil crosses over in the block behind the upper main bearing shell and feeds the passenger-side oil gallery, which feeds the passenger-side lifter bank. At the end of the

The Melling high-volume oil pump works great right out of the box in 99.99 percent of high-performance Oldsmobile applications. I do not recommend shimming the spring on the pumps because it is factory-set at 65 psi, which is plenty of oil pressure for any engine.

OILING SYSTEM

passenger-side lifter gallery is the 3/8-inch pipe plug with the spit hole to lubricate the distributor gear.

It appears that there are many components for the driver-side oil passage to feed. That is true, but as long as all related components are positioned and clearanced properly, there is no issue with this method of oiling. Certainly a priority main oiling system is a better method of feeding the lower end, but over the years I have proven that this method of oiling is satisfactory if you pay attention to detail.

1 It all starts at the oil pump. Pressurized oil flows through this hole in the main cap. I haven't found the need for porting this area.

2 From the main cap, oil is transferred to this hole in the block, which leads to the oil filter.

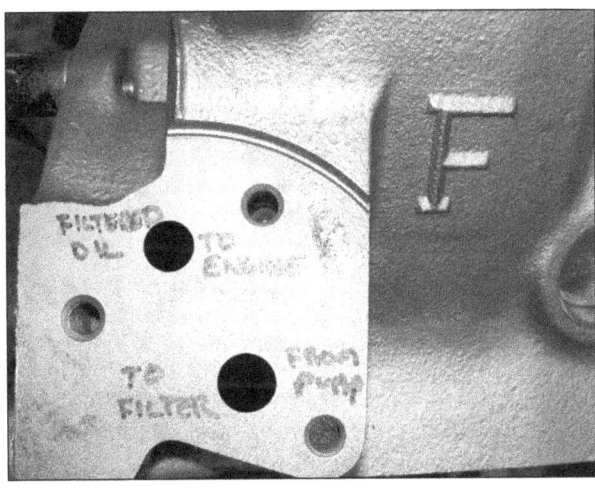

3 Engine oil travels from the pump passage shown previously, which is the lower of the two holes shown.

4 The lower hole is connected to the outside portion of the oil filter, which is where debris is captured.

5 Plugging the bypass is done by drilling and tapping for a 1/8-inch pipe plug. It is commonly thought that you always have unfiltered oil because the bypass spring is set at 12 psi or so. The filter inlet passage and bypass passage are connected therefore it is closed under pressure. But if the differential of pressure between the inside and outside of the filter media is greater than the spring pressure, the bypass opens and allows the engine to receive oil.

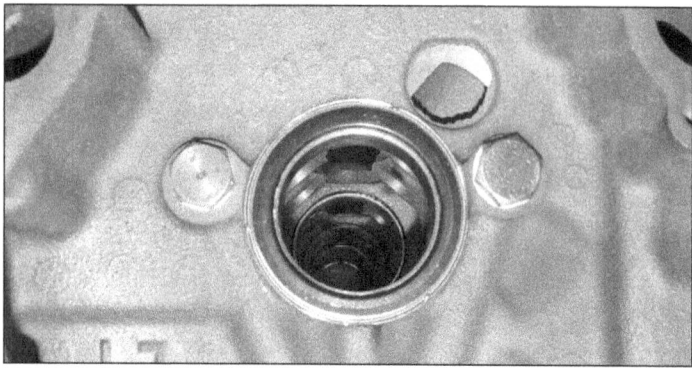

6 Filtered oil that enters the top hole in the passenger-side rear of the engine block travels through the passenger-side oil gallery, which feeds the mains, eight passenger-side lifters, and cam bearings. Although it seems to be an awful lot of items to feed oil to, I have not found it to be an issue.

7 This main-bearing feed hole is connected to the passenger-side oil gallery only. Cam bearings receive oil through an open area between the drilled cam-bearing feed hole and the drilled main-bearing feed hole.

8 When oil arrives at the front of the passenger-side oil gallery and feeds the front main and cam bearing like the other four, it then transfers through that common passage and feeds the driver-side oil gallery.

9 This passage feeds the driver-side lifter bank. If you choose, you can restrict that lifter bank by inserting a restrictor here, although I don't feel it is necessary.

Oil Restrictors

Oil is the lifeblood of any engine, but it's particularly valuable in a high-performance Olds V-8. Directing where it should be routed could mean the use of oil restrictors, but do you really need them?

Cam-Bearing Restrictors

According to all the experts, the first area that needs oil restrictors is the cam bearings. Available for purchase through a few companies are cam bearings with smaller oil-feed holes, screw-in type, or pound-in aluminum cam-bearing restrictors. The cam journal riding on a babbit bearing surely doesn't need any oil, with all the valvesprings pushing on the camshaft, right? In the past I have seen enough wasted cam bearings to figure out that lack of oil was the culprit.

Years ago, I ran aluminum pound-in cam-bearing restrictors, and I found them loose on occasion and resting against the main bearing shell, partially blocking oil flow to the main bearing. I started using screw-in-style restrictors to eliminate that issue. Once, I purposely left the restrictors out of one of my own engines to see if it made an oil-pressure difference, and it didn't. I did notice, however, that my cam bearings looked better. They need a cushion of oil, just like all rotating parts that have metal-to-metal contact. I since have had specially made cam bearings that have a slot machined into the back side, which allows the cam bearing feed hole to be rotated in a position that better oils the journal. This actually oils the cam bearings more for better bearing wear and does not affect engine oil pressure.

Lifter-Bore Restrictors

I haven't found a need for these, either. I have also restricted the oil-feed holes in the lifter bores and left them out on purpose after a freshen-up and never noticed a difference in oil pressure or oil flow to the top of the engine. The lifter internals and lifter-hole placement have designed in them a method of restricting oil that seems to be more of a restriction than your typical .030- to .060-inch feed hole that builders typically use for their lifter-bore restrictors. Flat-tappet lifters, whether solid or hydraulic, have highly restrictive orifices inside that allow minimum oil flow through.

Roller lifters do not have any restricted internals and have the machined oil-feed hole on the body of the lifter instead of the oil band like its flat-tappet-style counterparts. The way the roller lifter passes oil to the pushrod is through the clearance between the lifter bore and the body, which is usually about .002 to .003 inch. When the lifter is resting on the camshaft's base circle, there is little or no flow of oil because the lifter oil band is below the lifter-bore feed hole. As the cam lobe lifts the roller lifter up the lifter bore, the recessed oil band is then exposed to the lifter-bore feed hole and is pressurized. Oil moves through the clearance between the lifter body and the bore to the pushrod. It is actually a pretty simple and ingenious way of metering the oil to the rockers because there are no tiny orifices to plug up with debris.

Main-Bearing Modifications

This is yet another so-called must-do modification that does not need to be done. In fact, it could actually be a negative. Just like a fire sprinkler system, the main feed pipe must have enough size and volume to be able to feed each sprinkler head. If the first few sprinkler heads consume too much water due to incorrect sizing, the last heads in the main receive less or no water. Drilling out your main bearing holes larger can provide a greater leak, which creates the same scenario.

All Clevite main bearings manufactured for the Oldsmobile engine have a 3/16-inch-wide feed hole and a 3/16-inch full groove, which allows

This threaded main bolt hole is connected to one of the oil filter galleries. I have found that sealer is not required.

the engine oil to flow 360 degrees around the main journal. Drilling the feed hole in the main bearing to 5/16 inch (as many people do) only provides a greater leak over the top of the journal, but doesn't send any more oil around the journal due to the groove width remaining at 3/16 inch.

Some builders, myself included, have slotted the hole with a 3/16 endmill, creating a larger area for the oil to flow into the groove. I do not perform this modification anymore because I have found that it does not reduce main-bearing wear. The original designs of the main bearings are perfect the way they are. I build all my engines with unmodified oil-feed holes. Leave them alone; they are perfect the way that they were originally manufactured.

Lifter Gallery Plugs

Two lifter gallery plugs are located in the front of the block behind the timing chain, one of which has a tiny spit hole to lubricate the timing chain. I usually plug this hole; the timing chain gets plenty of oil without it. I have left the spit hole in there also, and never found it to affect oil pressure. It's your choice but I would plug it, whether you weld it shut or

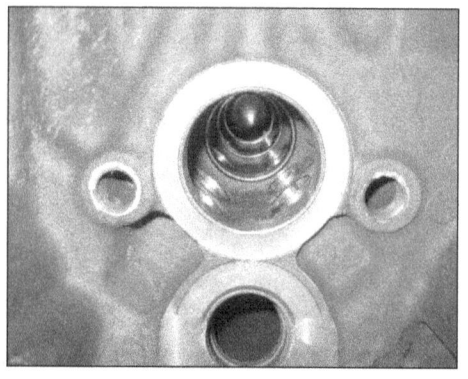

The DX blocks take a 3/8-inch pipe plug rather than the straight-thread hex plugs on every other Olds engine.

The most commonly used oil pump is the Melling MHV-22 high-volume oil pump with bolt-on pickup. If this pickup matches the depth of the pan, it does an adequate job. Deeper pans require the use of extended pickups available through Olds Performance Products and Moroso Performance.

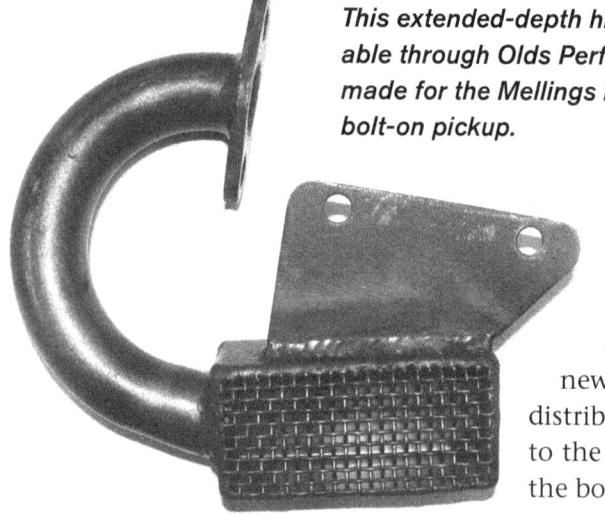

This extended-depth high-flow pickup is available through Olds Performance Products and is made for the Mellings high-volume oil pump with bolt-on pickup.

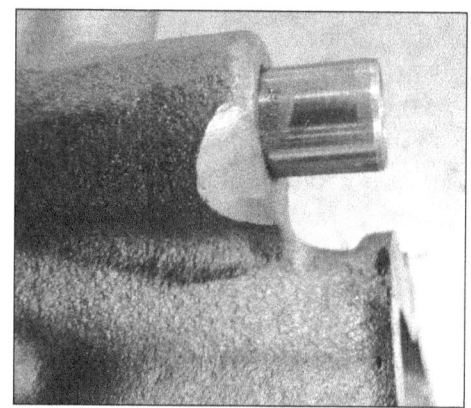

When using six-point nuts and studs, you more than likely have to clear the Melling pump to clear the nut. Many people have an oil pressure problem because the pump is held up by the nut and is not seated on the main cap.

just fill the back of the plug with silicone.

The lifter galleries in the back of the engine have one 3/8 pipe plug in the bellhousing area, which is to remain plugged, and one behind a 29/32 cup plug that has a small spit hole to lubricate the distributor gear. I recommend keeping the hole to lubricate the distributor gear. If your engine is not equipped with one of these 3/8-inch pipe plugs with the distributor gear spit hole, the easiest thing to do is get a 3/8-inch brass hex pipe plug (brass is the easiest to drill) and drill a .020- to .030-inch hole in that plug.

When installing the pipe plug in this passage, make sure that the head of the pipe plug does not protrude into the distributor-housing bore. You will not be a happy camper if you have your new engine installed and the distributor doesn't drop in due to the pipe plug protruding into the bore.

Oil Pumps

You have basically two choices for high-performance oil pumps in Oldsmobile engines: the Melling-manufactured M-22FHV high-volume oil pump with the bolt-on pickup and the Titan gerotor-style high-volume pump. The Melling pump produces about 20 percent more volume than a stock Oldsmobile oil pump, due to its taller gears and larger housing. I do not recommend modifying these pumps; I have not seen any of these modifications improve the pump. The common modifications include making the inlet larger, shimming the spring for more pressure, and porting the flow path.

Every oil pump has a relief valve, and the pressure on these pumps is set between 60 and 65 psi. This means that when the oil pressure meets that 65-psi threshold, the relief valve opens, and the pump stops producing pressure. It is a common belief that shimming the spring on the pump increases oil pressure. That is only partially true. This increases your oil pressure when your engine oil is thick or cold, but when the oil thins out (at operating temperature), the oil pressure isn't enough to open the relief valve. Shimming the spring doesn't increase hot oil pressure.

OILING SYSTEM

Many two-bolt flanges on this and other Oldsmobile high-volume pump pickups are not flat. You may have to hit it on the belt sander. Be sure to check it.

I made this tool out of an old main cap to measure and set oil-pump relief pressure. I bolt an oil pump on the main cap and spin the pump with a hand drill above a bucket of oil. As I close the ball valve to simulate a restriction (such as clearances in the engine), the pressure rises. When I fully close the valve, the relief valve in the oil pump opens, causing the outlet pump pressure to go no higher than I set it. Titan and Melling pumps are set at 60 pounds. There is no reason to set your oil pump any higher than that unless you enjoy cleaning engine oil off everything when you blow an oil filter apart.

A word of warning: On more than one occasion I have seen where a person had shimmed the pressure relief valve so much that the cold-oil pressure was high enough to blow the oil filter apart. The only way to create more oil pressure is to have a larger-volume pump.

Titan oil pump is the best oil pump for the Oldsmobile engine. They are rather pricey but are a top-quality pump that has tremendous volume, an adjustable pressure-relief valve, and an anti-cavitation gerotor design. I use the Titan pump in all serious engine builds, because you can't have too good an oil pump for your engine. You can purchase these oil pumps with a few different choices of pump gear widths, which affects the output (volume). These ultimate-high-performance Oldsmobile oil pumps are usually made to order, so your pan depth needs to be determined when that order is placed. These pumps are rather large and require oil-pan modifications for them to fit, unless you purchase one of the BTR/Moroso aluminum pans.

Oil Pressure

A common belief is that engines need 10 psi of oil pressure per 1,000 rpm. I have not found that to be that

The Titan oil pump has an adjustable pressure regulator and a tremendous flow rate.

The Titan oil pump is a very bulky unit and doesn't fit stock pans or any pan that is not designed for it.

case at all. I have built many successful Oldsmobile engines that have had no more than 35 to 40 psi of oil pressure, maximum, at elevated engine RPM. I consider 40 psi of hot oil pressure to be the norm for any of these engines with proper clearances. A few engines I have built had a hard time achieving 35 psi of hot oil pressure. They have been inspected after dyno pulls or after a period of street miles and the bearings did not have a scratch in them. The only time low oil pressure indicates a problem is when that low oil pressure is different than what the engine normally has. Don't be hung up on achieving high oil pressure numbers on an Oldsmobile engine.

Oil-Pump Drives

You don't need any special oil-pump drive. Melling manufactures an inexpensive stock replacement (PN IS22F), which has never failed me in any application. High-strength shafts are not required. Spend your money on something more important that gives you something on an ET slip.

Oil-Filter Adapters and Oil Filters

The factory oil-filter adapters work rather well. The only modification worth considering on these is to block the bypass passage to prevent unfiltered oil from reaching the engine. Normal operation with the factory bypass actually filters all of the engine oil. The bypass only opens when the pressure differential between the outside and the inside of the filter is increased due to restricted filter media. When this occurs, there is no loss of oil pressure at the gauge so the engine receives unfiltered oil and you never know there is an issue.

However, if the bypass is plugged, and the filter media gets clogged with debris, there is a loss of oil pressure at the gauge and you know something is going on immediately. The only negative in this situation is that if you are driving a long distance, you cannot just pull to the side of the road and change an oil filter. But in reality, if the filter gets plugged enough to cause a drop in oil pressure, it's probably too late at that point anyway. To

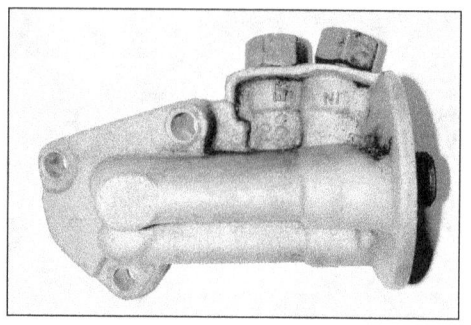

This oil filter adapter is from a 350 diesel engine and has oil cooler provisions. If you need an oil cooler, it works and is even marked so that it is plumbed correctly.

block the bypass, pry the sealing disc out with a screwdriver and remove the assembly. After that, drill and tap the hole for a 1/8-inch pipe plug, and you are good to go.

The oil filter I prefer to use is the WIX PN 51258, which measures 3⅜-inch OD and is 4¼ inches tall. My second choice is the WIX PN 51522. It's ideal if you have some clearance issues with your headers. It has a 2⅞-inch OD and it's 4⅜ inches tall.

I recommend that you avoid using Fram and AC oil filters. I have had issues with these but have never had an issue with the WIX brand. I think a media filter is better than a screen-type; the paper media filter

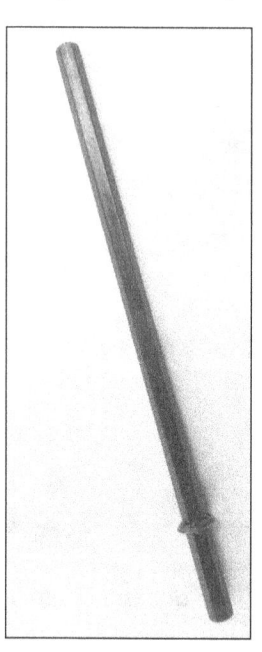

The Melling oil pump shaft works great in any application and is very inexpensive. No need to spend your hard-earned money on anything else.

Oil-filter-adapter gaskets are available through FelPro.

The PN 51258 WIX Oldsmobile filter fits most applications and is the best one to use. The PN 51522 works well in tight header clearance applications.

I have never had an issue with a WIX filter; therefore, I use one on every BTR engine. Oil enters the outside portion through the little holes around the outside, passes through the media, and then supplies filtered oil through the center hole and back to the oil filter adapter.

has a finer micron rating and does a better job.

The best piece of advice I can give regarding oil filters is to buy an oil-filter cutter and use it. It is a good practice to cut open the filter during oil changes to help inspect the engine. It is especially important to cut filters at the first sign of anything going wrong with your engine. If you hear a noise that you've never heard before, cut the filter and inspect it. If the engine suddenly begins running hot for some reason, cut the filter. Did you lose some ET at the track for no reason? Cut the filter! If you inspect your oil filter at the first sign of anything out of the ordinary going on with your investment, you can catch evidence of a problem before it turns into an expensive disaster.

Oil Pans

Most of the oil pans made for Oldsmobile engines are basically stock oil pans with a deeper rear sump to hold

The best tool you may ever own is an oil filter cutter. I can't stress enough how important it is to monitor your engine oil. When you get in the habit of looking to see what the oil filter traps, you see a pattern. After some experience, you know right away what is normal and what is not. There is virtually no reason for disastrous engine failure if you monitor the engine oil filter.

an extra quart or two of oil. I have not seen any performance improvements with these. Most of the performance that is to be gained in an oil pan is in the front portion. There is simply not enough volume there, and the pan is way too close to the spinning assembly. Unfortunately, the front crossmember is fairly close in most stock chassis, which does not leave much room for increasing oil pan volume at that point.

I recommend against using the Oldsmobile Toronado pan. Years ago I was dyno testing with my NHRA Stock Eliminator 455 W-30 engines and was going nuts trying to figure out why the engine was down about 15 hp. After some thought, I remembered that changing to the Toronado pan was the only change, but I refused to believe that it could kill the horsepower by that much. After many pulls and getting nowhere, I drove home, grabbed the old standard 5-quart pan, went back to the dyno facility and changed pans. After the installation, the power was right back to where it had been previously. I would have bet anyone a great deal of money that it wouldn't have changed the power, but it sure did!

The bottom line with oil pans is to increase volume as much as possible. In my opinion, the best oil pans for the maximum-performance Oldsmobile engines are made of aluminum by Moroso Performance and are designed by and are available through BTR. There are basically two styles available.

The first barely fits factory crossmembers, but does not work with factory-style motor mounts. This oil pan has increased volume in the front, has a side kick-out, and fits a Titan oil pump. This pan is as large as you can get without cutting a crossmember. Steering linkage may hit slightly when making a tight turn. If you want to have a completely bolt-in pan that fits perfectly and has clearance everywhere, run a stock pan.

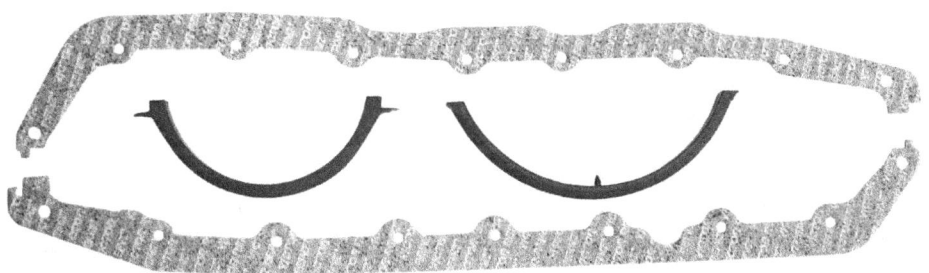

The Victor Tuff Cork oil pan gasket is the best I have used in my Oldsmobile builds.

The second design is the Moroso high-performance aluminum oil pan; the style used on my Starfire and all of the highest-horsepower BTR Oldsmobile engines. I consider this to be the best wet-sump oil pan available for the Oldsmobile engine, period. This pan has tremendous volume, good oil control, and fits Titan oil pumps. However, front motor plate and crossmember modifications are required. If you want the ultimate in wet sump performance, this is the oil pan for you.

This BTR-designed Moroso aluminum oil pan fits the BTR and Jeff Smith girdles, a Titan oil pump, and stock chassis with a motor plate. It is also available for the Program Engineering girdle or no-girdle applications. It's as big as you are going to get without completely cutting the factory crossmember. But you may have to do a little nip or tuck.

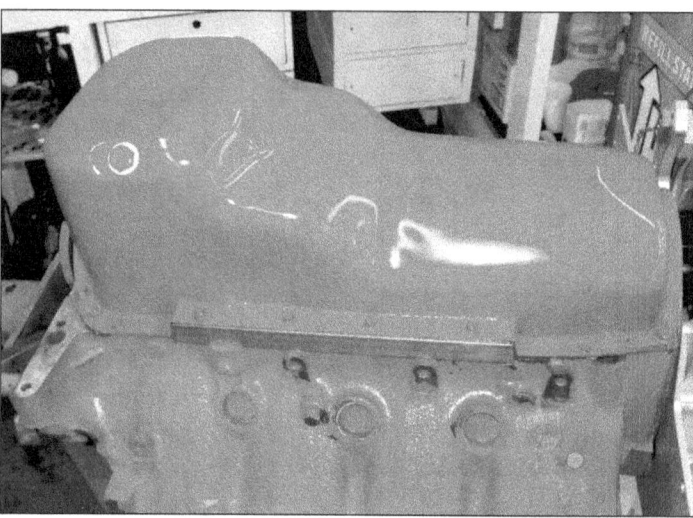

This stock steel pan has been modified for the BTR girdle.

The oil pan for the 2008 and 2009 PHR Engine Masters Challenge engine was as wide as the pan rails and a maximum of 12 inches deep, which is the maximum volume that the rules allowed. The tech officials measured that a couple of times; it's huge! I'm sure it's worth some horsepower. You can't have enough oil pan volume!

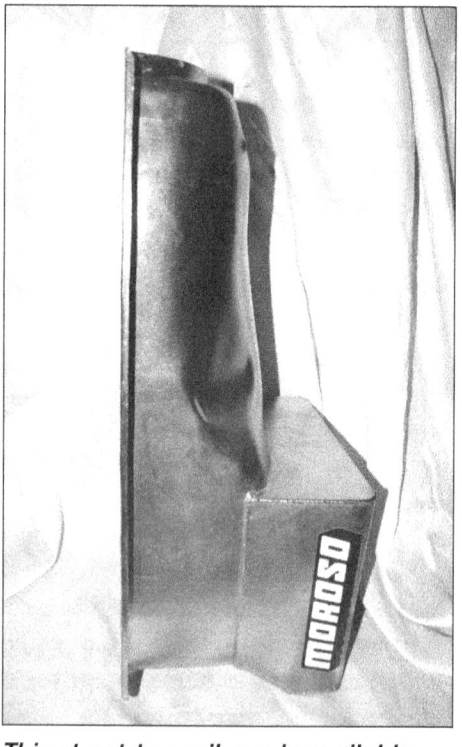

This street-type oil pan is available through Moroso Performance, Olds Performance Products, and Milodon. It holds extra oil in the rear sump, but the front portion is stock and clears just about any chassis.

OILING SYSTEM

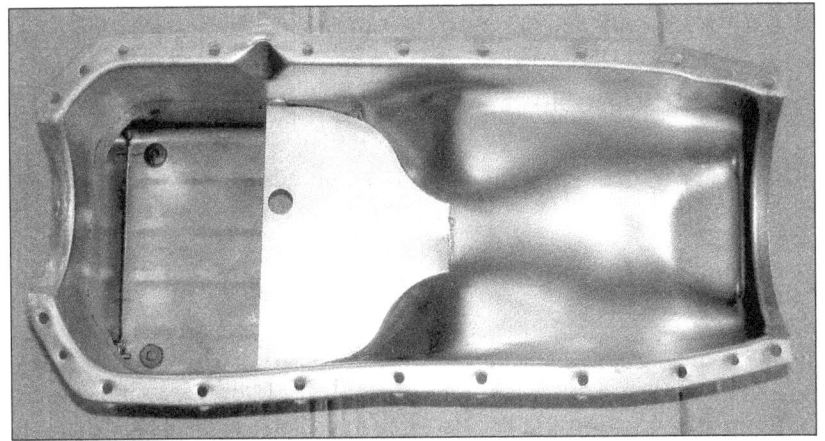

The baffle in these pans prevents oil from uncovering the oil pump pickup upon deceleration. I have seen some stock pans without this baffle. Do not use one with no baffle.

This BTR-designed Moroso aluminum oil pan is about as good as it gets without going to a dry-sump system.

The funny-looking kick-out on the backside of the rear sump is there to clear a Titan oil pump.

The inside of this Moroso pan has a unidirectional windage screen and has as many tricks as can be done in a wet-sump pan. If you want the best oil pan for your Olds engine, it's a Moroso.

Windage Trays

Most of the bolt-in windage trays available are not worth anything. It seems that anything mounted close to the crankshaft just robs horsepower. I don't recommend bolting any devices in your lower end with small-volume, stock-type oil pans. No stainless trays, no rear-pan baffles, no crank scrapers, no nothing. If you increase oil-pan volume by making your own pan, the only thing I suggest to use is the Moroso uni-directional windage screen.

Engine Oils

As you should be aware by now, zinc and some other things have been removed from engine oils, making these oils not compatible with flat-tappet camshafts. There are some alternatives. ZDDPlus is a relatively easy-to-find zinc additive in an 8-ounce bottle, and one of these bottles supposedly adds enough zinc for 5 quarts of oil to get the zinc levels back to where they need to be. You can also purchase racing or non-street-legal oils that already have the proper zinc levels for your engine through Joe Gibbs Racing, Brad Penn, Valvoline, Mobil 1, AMS Oil, and others. Just do your research.

In the 2009 *Popular Hot Rodding* Engine Masters Challenge, I used new Mobil 1 racing 0W-30 oil and noticed the rather dark color. This oil has high levels of zinc and

The newest Valvoline Racing Synthetic is available at Advance Auto stores and seems to work well in the limited time I have been using it. I have used it in brand-new engines and have not found that it caused any ring sealing issues because it's synthetic oil.

OLDSMOBILE V-8 ENGINES: HOW TO BUILD MAX PERFORMANCE

CHAPTER 6

Mobil 1 racing synthetic is the ultimate in performance oil. It contains everything nasty you can think of, and it really stinks so you know it's good stuff! I'll make an educated guess that if you poured this oil into your performance Oldsmobile engine, you would pick up about 25 hp or at least a tenth in the quarter-mile.

This Valvoline racing oil is not available in your average auto parts store; the elevated zinc levels supposedly harm catalytic converters. I have been using this oil in all of my high-horsepower builds.

The standard Mobil 1 oil is a great all-around oil for street/strip applications, and is available just about anywhere.

This new Mobil 1 racing oil was used in the 2009 Popular Hot Rodding *Engine Masters Challenge engine. During a seminar at the Performance Racing Industry trade show in 2009, the claim was made that the oil reduces friction and increases horsepower. I have not heard of a brand of engine oil that didn't claim that. One day soon, I will make some back-to-back dyno tests.*

phosphorus, which some of the others do not have. One other thing I noticed about this particular oil was that it was very clingy, meaning that it didn't run off any of the engine parts like some of the others do. I will be testing this oil more in the future.

The biggest horsepower gains you find in engine oils are not in brands, snake-oil additives, or synthetic versus conventional. Rather, it has to do with the viscosity. The bottom line here is: Thinner oils make more horsepower. I have seen as much as a 15- to 25-hp difference on my engine dyno by switching from conventional 20W-50 oil to the 5W-30 Valvoline synthetic numerous times. Years ago, I did a back-to-back change at the racetrack with my old red 1970 Cutlass, switching between 20W-50 oil and 10W-40 oil, and saw about .1-second ET difference between those two oils.

Some of the oil manufacturers recommend different weight oils for engines with tighter or looser bearing clearances. I have not found that to be true. I have run some high-horsepower engines with very loose bearing clearances with 5W-30 engine oils with 100-percent success. If everything is right in your engine, you don't have a problem with the thin engine oils. My 1,200-hp 403 Oldsmobile Starfire engine has some pretty loose bearing clearances and used the V-853 5W-30 oil, which shouldn't work. Some engine-oil experts tell you that the oil is too thin for this application. Don't be afraid of thin oils if you have paid attention to all the details. If it works for me, chances are it will work for you.

Vacuum Pumps

Belt-driven vacuum pumps are a great addition to your Oldsmobile ride. The original vacuum pumps that were used on racing engines

OILING SYSTEM

derived from factory smog pumps that blew air into exhaust manifolds. Some ingenious racer figured out that if you plumbed the inlet of the pump into the engine, and the outlet to a canister with a breather, it produces a negative pressure in the crankcase and makes more horsepower.

Since then, some manufacturers, such as Moroso Performance, have designed pumps that survive at racing speeds. I have dyno tested with these pumps and it seems to be worth anywhere from 10 to 20 hp, depending on piston ring seal and the amount of vacuum (or negative pressure) in the crankcase. The other advantage is, with that negative pressure in the crankcase, oil leaks are less likely. Rather than a positive crankcase pressure trying to push oil out of every little nook and cranny it can find, it is quite the opposite with the negative crankcase pressure. Another good deal with these pumps is in street applications, where power brakes and the amount of engine idle vacuum is an issue. Just tee into the inlet side of the vacuum pump and voilà! Power brakes!

If you want to use a vacuum pump on your performance Oldsmobile engine, the Moroso enhanced-design pump and bracket fits well in multiple spots on small- and big-block engines. It even can be mounted on an Oldsmobile application using a complete March Serpentine Conversion Kit such as Doug Lang's 496 pump-gas street engine that has all the toys, including air conditioning.

The Moroso four-vane vacuum pump (PN 22641) is a great choice for street/strip applications. It produces plenty of vacuum and is a great addition to just about any ride. Usually, 8 to 12 in Hg (inches of mercury) gives significant horsepower and oil-leak reduction. Keep in mind that the more vacuum, or negative pressure, the lower the oil pressure will be due to matching negative pressure at the inlet of the oil pump.

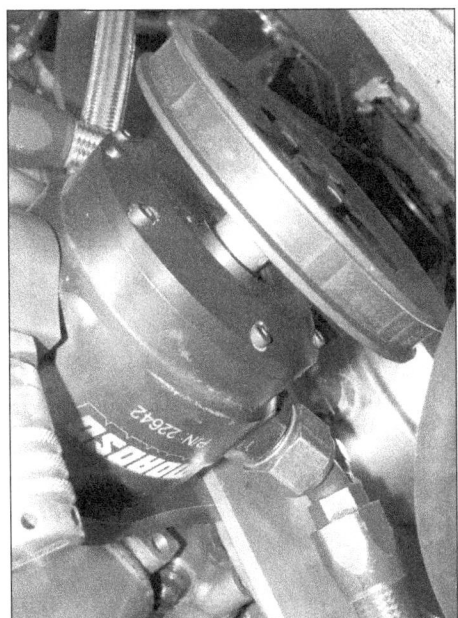

The Moroso Enhanced Design vacuum pump (PN 22642) sucks the sides of the block if you are not careful. This pump has produced 23 in Hg negative pressure on my 403-ci nitrous engine. The amount of vacuum on your engine basically tells you how good the ring seal is. If crankcase vacuum is lower than it is normally on your engine, it means that your engine has a leak somewhere, or there is an issue with the piston rings.

CHAPTER 7

CYLINDER HEADS AND INDUCTION

The wide range of both factory and aftermarket cylinder heads and intake manifolds offer many potential combinations for Olds performance enthusiasts. The proper combination for you will depend on many factors, and this chapter outlines how to best feed your angry Rocket.

Factory Small-Block Cylinder Heads

The Oldsmobile factory-production small-block cylinder heads are identified by a number cast into the front lower portion of the head next to the number-1 and number-8 cylinders. The oldest castings have a lower number and the latest production castings have a higher number. All of the small-block combustion chambers have roughly the same shape, but vary in volume. The same goes for the intake and exhaust ports on the muscle-car-era castings. They did change quite a bit in the later smog engine years. These castings are undesirable for performance use. These cylinder heads can certainly be made better with some work, but it is generally best to use the older castings.

The most desirable small-block Olds cylinder heads are the number-6 and number-7 castings.

The most common modification done to these small-block Olds castings is to install the 2.000-inch-diameter intake and 1.625-inch-diameter exhaust valves from the big-block. With the right seat cutters, the bowl is larger and the bowl shape allows a better transition for the air/fuel mixture to exit the valve, thus increasing available horsepower. Installing these larger valves should be standard procedure, even for stock rebuilds. Stock-type steel

The Edelbrock Performer RPM is by far the most popular Oldsmobile cylinder head ever produced in the aftermarket. They will work in Oldsmobile applications ranging from mild small-blocks all the way up to max-effort big-block engines of more than 800 hp.

Cylinder Head Chamber Size

Engine (ci)	Cylinder Head	Chamber (cc)
330	3	60
330	4	60
350	5	64
350	6	64
350	7	64
350	7a	64
350	8	79
350	3A	75
403	4A	83
307	5A	67
307	7A	64

CYLINDER HEADS AND INDUCTION

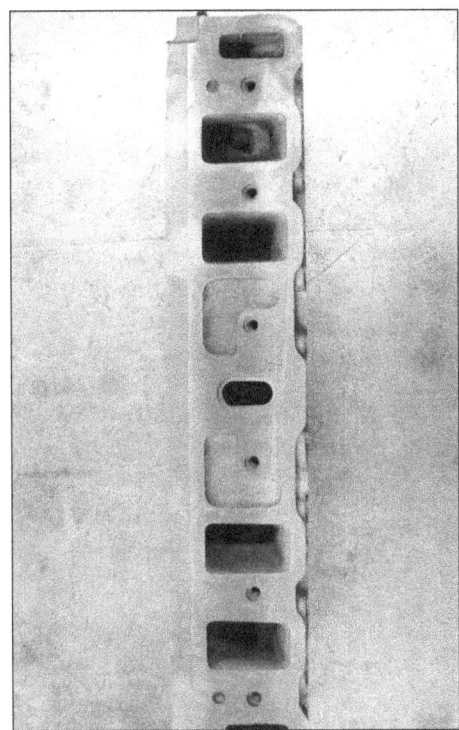

The factory iron small-block cylinder head has some very small intake ports that are easy to see.

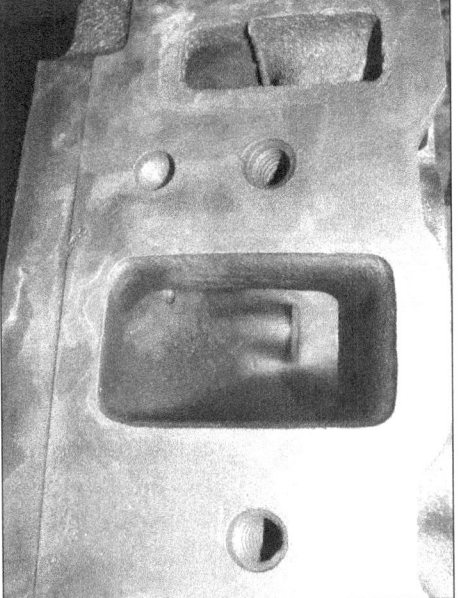

If you want a free port job on your small-block Olds heads, put the die grinder down. Get big-block heads, mill the deck surface so you can get the combustion chamber volume, and presto! you have a ported head.

This factory iron big-block "A" cylinder head has the largest ports I have seen. If you bolt a set of big-block heads on a small-block, it's like bolting on a ported head. Some manifolds may not have enough material and runner volume to match, but the Edelbrock Victor (PN 2812) does.

Oldsmobile small-block cylinder heads have a number, such as this popular number-7 casting.

big-block Oldsmobile valves are available through SBI and other sources and are relatively inexpensive. This modification is easily performed during the valve-job operation and turns an old, rusty, worn-out cylinder head with pitted seats into a set that is in brand-new condition.

Factory Big-Block Cylinder Heads

Oldsmobile factory-production big-block cylinder heads are identified by a letter cast into the front lower portion of the head on the number-1 and number-8 cylinders. The oldest castings (used on the 1965 400- to 425-ci engines) have the letter "A," and the latest big-block production castings have the letter "J." The series ended there. I have not found any considerable difference between the castings, with the exception of the "J" heads. They definitely have the smallest runners of the bunch and are a poor choice for performance use, even with porting. So remember: "J" is for junk.

In years past, I measured intake runner volume in a bunch

CHAPTER 7

These Hurst Olds "D" heads are very rare. The 1972 W-30 "H" heads are probably the rarest; the 1970 W-30 "F" heads are not quite as rare.

Filling the exhaust heat crossovers can never hurt. Steve Curry did a nice job on these "C" heads by pouring in melted aluminum from the port side and then porting the bowl properly. Notice the shape of the port under the intake seat.

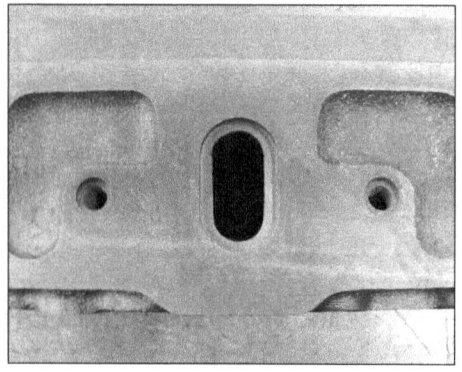

Another method of blocking the exhaust crossover is to machine a pocket on the intake side and press fit or silicone a piece of metal in there.

Cylinder Head Identification

Cylinder Head	Year	Engine Size (ci)	Chamber Size (cc)	Casting Number
A	1965	400/425	82	383821
B	1965–1966	400/425	82	383821
C	1967–1969	425/455	82	394548
Ca	1967–1969	425/455	82	394548
D	1968–1969	455	69.75	400370
E	1968–1970	455	82	403686
F	1970	455	82	404438
G	1971	455	82	409100
Ga	1972	455	82	409100
H	1971	455	82	409160
J	1973–1976	455	82	411783
K		Replacement 455	82	413191
Ka	1973–1976	455	82	413191

of different-lettered iron cylinder heads and found that the "E" castings were second in line to the "J" heads in small runner size. The "E" castings are smaller than the others, but only by a few cubic centimeters. The famous "C" head is well known for being the best factory iron cylinder head to use, but I have not found that to be the case.

Of all the factory iron heads I have played with, I have found the "A" heads to be the best in stock form. In my experience, it seems that the rest of the factory cast-iron cylinder heads (A through H) are close enough in runner shape and size so that it does not really matter which one you select for your high-performance Oldsmobile project, especially if you are porting them.

Head Gaskets

When I ran the NHRA Stock Eliminator W-30 engine, I used the factory .017-inch embossed steel shim head gasket. That gasket performed very well at 11:1 compression and I never had a gasket failure. Unfortunately, they are not available anymore and have not been for quite some time. Luckily, I saved all of my used ones and reused them at a later date by glass-bead cleaning them and gluing a .015-inch-thick soft copper wire around the raised combustion ring. They worked like a charm.

A number of head gaskets are available for the Oldsmobile engine. The most popular head gaskets for street applications are the FelPro PN 8171 PT1, the FelPro PN 1155, and the Corteco PN 55660HG in .040-inch-thick and PN 55661HG in .028-inch-thick versions.

I wouldn't say these gaskets are the best choice for aluminum heads. I have had various issues with them. I don't know whether the power levels just happened to be greater on the aluminum-headed engine, which makes that the ultimate cause of failure, or if it was the fact that the heads were aluminum. I don't really know, but when I have an issue with something, I don't use that product again. I don't have time to figure out why some company's product failed, especially when there is something else I can get my hands on that performs reliably. However, I have not had a failure with these gaskets on cast-iron–cylinder-head engines.

The best head gasket in 98 percent of high-performance Oldsmobile applications right now is the Cometic MLS head gasket (MLS stands for multi-layer steel). These gaskets basically consist of two layers of embossed hardened steel and a shim of desired thickness in between. This design allows the builder to select a wide array of thicknesses for the application. I have seen many engines use these in very-high-horsepower turbo and blower applications with varying degrees of success. When they do fail in these applications, it usually ruins something like the block or the cylinder head.

These MLS gaskets are made to order from Cometic and take about four weeks to get your hands on them from time of order. These gaskets are pretty much available in any thickness and bore size when you custom-order them. BTR stocks the commonly used thicknesses, and they are available in .027-, .030-, .036-, .040-, .045-, .051-, .056-, .060-, .065-, .071-, .074-, and .120-inch sizes.

The ultimate setup in cylinder sealing is the copper head gasket with a stainless O-ring embedded into the cylinder head, with a corresponding receiver groove machined in the block. When a Top Fuel car uses a method other than this to seal combustion pressure, I'll try it. Until then, my serious engines are sealed by this method. Copper head gaskets get a bad rap from people, mostly because the O-ring job was performed incorrectly, allowing coolant into the engine. This happens either because the combustion seal is compromised or the head does not sit flat due to improper machining. Trust me, when the job is done properly, there aren't any sealing issues in the highest-horsepower applications.

Copper head gaskets can be purchased from numerous suppliers such as Clark, Hussey, SCE, and Flatout Gaskets and should be ordered with a gasket-bore size .050-inch larger than your engine bore. I prefer the gaskets

The obsolete factory Oldsmobile big-block .017-inch-thick steel shim gasket worked very well in my 11:1 NHRA Stock Eliminator engine.

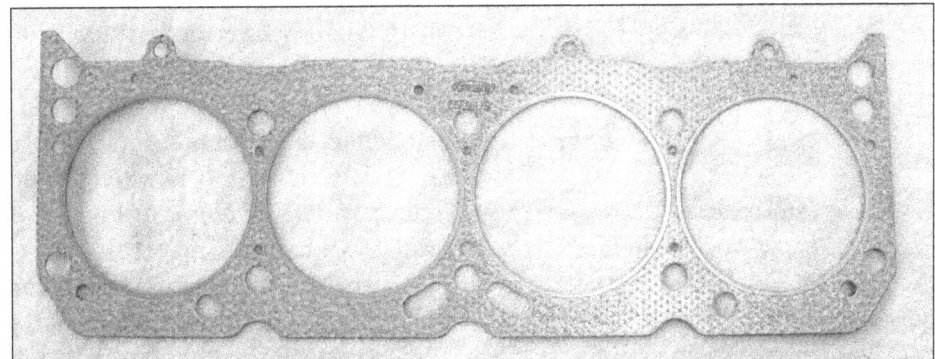
Corteco makes high-quality gaskets. They are available in .028- and .040-inch thicknesses. I only use these on cast-iron head engines. I have seen very slight water seepage on engines using aluminum heads.

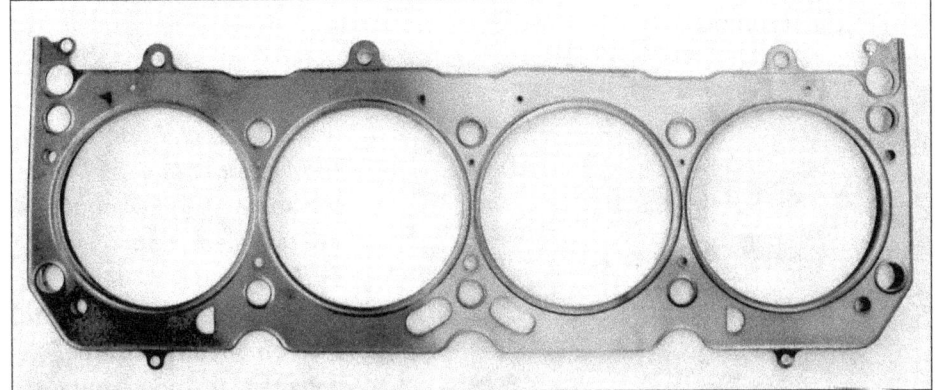
Multi-layer steel gaskets made by Cometic are the ultimate in combustion sealing. They require that the decks be flat and smooth. Don't stress out over the finish; just leave no rough cuts. I have reused them multiple times by carefully cleaning them and applying a very light layer of silicone over the entire gasket.

CHAPTER 7

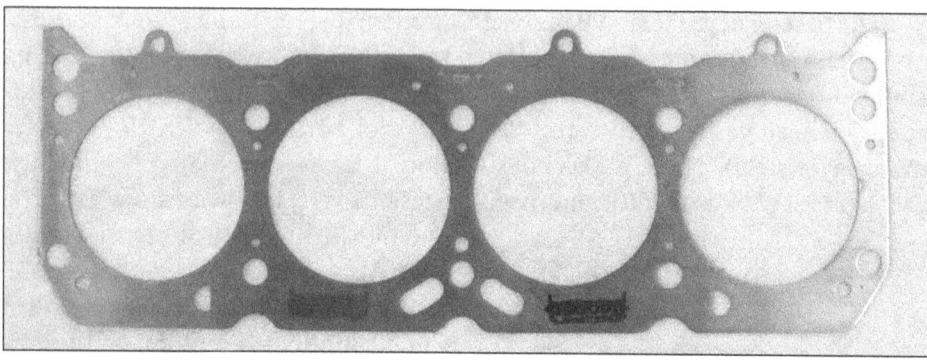

There is no better method of sealing combustion than the copper head gasket with the proper O-ring and receiver grooves machined into the head and block. It is the same method used by 5,000+-hp NHRA Top Fuel cars.

O-rings can be installed in the head or the block. The cylinder head location is preferable.

from Flatout; they are made to order with any bore size and configuration and are made and shipped within a few days.

When performing the O-ring and receiver-groove operation, the locations of the O-ring and receiver groove are absolutely important. They must line up perfectly to each other. When BTR performs this operation, the O-ring and receiver grooves are located off of the cylinder head and block dowel pins, and they are machined on a Cincinnati CNC machine, which makes it easy to get perfect. The cylinder head is machined so that the stainless .041-inch-diameter O-ring protrudes .015 inch from the deck, and the corresponding .040- to .060-inch-wide receiver groove is machined at the same depth into the block.

When you remove a cylinder head torqued up with a copper head gasket, you literally have to pry the gasket off the block because the soft copper embeds into the receiver grooves, which is what seals the combustion pressure. Don't ever let anyone tell you that you don't need a receiver groove in these copper head gasket/O-ring applications. You do.

The Milling Process

Milling cylinder heads for increased compression is a relatively easy operation because Oldsmobile cylinder heads are square and can easily be cut without any special fixturing. I have milled factory iron, Batten, and Edelbrock Performer RPM heads as much as .100 inch for certain applications. The lowest combustion chamber volume I ever had on an Edelbrock Performer RPM head with the standard combustion chamber was on the 2009 Engine Masters Challenge engine at 46 cc. With a range of 77 cc to 46 cc, you should have a variety of compression ratios available for your simple mill job.

Even at that small 46-cc level, the cylinder head seemed to have adequate deck thickness for the 640 hp that the particular engine produced. The deck thickness and stiffness required on the cylinder heads has to be determined according to the amount of horsepower the

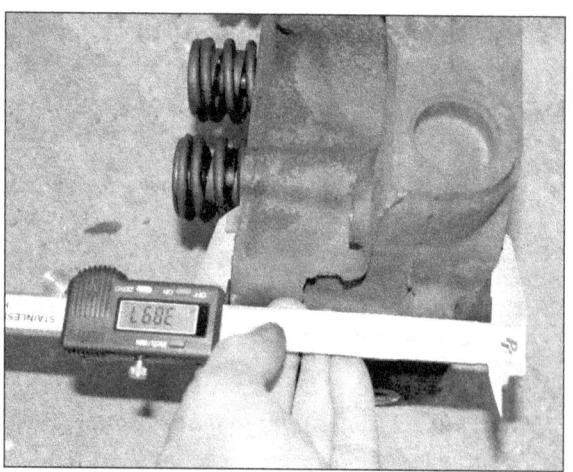

Factory iron heads, Batten, and Edelbrock Performer RPM cylinder heads all have the same height when they are unmilled. A good way to determine if a head has been milled and to estimate the combustion chamber volume is to know what the stock chamber volume is and then calculate .006 inch removed per cubic centimeter reduced.

CYLINDER HEADS AND INDUCTION

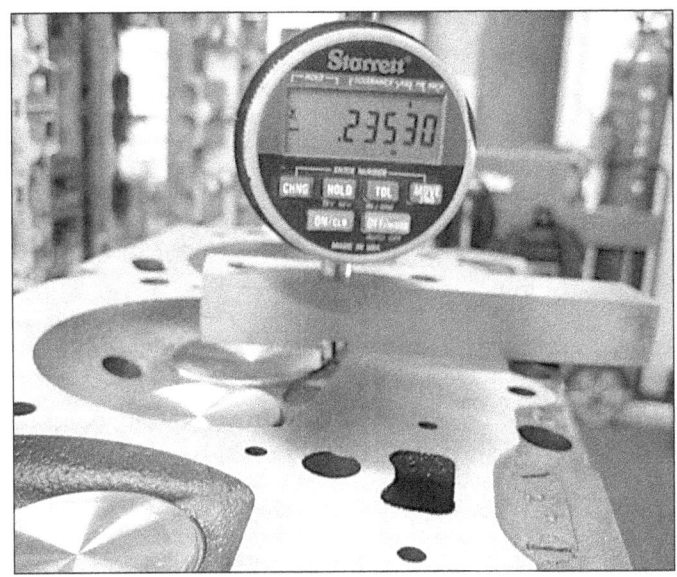

The valve free-drop measurement is from the cylinder head deck surface to the highest point on the valve head. When performing a valve job, the machinist should try to get the valve heights as equal as possible. All intakes should be the same, and all exhaust valves should measure the same to all exhausts.

engine can produce. When milling your cylinder heads, make sure that the machine shop machines the deck surface parallel to the valve-cover rail. This ensures that the valve free-drop and combustion chamber depth is even. I have seen many heads that have been milled unevenly, which throws everything off. So give your heads a check with a set of vernier calipers to make sure that the deck surfaces are parallel to the valve-cover rail and the same as each other. This tells you if both heads are milled the same amount and if those decks are straight.

When milling to reduce the combustion chamber volume, it takes approximately .006 inch of deck surface removed per cubic centimeter of reduced combustion-chamber volume. This method brings you pretty close. If you need it to be more exact, you have to check multiple times because the head is shaved.

Aftermarket Cylinder Heads

Over the years, a number of different Oldsmobile aftermarket cylinder heads have been produced. At one time Edelbrock, Rocket Racing/Wenzler, Batten Performance, Bulldog Cylinder Heads, Mondello/Knowlton, ProComp, and Wise Performance manufactured these cylinder heads. Current aftermarket aluminum heads are manufactured by Edelbrock (Performer RPM), Rocket Racing/Wenzler, Batten Performance, and Pro Comps.

Edelbrock

I am a big fan of the Edelbrock Performer RPM-series cylinder heads for the fact that the quality is nearly 100-percent perfect. They are ideal street replacement cylinder heads and you can trust them to be perfect when you take them out of the box. I have found that all of the accessories that come with the complete cylinder heads are of the best quality also. The valve sizes that come with the PN 60519 heads are 2.072-inch head diameter x 4.750-inch-long x .341-inch stem diameter for the intake and 1.680-inch head diameter x 4.750-inch-long x .341-inch stem diameter for the exhaust.

All Performer RPM-series cylinder heads are essentially an upgraded version of the original factory design. Even though they are similar to the stock design and the flow numbers are similar to factory iron heads, there is considerable performance improvement just by bolting them on out of the box.

I have dyno tested numerous 455-ci Oldsmobile big-block engines with basic street components, like an out-of-the-box Edelbrock Torker intake manifold, a 10.5:1 compression with stock factory cast-iron cylinder heads, and a hydraulic flat-tappet camshaft. These engines typically make 400 to 425 hp on my Superflow 901 engine dyno. The same-style engine with a set of out-of-the-box

The original Edelbrock Performer RPM and the newest version with a "heart-shaped" chamber. The combustion chamber has a different shape, but it does not provide a performance gain. The newer casting is, however, improved in many other areas, including larger, better flowing ports as cast and revised cooling passages, which allows you more room before hitting water.

The stock Edelbrock Performer RPM combustion chamber.

The intake ports of the Performer RPM are port matched to a Mr. Gasket 404 intake gasket. The intake port opening is the largest part of the port. It shrinks considerably as it approaches the intake valve. The place to remove metal is not at the port opening, but the area most difficult to get to, which is the short-side radius at the valve opening.

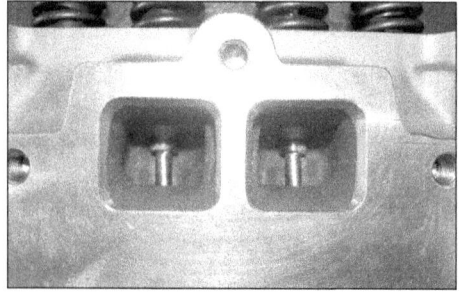

The Edelbrock Performer RPM cylinder head is a quality street replacement cylinder head. It makes about 50 hp more than a factory iron big-block head right out of the box.

I have always found the Edelbrock Performer RPM deck surface to be flat and requiring no additional machining to seal properly. The combustion chambers are a double-quench design with 77 cc out of the box. I have milled these deck surfaces to the spark plug boss in the combustion chamber, which achieves a volume of about 45 cc.

We built three sets of maximum-effort Performer RPM cylinder heads from raw castings. You can see the difference in shape and volume in these two pairs of modified exhaust ports.

The Performer RPM exhaust ports are better than those on the factory iron head, but not by much. I don't care how much work you do to these, they are only going to flow about 215 cfm on a flow bench. Don't stress though, it doesn't mean anything for power.

CYLINDER HEADS AND INDUCTION

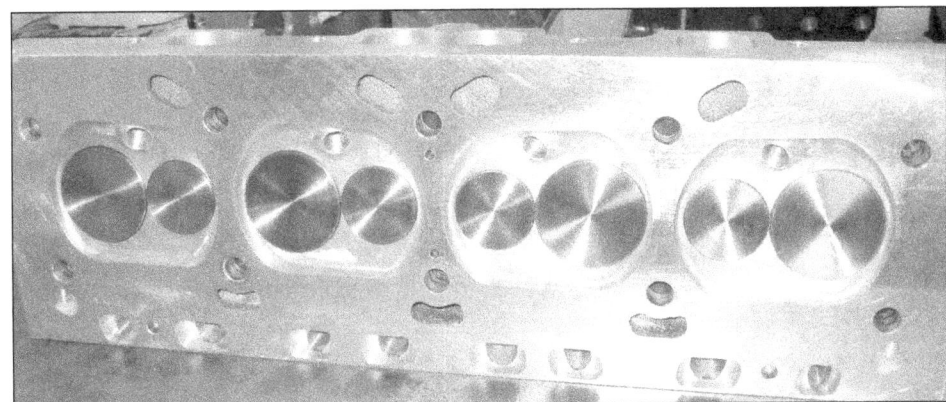

The combustion chambers are machined slightly differently than they were as stock on these highly modified Popular Hot Rodding Engine Masters Challenge *cylinder heads.*

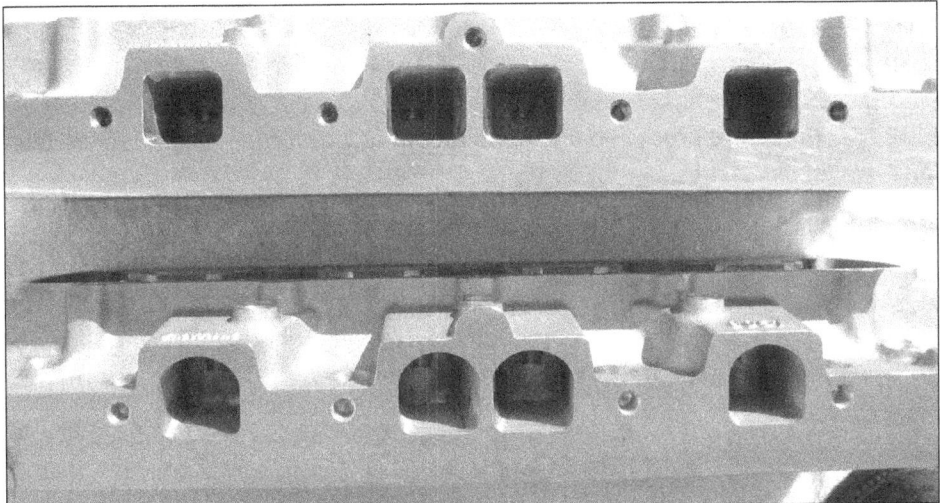

Although they are still very small compared to an off-the-shelf Performer RPM head, these exhaust ports can support 820 hp on a 506.

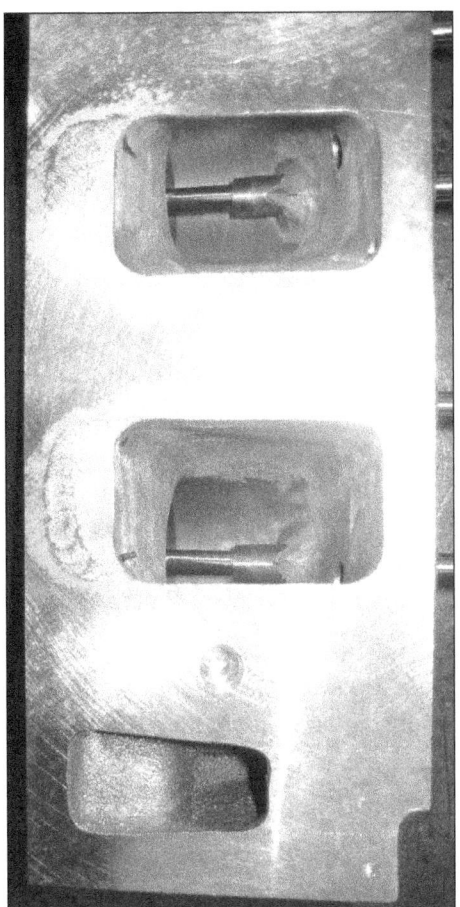

The intake ports on the ultimate BTR Edelbrock head have been raised to the maximum. The floor has been welded, the pushrods have been taken out of the intake ports, and there is a constant cross-sectional area.

Edelbrock Performer RPM cylinder heads makes anywhere from 490 to 510 hp with all the same components. Regardless of the flow numbers, the Edelbrocks increase performance.

Compared to their cast-iron counterparts, the intake ports are not much different in shape and size, but the bowl area has a considerably better shape with nice seat angles. In fact, the shape and size of the bowl is better as cast compared to the best-ported bowl you can achieve in an iron head.

On the subject of the bowl area in this head, the reason it is so good, compared to the factory iron heads, is the roundness of it, the diameter, and the depth below the valveseat. Because the diameter of the bowl is a little on the large side for the 2.072-inch-diameter intake valve that is supplied with the completely assembled heads, the intake side responds rather well by installing a larger valve. A 2.125-inch-diameter valve is a common size that is available off the shelf in various lengths that work in Oldsmobile applications. If you are going to port the cylinder head, the intake-valve head diameter that best suits the Edelbrock Performer RPM bowl size is 2.165 inches.

Unfortunately, all 2.165-inch off-the-shelf parts are designed for engines that use very long valves. Therefore, they are too long for use in an Oldsmobile cylinder head. If you want to use this diameter valve, it has to be custom made or purchased through BTR (I stock them). Intake-valve diameters larger than 2.165 inches require considerable opening of the bowl and a correspondingly larger OD valveseat than is factory installed in the Edelbrock head.

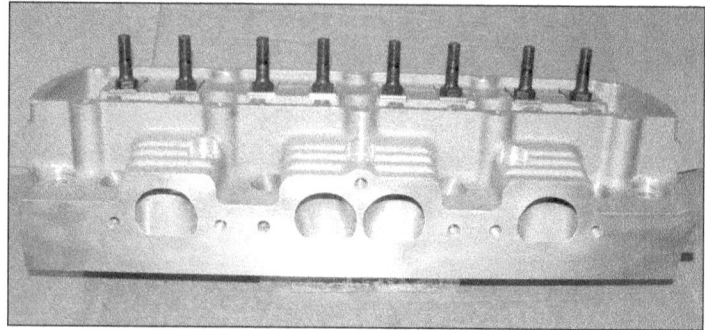
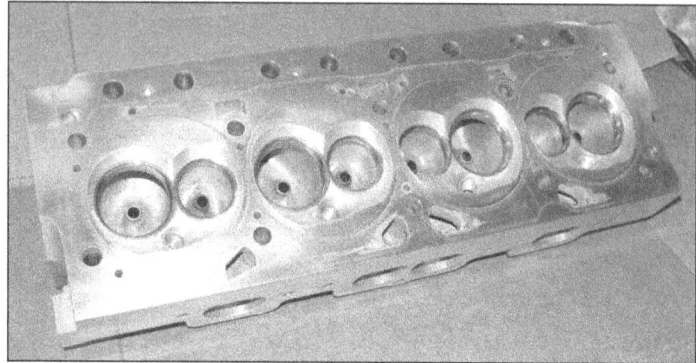
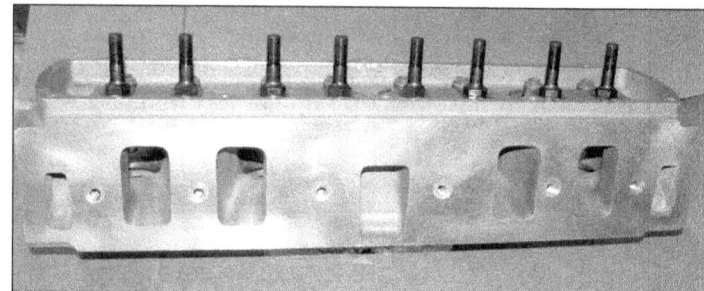

Here are four views of the Bulldog cylinder heads. They were produced in a limited quantity. Unfortunately, there were many unhappy customers due to casting and availability issues.

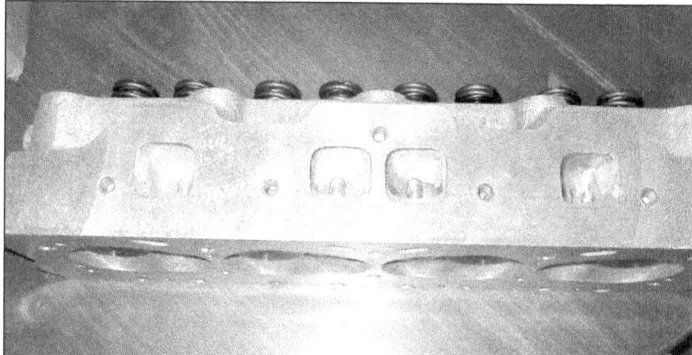

The exhaust side of the Mondello/Knowlton cylinder head.

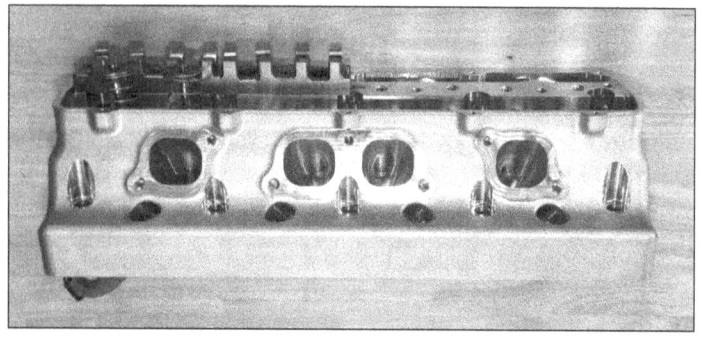

The Mondello/Knowlton cylinder head is a limited-production head and has been known to have casting flaws. It claims some very large CFM ratings, but I don't buy it.

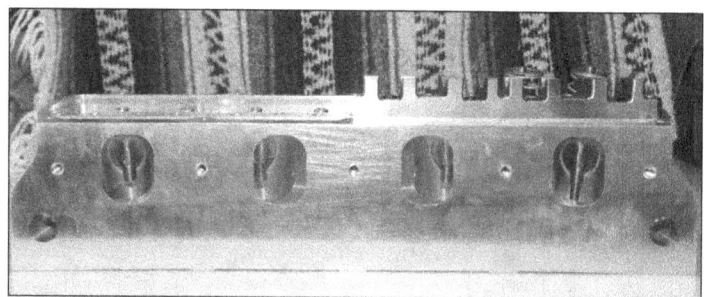

This one-of-a-kind Oldsmobile billet cylinder head was made by Marty Zimmerman. The port layout, port centerline, and every other aspect are everything a hardcore Olds enthusiast could ever want.

Exhaust gases have no problem getting out quickly!

CYLINDER HEADS AND INDUCTION

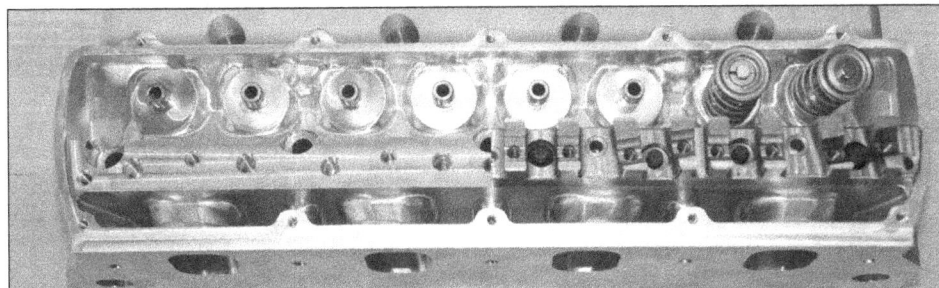

Take notice that the rocker-stand pedestals are at unusual angles because the valves have some side cant to direct air to the center of the cylinder.

BTR purchases special Edelbrock Performer RPM castings with pushrod and rocker stud holes deleted. We strategically locate the holes so that the pushrod pinch point is virtually eliminated when ported. In stock configuration, you can hardly touch the pushrod pinch point with a cartridge roll without breaking through. With the relocated pushrod holes, you can widen that area about 3/8 inch.

These copper beryllium seats are the best seats for titanium valves. This billet head even had provisions for water.

Rocket Racing/Wenzler

I have worked with a few sets of these cylinder heads and have seen some things I like and some things I don't like. On the positive side, the intake and exhaust ports are raised, and the port shapes are conducive to making horsepower. I have seen some fast-running cars using these cylinder heads (like John Stolpa's 1965 Cutlass from Rocket Racing and Performance) and cannot dispute the performance potential in them. Though I have not been completely satisfied with the casting quality and as-delivered machining on the heads I have had in my shop, it appears that most customers are generally happy with them. I do not recommend installing them out of the box, but encourage you to take them to an Olds cylinder-head expert for review first. Once they've been inspected, it's apparent they can make big power.

Batten Performance

As of this writing, the fastest, most powerful Oldsmobile engines in the world use Batten cylinder heads.

In the late 1970s, Batten Performance cast the first-ever aftermarket Oldsmobile cylinder heads for Oldsmobile. These heads were originally produced in cast iron and then, later, in 356 T6 aluminum. The first aluminum models actually had a GM PN 22505805. Three revisions were commonly known as Stage 1, Stage 2, and Stage 3. The Stage-3 Batten castings are the most robust and the

The Rocket Racing/Wenzler cylinder head.

CHAPTER 7

The Batten cylinder head combustion chamber.

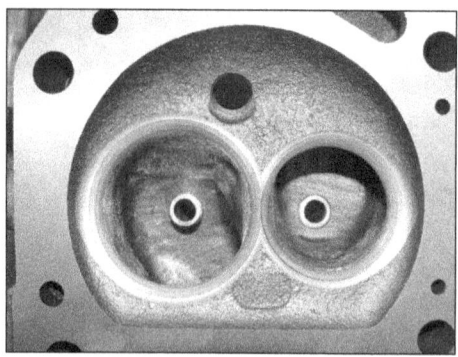

The factory iron big-bock combustion chamber.

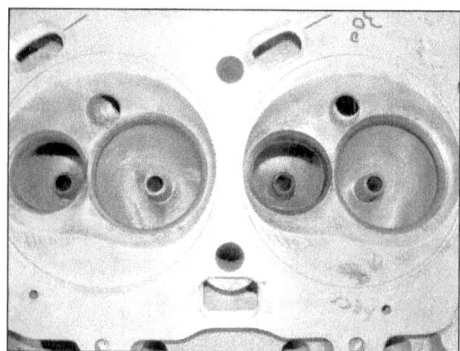

The EPD-designed Batten cylinder head combustion chamber.

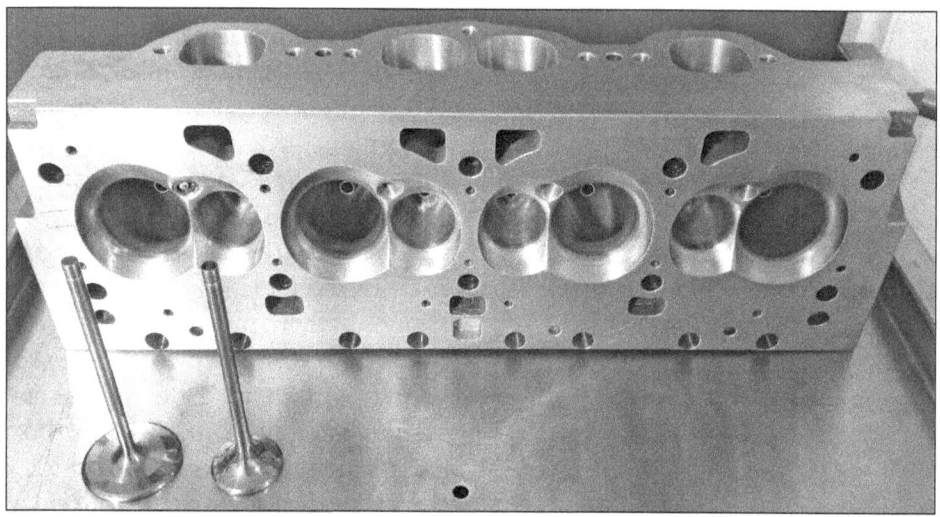

The Wise Performance Engineering "Z head" is currently in prototype stage and should be available in the future. If the project is completed, it may take Oldsmobile performance to the next level.

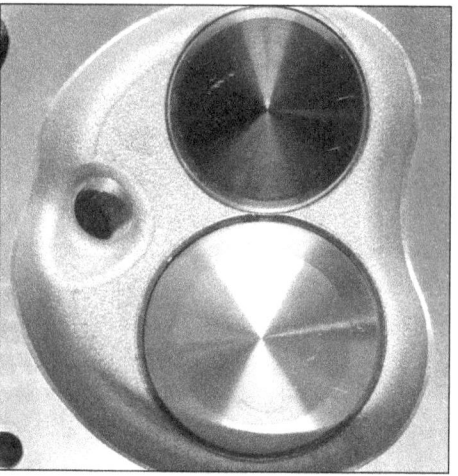

This is the very latest Edelbrock Performer RPM combustion chamber (PN 60519). It differs from the original design as shown.

most desirable. The casting quality is mediocre at best on all of them, but the best of them are the latest Stage-3 castings. I have used a number of the Batten heads throughout the years with great success, but not without a price. Every single Batten cylinder head I have had my hands on has had a multitude of issues, including poor machining quality, casting quality, and valveseats that are too hard for any valve.

Many of the machining issues cannot necessarily be blamed on the manufacturer because way too many people have had their hands on them throughout the years. The first area of concern is perpendicularity. I have found decks milled crooked from end to end, causing chamber sizes and valve-head-to-deck relationships (free-drop) to be different from end to end and from head to head. I have found intake surfaces that were not square to the deck surface, or parallel to the dowel-pin locating holes on the deck surface. The valve centerlines are almost always not exactly the same between one another. Every single machined surface of the cylinder head needs to be checked.

The second area of concern is casting quality. Pressure testing is always suggested on these. I have found many that didn't have issues, but have also found many that did. It just isn't worth it to do a bunch of work to these heads, install them on the engine, fire it up, and find out you have to fix leaks.

The third area of concern is the valveseats. I am not sure what types of valveseats were installed in these heads, but they are incredibly hard. They are very hard to machine and dull your cutters in a hurry. They are very hard on stainless valves and absolutely destroy a set of titanium valves within a short amount of time. If you run stainless valves, you can get away with it for a while but requires a valve job sooner than normal. If you require titanium valves in your application, you have to remove these seats and replace them with ductile iron or copper beryllium.

If you plan on using a set of these Batten heads on your Olds engine, know ahead of time that it is not an inexpensive task.

ProComp

The ProComp cylinder heads are becoming very popular because they are about half the cost of an American-manufactured Edelbrock cylinder heads, which they closely resemble. These cylinder heads and the ports are a bit smaller than the Edelbrocks and not quite as nice.

I have had only one pair of these in my shop that had some run time on them. There was some crazy guide wear to the point that the bronze dust mixed with oil accumulated on the backside of the valves on one head. I do not know if this was a

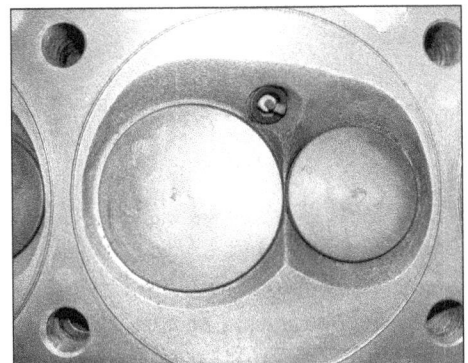

The BTR 403-ci nitrous-injected Oldsmobile Starfire combustion chamber.

This is a Stage-3 Batten cylinder head and can, which can be identified by the rocker stud pads being all tied in together, unlike on the Stage-1 and Stage-2 castings.

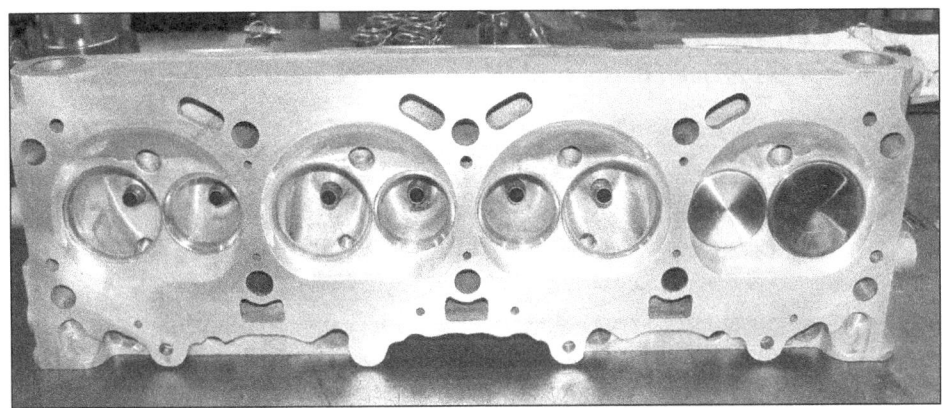

The deck surfaces of the Batten aluminum cylinder heads are very similar to factory castings.

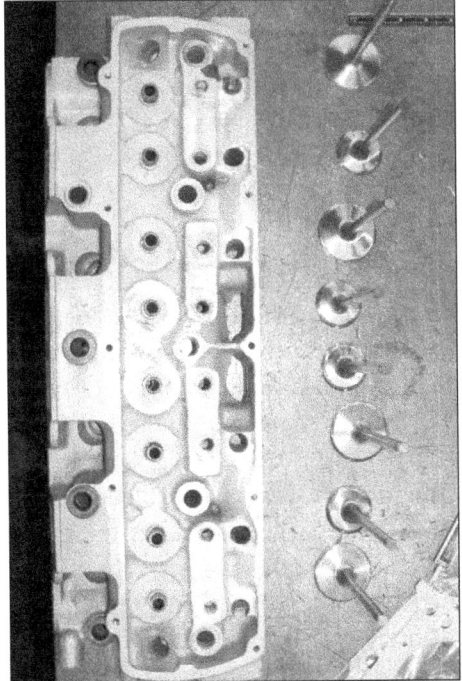

This is a Stage-1 Batten aluminum head. You can determine that by the very thin rib in the center connecting the center head bolt to the intake surface. A Stage-2 head is thicker in that area.

The Batten cylinder heads are the most powerful to date. CJ Batten was certainly ahead of his time; 30 years later these heads can compete in racing classes with 2015 technology.

CHAPTER 7

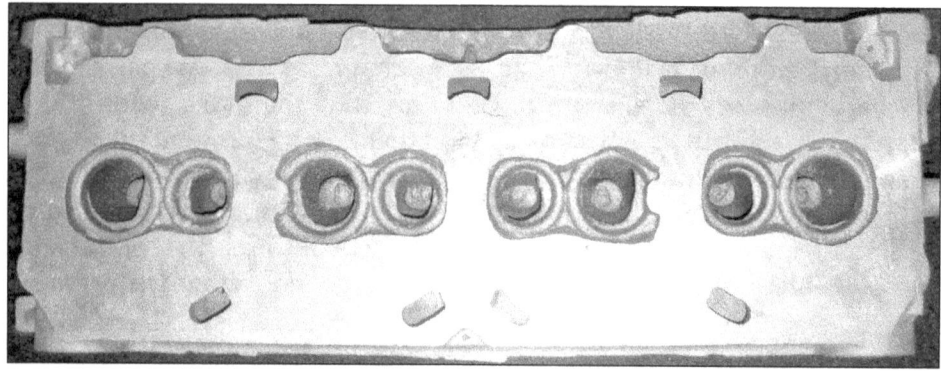

Some of the later-produced Batten aluminum heads were cast with no combustion chamber. This allows an up-to-date head to be machined instead, without major welding. This cylinder head just happened to be what the Starfire heads started as.

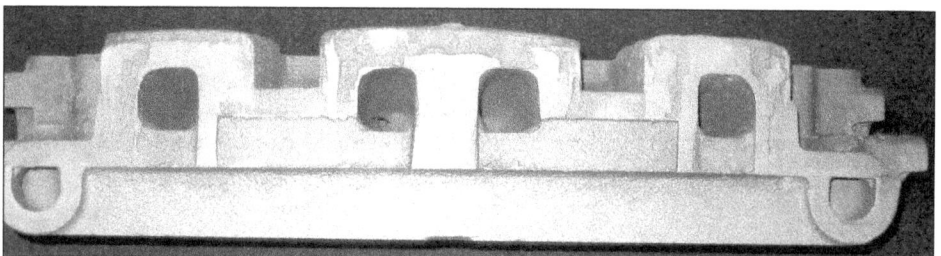

This is the exhaust side of the raw Batten head. The ports were considerably shrunk so that the head porter could do anything he wanted without welding.

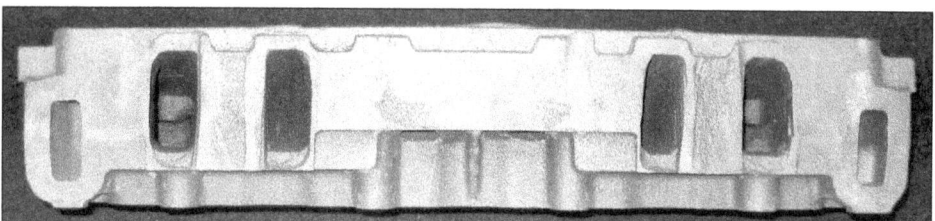

The intake side of the raw Batten aluminum head has been specially cast with small ports. This head allowed me to move the center port back to the stock Oldsmobile location so that it is a mirror image to the outer ports. It now fits a standard intake manifold, such as the Edelbrock Victor.

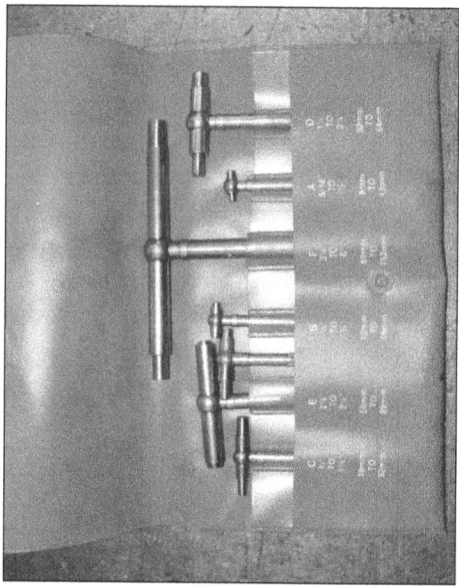

These Starrett telescoping gauges are ideal for measuring the size of the cross-sectional area of a port.

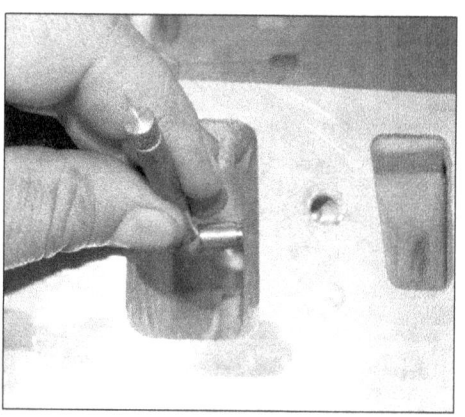

To get a good idea of what is going on inside a port, use a telescoping gauge to measure width and length every 1/2 inch or so, including the bowl.

quality issue or an issue due to incorrect assembly by the previous engine assembler, but it was definitely something I have not seen before on any cylinder head.

This example, as well as discussions on Internet forums about quality issues with ProComp cylinder heads makes me think that it's just better to stick with the American-made Edelbrock cylinder heads.

Porting Tips and Tricks

Porting an Oldsmobile cylinder head is not any different than porting any other brand of cylinder head when you understand how air behaves. Air flowing through a passage (whether it is a furnace duct, a pipe, or an intake port) does not like to turn, and doesn't like changes in volume. When there is a change in volume, one of two things occurs:

The area of the passage gets smaller or it gets larger. When the square area at a given point gets smaller, it becomes a restriction. When an area of a passage becomes larger, the air expands and slows down. The ultimate way of preparing an intake or exhaust port is to maintain a constant cross-sectional area.

The easiest way to get an idea of what is going on in the port, and where to work on it, is to get a pair of

You don't have to get real fancy with the measurements (I realize that you are not measuring corner radiuses), but when you map out the port as shown, you see very quickly where metal needs to be removed.

snap gauges. Measure the port from one end to the other every 1/2 inch or so, and record your cross-sectional area dimensions.

You quickly see that the port shrinks and expands quite a bit, whether it is a factory iron head, an Edelbrock Performer RPM, or a Batten cylinder head. With an Oldsmobile head in particular, there are some things in the way (such as pushrods and head bolts), preventing the cylinder head from achieving constant cross-sectional area, so you can only do so much to an existing Olds head without moving these items.

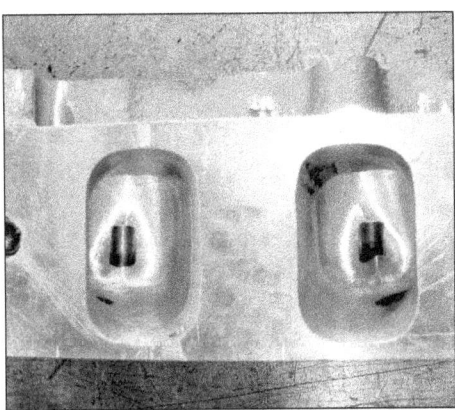

These are the intake ports from my 7-second Olds Starfire. The inner port is a mirror image to the outer.

The Batten intake ports are raised considerably and the inner ports are moved closer to the outer ports. With those inner ports moved away from the factory location, it is difficult to fit a factory manifold, such as the new Edelbrock Victors.

These EPD-prepared Batten heads had a weird, stepped exhaust port that went from the normal rectangle shape to round. I can only guess why the builders did it, but I would not copy this on a new set of heads; there is too much sudden expansion of the exhaust charge.

These are the exhaust ports of the Starfire cylinder heads.

On a mild port job on the Edelbrock Performer RPM cylinder head, the bronze guide must be removed first.

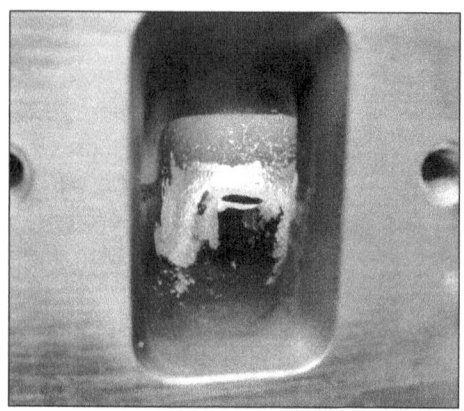

The places to start removing metal are on top of the guide boss and on either side of that valveguide boss.

You can tear-drop the front portion of the guide boss and straighten the areas leading to the bowl.

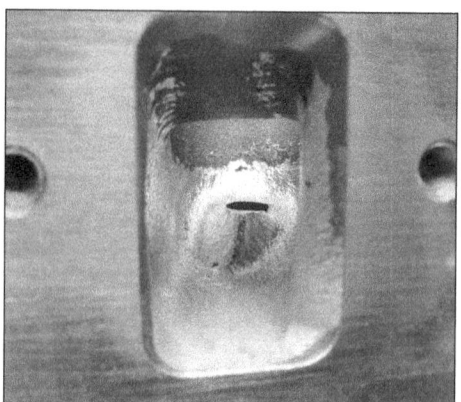

Work your way from the guide area to the outside of the port, not from the outside in. Stay away from the area surrounding the pushrod hole. It is thin as paper, so don't even breathe on it or you will be installing thin-wall sleeves in the pushrod holes.

Stay away from the port entrance until the final polish. This keeps a nice, square shape that is appealing to the eye and allows you to lay out the port easier on the intake manifold for port matching.

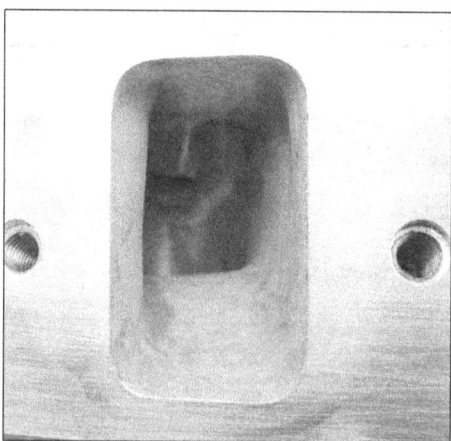

The best finish is provided by 80-grit cartridge rolls. Keep the RPM on the low side or they wear out quickly and don't receive a good finish.

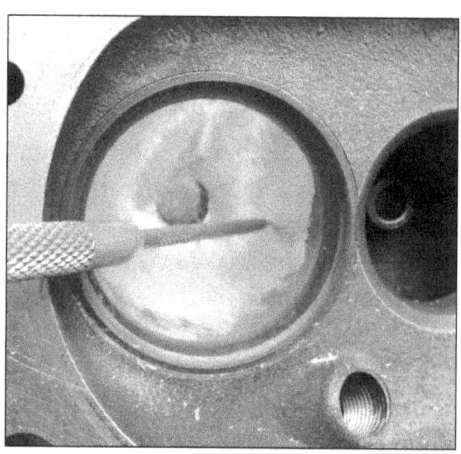

The bowls need to be widened in this area on both sides of the guide boss. These bowl walls should drop vertically from the bottom undercut on the valveseat.

Keep the bowl round and concentric to the valveseat throughout. You can finish-blend this area with the cartridge roll and perform the valve job last, to which the bottom angle of the multi-angle valve job should blend right in. The bowl is plenty big for a 2.072-inch valve; when you install larger valves, the bowl diameter is increased accordingly.

CYLINDER HEADS AND INDUCTION

These 307 cylinder heads on Dale Robinson's 2008 Popular Hot Rodding *Engine Masters Challenge engine show extensive work, such as raising ports and filling dead areas of the ports.*

This "ported" head is a good example of an engine that lacks performance. Someone wastes time or, worse yet, charges you to open up and polish the part of the intake port that is the largest and easiest to get to; they ignore the small portion of the port that is more difficult to reach.

Removing the guide boss entirely on a factory iron head is a good modification to perform and increases volume and flow in the areas that need it. Using a solid-bronze guide supports the valvestem properly and allows tight stem-to-guide clearance, whereas .015-inch-thick bronze liners don't.

The ultimate port runner is one that has a straight shot at the valve, has no turns or bends, and has a constant cross-sectional area with a minimum of shrinkage up to the short- and long-side radii. These are the sections of the port where the air/fuel mixture needs to turn at its sharpest angle as it enters into the bowl.

The shapes of short- and long-side radii are especially critical in Oldsmobile cylinder heads because of the shallow 6-degree valve angle. This means the air/fuel at that point needs to make a nearly 90-degree turn! Remember, air does not like to turn or change direction, and turning less than 10 to 15 degrees does not seem to affect airflow much. To get that air to turn from the port into the bowl, the short-side radius and the long-side radius both need to have as gradual a turn as the port walls allow.

Going into the bowl area, just before the underside of the intake valve, the cross-sectional area still needs to be maintained as much as possible, but should be 90 to 95 percent of the square area of the runner. This is because of the maximum allowable intake valve size, due to interference with the exhaust valve.

For this reason, in general, bigger intake valves in a cylinder head make more horsepower as long as

CHAPTER 7

One of the best modifications you can do to the Edelbrock Performer RPM exhaust port is to deepen the bowl for more volume so the exhaust gases can turn more than 90 degrees to get into the port outlet. Removing the portion of the valveguide throughout is acceptable, as there is enough length left to support the valvestem.

 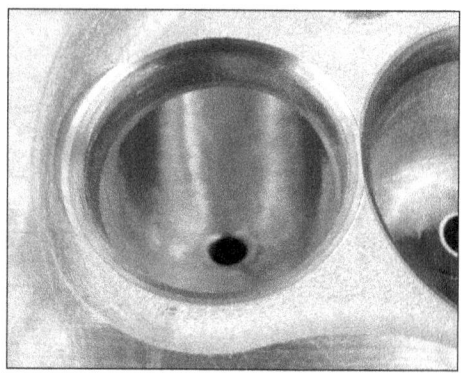

Bowls are ported for a 2.165 intake valve and a 1.680 exhaust valve. This is about as large as you can set the inner bowl diameters without replacing the seats to a larger OD. You have to be careful not to reduce the radial thickness of the seats too much because a little interference fit will be left and a seat could potentially fall out.

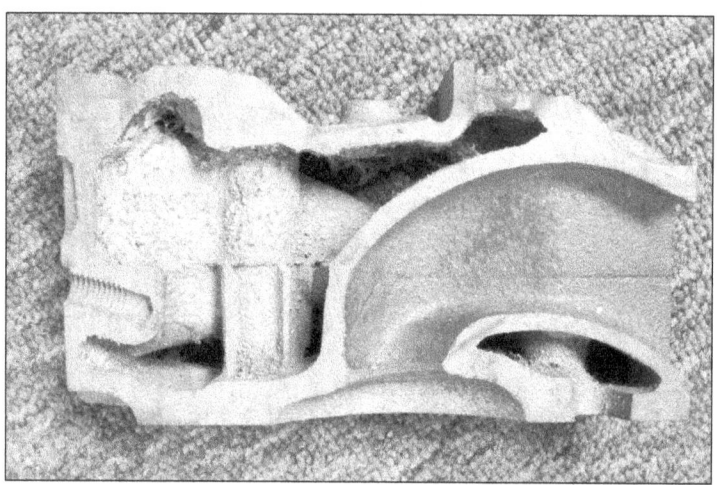

This cutaway of an old factory iron "C" head shows the inner workings of the ports and cooling passages.

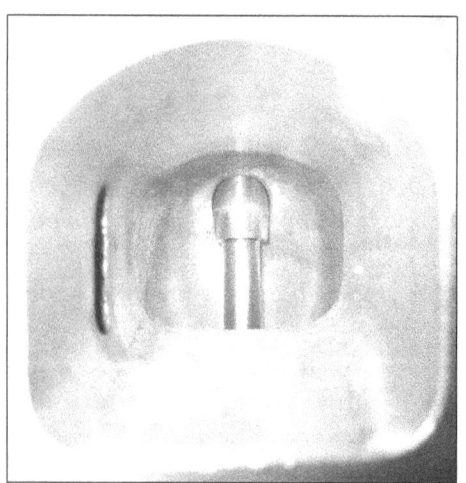

Removing the humps surrounding the head bolts in the center exhaust ports is another modification that is an improvement, but it requires a rigid steel insert, not a thin-wall sleeve, to prevent the head from collapsing when torquing the head bolt. Don't worry about the head bolt being exposed.

the bowl area beneath the valveseat is sized and shaped properly for that valve size. It seems to be best to sacrifice exhaust-valve size to achieve the largest correct intake-valve size for the intake port. I have built some larger-cubic-inch Olds engines with large intake valves and relatively small exhaust valves with great success, so don't be hung up on the 1.710-inch-diameter exhaust valve.

Spend most of your time on the intake side of the cylinder head, and match the size of the port to the size of the intake valve. Whatever room is left over, use that size for the exhaust valve for maximum performance.

Valveguides

The valveguides must be straight and round, in order to cut a good valveseat in the cylinder head. The greater the clearance between that valveguide and valvestem, the more that the valve head beats the seat out of shape over time. Unless the valveguides are absolutely perfect, brand-new solid bronze valveguides should be installed in your cylinder heads before cutting the valveseats.

Be aware that not all bronze guides are created equal. When I perform this operation in the shop, I use only solid bronze guides; they are stable, have good wear characteristics,

CYLINDER HEADS AND INDUCTION

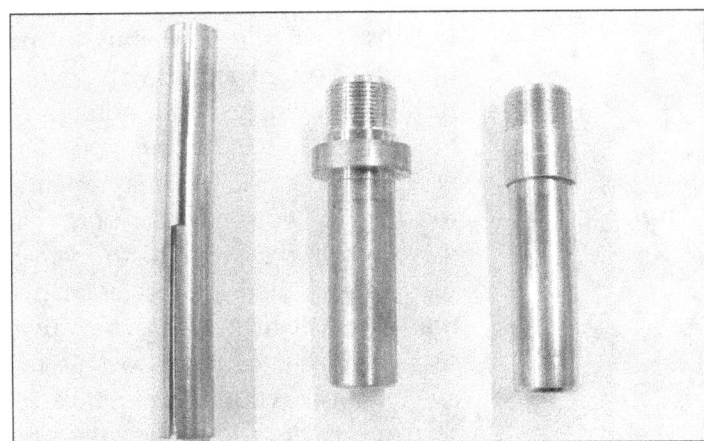

Left to right are a .015-inch wall bronze insert, a flanged guide, and a commonly used solid bronze guide.

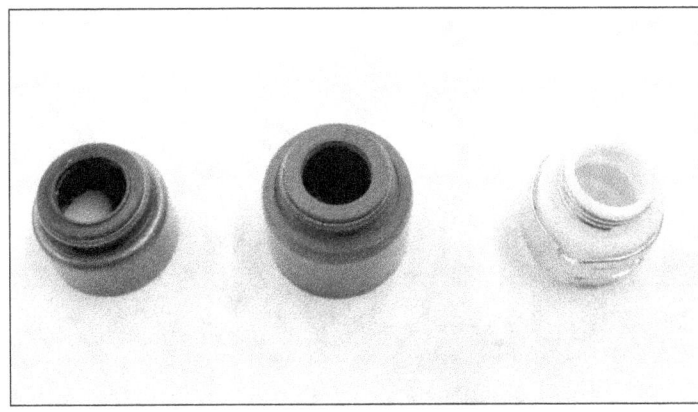

The best valve seals to use are these positive types. Left to right are a poly seal, a more expensive Viton seal, and a Teflon seal. I prefer the Viton seal with metal jacket.

and are easily replaceable. I don't use the .015-inch, thin-wall bronze guides. I have found that, in contrast to the solid guides, they make the valve stick if you do not give them extra clearance. The whole point of paying for new valveguides is to keep the stem-to-guide clearance at a minimum so that they can maintain oil control, and to keep the valveseat in shape longer. As always, the better solid-bronze guides are much more expensive than the thin-wall inserts. Most shops use the insert method because there is more profit margin in using them; they are about 50 cents each, rather than about five dollars for the solid-bronze guides.

The best way to get valveguides round and straight to size is to hone them. On aluminum heads, with solid-bronze guides, you should shoot for .0013- to .0015-inch clearance for the intake stems, and another .0004- to .0006-inch extra for the exhaust stems. On cast-iron cylinder heads with solid-bronze guides, you should shoot for .0015 to .0017 inch on the intake and an additional .0004 to .0006 inch on the exhaust for stem-to-guide clearance. On occasion, I have had the center exhaust valves stick, so I give the center guides an extra couple of tenths, although I have never had that issue with aluminum heads.

The Valve Job

Performing what is known as the valve job is usually done with machining equipment like my Serdi 100. This piece of equipment is considered by most builders to be one of the best machines for this operation. The Serdi machines use a single-point carbide cutter that has the exact shape of the seat angles and widths you are looking for. These carbide cutters are available in a multitude of sizes, shapes, and angles. The cutter is attached to a tool holder that houses a carbide pilot that slips into the valveguide, which holds that cutter so that it can machine the valveseat without chatter. Most shops have this style of machine now, manufactured by Serdi, Sunnen, or others. Do not let anyone touch your heads with the old grinding-stone method. I have used the stones in the past to grind seats and know that you cannot do as good of a job as with the single-point cutter method.

Before porting a cylinder head, the valveseats should be roughed in at a slightly smaller diameter for two

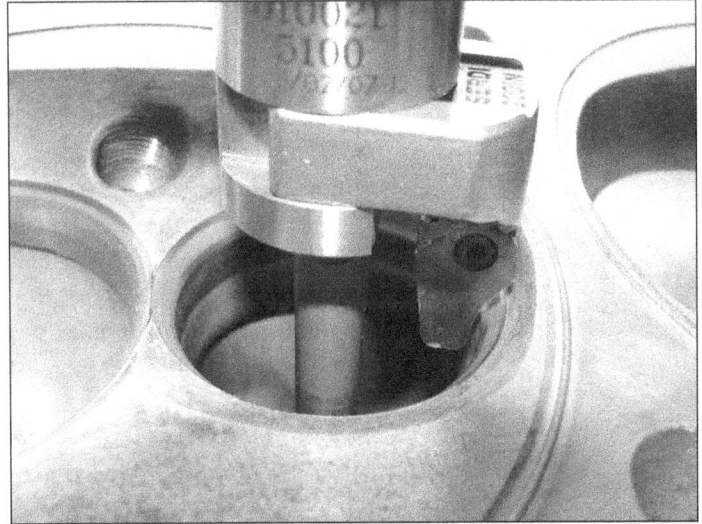

The Serdi 100 machining center uses a single-point cutter system that cuts valveseats to multiple angles in one operation. Hundreds of different cutter inserts are available, but most of the ones I use are custom-made by either Sunnen or Serdi.

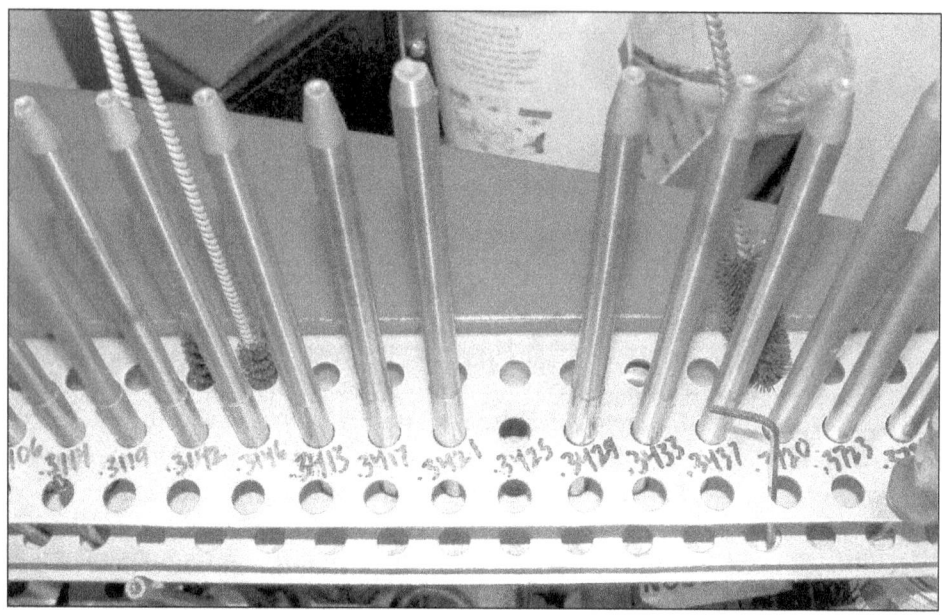
Carbide pilots, which locate the cutter to the valveguide, are in .0004-inch increments. Using the pilot that fits tightly in the honed guide keeps the valveseat concentric to it.

The bowl, which is the area below the valveseat, should be round and concentric to the valveguide. Notice that the cutter is hitting the right side and not the left side.

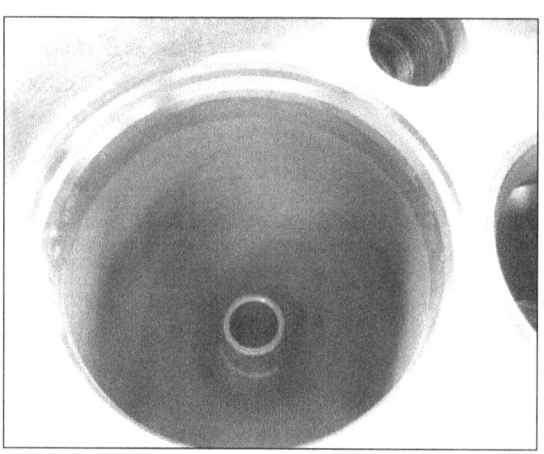
This finished valve job and bowl blend shows the proper shape. In this cylinder head you have a 45-degree seat, a 40-degree top cut, and 60- and 75-degree undercuts. After the 75-degree bottom cut, the bowl should drop about .100 inch before the short side and long side radii are initiated. The side walls should drop all the way to the bottom of the bowl.

reasons. First, the bowl must blend into the bottom angle without disturbing that angle. If you don't have the valveseats cut before you start porting the bowl, you may open it too large or you may not port that valve bowl concentric to the valveseat. Second, there is a greater chance that you will nick or hit the valveseat with your cutting tools. When all your work is done, the final valveseats are cut to the proper diameter and blend into your work perfectly.

Typically, the seat angles are selected by the amount of valve lift planned for the engine. The high-performance factory Oldsmobile engines that used the large 2.072-inch intake valves had 30-degree valveseats. At low lift, the effective open area is greater than with a steeper angle (such as the 45-degree seat). When I was playing around with the NHRA Stock Eliminator W-30 engine in the early 1990s, I was limited to .475-inch valve lift, according to the rules for the class, and found the 30-degree valveseats work rather well.

I use a 30-degree intake seat in low-lift applications or, at the very least, I certainly do not recommend converting to the 45-degree seat if you already have the 30-degree valves. I use 45-degree seats (intake and exhaust) on the other 95 percent of the street and high-performance applications having more than this limited (less than .500 inch) low-lift situation. I use 55-degree seats on certain very-high-lift applications.

The widths of the valveseats vary, depending on the application. For street and applications where longevity is a concern, I use intake seat widths of .060 inch and an exhaust seat width of .080 inch. Don't worry about the "flow." I have had plenty of hard-running engines with these wide seat widths. On the subject of longevity and valveseats, I don't feel it is necessary to install hard exhaust seats; 99 percent of the applications cruise around for only a limited amount of time. Also I have never seen an exhaust seat recessed severely on a cast-iron Oldsmobile cylinder head from the use of unleaded fuel.

Using thinner seats makes more horsepower most of the time because it opens the throat of the bowl or cross-sectional area, which provides a greater net area for the air/fuel mixture to escape. To explain further: The two cutter inserts have different seat widths. One insert has a .080-inch-wide 45-degree seat, and the other insert has a .039-inch-wide seat; both include the same-width 60-degree and 75-degree bottom undercut. The smallest effective diameter of the bottom 75-degree undercut is larger on the thinner seat angle. At this point, if the intake port cross-sectional area is 3.4 square inches minimum, and the minimum throat diameter at the bottom undercut is 3.2 square inches with a wide seat width, you will benefit from a thinner seat and a greater throat opening.

Get the point? This is where you get into 50- and 55-degree valveseats. The steeper the seat angles, the larger the effective throat area. With a typical ported cylinder head, the bowl's square area can often be the choke point, and unless you install a larger intake valve (and maybe you cannot install that larger valve due to interference with the exhaust valve), the only way to open this throat area is to use 50- or 55-degree seat angles. With higher-lift camshafts, the valve spends very little time at low lift and you can really benefit from these seat angles, but only if the choke point of the head is at the valve bowl.

With regard to top cuts (near the combustion chamber) and bottom cuts (near the bowl) from the intake seats: Air does not like to turn much more than about 15 degrees. So if you are using a 45-degree seat, a 60-degree undercut of about .060 inch, and a 75-degree of about .060 inch, then 90 degrees for about .100 inch before the short side radius is initiated works really well. The top cut for the intake side is not as critical in the flat Oldsmobile combustion chamber, as any top cut that may be conducive to aiding flow just sinks the valve deeper into the port. Use of a 30- or 35-degree top cut works fine for the intake side because you give it the absolute minimum of top cut anyway.

Regarding top and bottom cuts for the exhaust side: A wide 30-degree top cut works rather well with a 45-degree seat, and undercuts can be a little steeper than on the intake side. A radius cut also seems to work rather well in all of the cylinder heads that I have done. It is, however, not as critical as the intake side.

The Flow Bench

How does all of this relate to the flow bench? The flow numbers on a cylinder head are the industry standard of determining cylinder-head horsepower potential. Honestly, I have seen numerous engines (both Olds and non-Olds) that have proven this is not always the case. I have seen engines make good horsepower numbers with low flow numbers. I have also seen different-brand engines with the same cubic inch, and with cylinder-head flow numbers ranging from 360 to 420 cfm, make roughly the same horsepower on the dyno and near-identical performance at the racetrack. Don't be hung up on the flow numbers on a cylinder head.

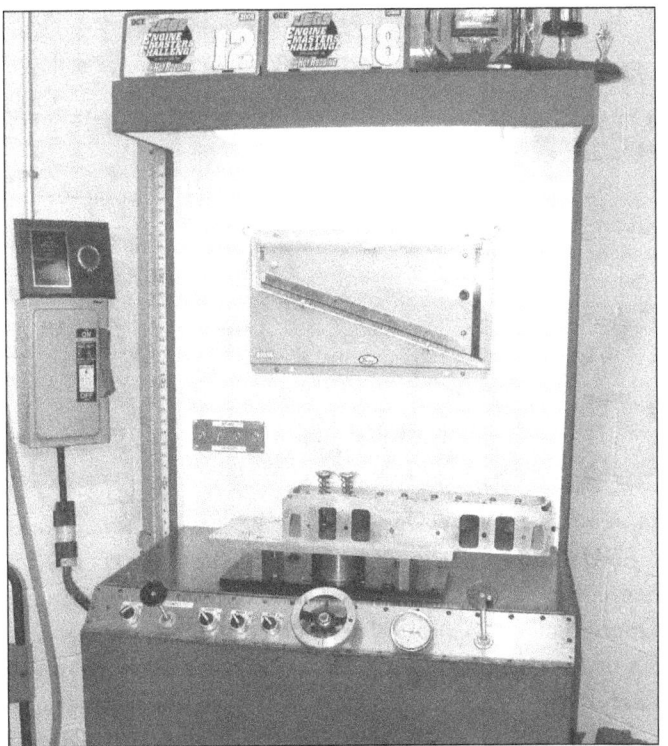

A flow bench simply works off the pressure differential. To operate, you select one of the calibrated orifices that flows a certain CFM rating, turn on the machine, and set the test pressure to 28 inches of water pressure. The inclined manometer reads from 0 to 100 percent and levels off at a certain reading. If you are using the 300-cfm orifice, and the inclined manometer reads 50 percent, your test port is flowing 150 cfm.

I have also seen way, way, too many inflated flow numbers on cylinder heads for the purpose of selling those heads. Oldsmobile cylinder heads seem to be the worst of the brands: big flow numbers but no performance. Or maybe I just pay more attention to them. Buyers, beware. My advice to you is to do your research regarding which cylinder heads with these wonderful flow numbers are actually performing at a racetrack. Dyno and flow bench numbers are far too easy to fudge. Reputed dynamometer and flow bench results sometimes lie, but a time slip at the racetrack cannot.

CNC-Ported Cylinder Heads

Porting by hand is not only time consuming, but it is very difficult to match your work from port to port and head to head. The best set of cylinder heads is a set that has fully CNC-machined ports. This should ensure that every port is the same and has the best quality. Having said

The max-ported exhaust ports of the new Edelbrock Performer RPM is as good as it can be within the limitation of the casting.

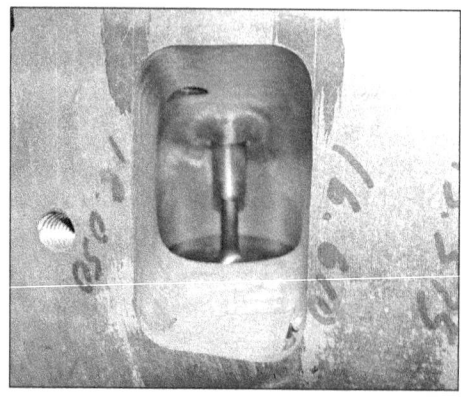

This intake port on Kurt Wich's 506 830-hp uses a highly modified Edelbrock Performer RPM cylinder head. The floor was welded and raised as much as the casting allowed.

Comparing the stock intake ports on the Edelbrock Performer RPM head to the BTR max-ported version, it is easy to see which one moves more air. The port opening size remains unaltered; it is already the largest part of the ports.

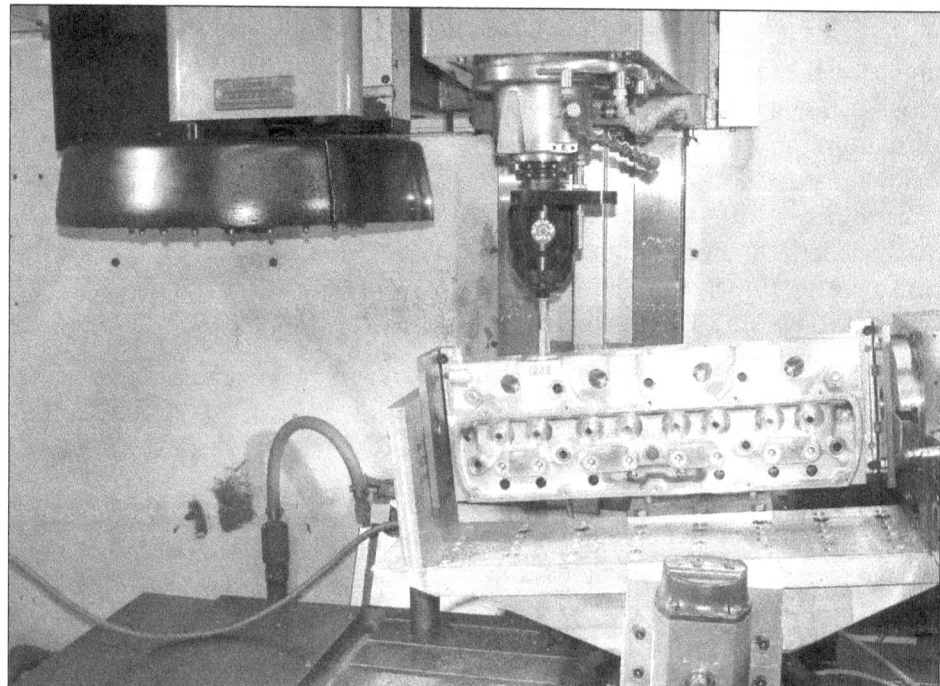

The Fadal VMC 40/20 five-axis CNC has the ability to digitize or probe ports and combustion chambers. The rotating fixture allows the cutter to machine around corners so that a whole port can be machined exactly the same as the original. Over the years we have developed cylinder heads for many different applications that have made plenty of power. This machine allows us to copy them and give the customer the right head for the application.

CYLINDER HEADS AND INDUCTION

The Renishaw probe creates a three-dimensional file of an exact copy of the prototype port. With this information, we can machine an exact copy for the customer.

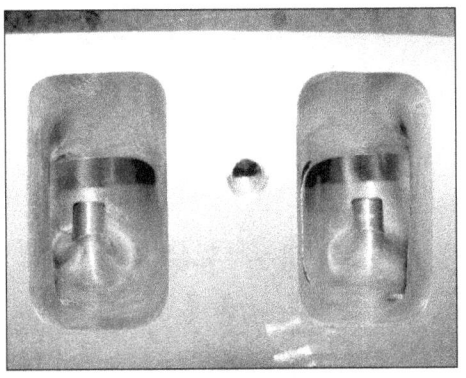
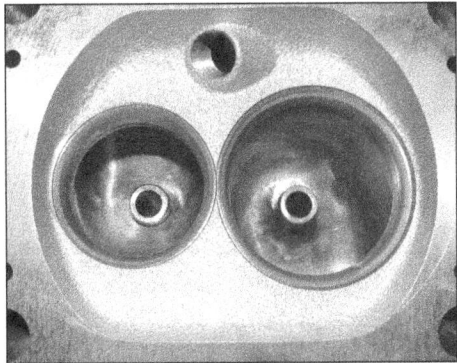

Not all CNC-machined heads are created equal. This is a gorgeous set of intake ports machine-ported by Joe Blow CNC Cylinder Head Company that didn't make any power on an engine that was being repaired in the shop.

set that cylinder head up in the machine, and probe the port with a stylus in the shape of the cutting tool. This gives a three-dimensional file on the computer. With that file, we can manipulate that port slightly to give us exactly what we want to cut into the cylinder head. Of course, it is a little more complicated than that, but that is generally how it all takes place.

Valves

Many U.S. companies offer Oldsmobile engine valves. I have found that Racing Engine Valves (REV) and Ferrea Racing Components have the best quality and price for Oldsmobile applications. I have found their valvestems to be straight and always the same size, the valve head diameters to be correct and consistent, and the valve faces to be concentric and machined to the specified angle. I can't say that about most of the other popular companies that sell valves for Oldsmobiles or even the custom valves available for our applications.

Ferrea has many different series of valves, depending on the application. The inexpensive 5000-series high-performance valve is a basic replacement stainless design for flat-tappet and hydraulic roller applications. Although inexpensive, I have found them to have good quality for their price.

Oldsmobile valve lengths are generally short when compared to other engines, so valve-head diameters and valve length sizes are quite limited. Chances are that if you want an oversize valve for your high-performance Oldsmobile application, you have to make a custom valve. REV is a very good choice for your custom stainless-valve needs. I

that, keep this in mind: If Oldsmobile Joe has a set of 350-cfm, CNC-ported heads by an Oldsmobile-expert CNC company, and his 3,500-pound, 455-ci Cutlass runs 11.50 at the racetrack, chances are that the highly touted CNC ported heads are not all that great. The CNC machine only does what it is told to do by the port designer.

Remember, just because a cylinder head is CNC-ported, it does not mean that the cylinder head is guaranteed to perform. I have had the so-called best-ported Oldsmobile cylinder heads money can buy in the shop and they didn't make any power on the dyno. Do some research to find CNC heads that are being run on cars that perform up to expectations of ET, not marketing or Internet hype.

BTR Performance owns a Fadal VMC 40/20 five-axis CNC machine, with Renishaw trace/cut software for digitizing our proven port designs. Over the years, we have ported enough cylinder heads that performed well to have learned what works and what does not. So with this type of machine, we can copy proven heads exactly for our customers. When I have an idea to do something different in a port or combustion chamber, for example, I complete one intake port by hand,

CHAPTER 7

Oldsmobile Valves

Ferrea Part Number	Function	Head Diameter (inches)	Stem Diameter (inch)	Valve Length (inches)	Tip Length (inch)	Style
F5141	Exhaust	1.710	11/32	4.668	.250	9-degree Flo-Dish Head
F5141B	Exhaust	1.710	11/32	4.735	.250	9-degree Flo-Dish Head
F5142	Intake	2.075	11/32	4.715	.250	9-degree Flo-Dish Head

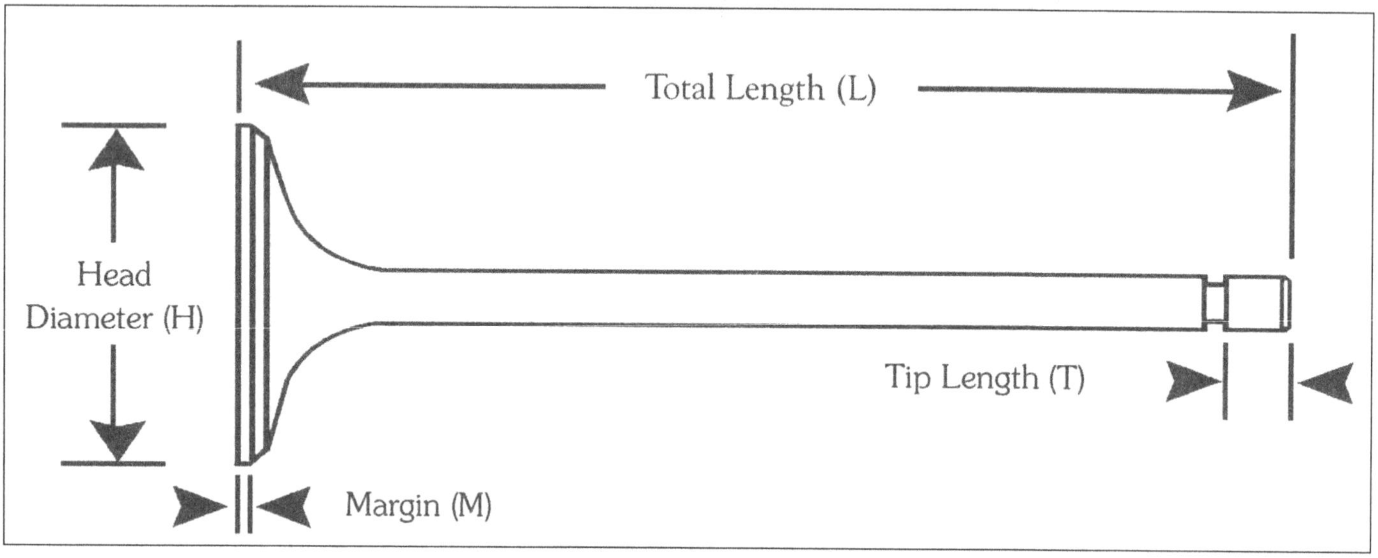

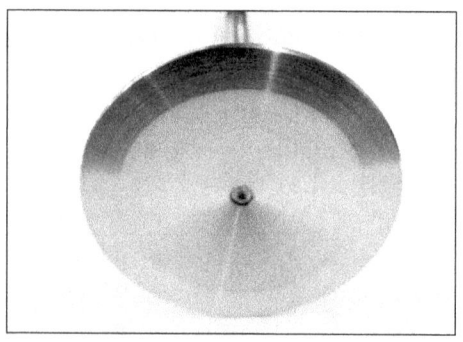

Stainless valves usually have a dish in the valvehead to reduce weight. Not all stainless valves are created equal. Some of the cheaper ones do not lap in because of shortcuts taken during the manufacturing process and, therefore, have to be reground before use.

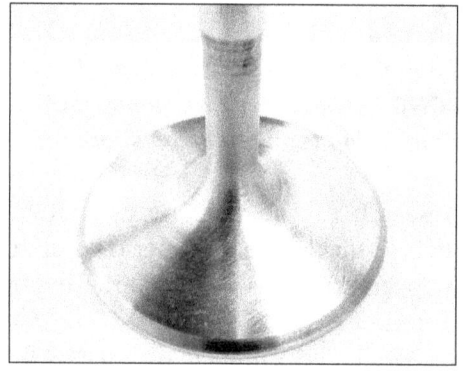

Better-quality stainless valves have an undercut stem, but more important, a thin valve face that requires no backcut.

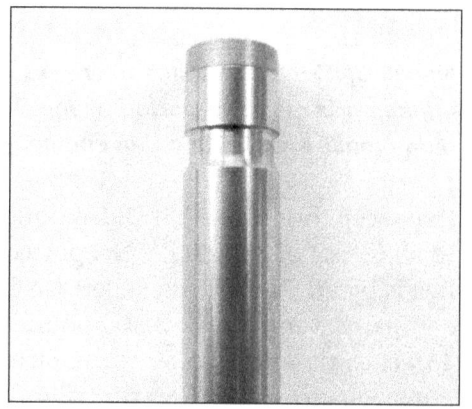

Titanium valves are relatively soft and require a hard tip (shown) or a lash cap, which is a hardened piece that fits over the valvestem tip. The square groove in the valvestem is simply a locator for the valve lock.

usually use Ferrea for my custom titanium valves.

One thing to be aware of regarding valves and valve locks is the fit between them. The groove in the top of the valvestem is simply a locator so that the retainers are all at the same height in relation to the valve tip. It has nothing to do with holding the valve in place; it is the wedge action between all those components that does that job. I have seen fitment issues between retainers, locks, and valvestems from various manufacturers. The valve lock must have the proper inside radius and the valvestem must have the correct outside radius in order for them to mate and hold tight. I have seen plenty that did not match properly.

The biggest problem is when the diameter of the valvestem above the keeper groove is not the same diameter as the valvestem below the keeper groove. Check some of valves with a micrometer and you'd be amazed at what you find. I have not had these issues with Ferrea and REV products, which is the reason I use them.

I have found Comp Cams retainers and valve locks to fit well to most components, but it is a good idea to check the fit of all these items together by installing the valve, lock, and retainer in your hand and pulling them together with some force. The valvespring retainer should lock itself to the valvestem and should not fall off without you pushing it off with some force. If you let go of the assembly after pulling the components together, and the assembly falls apart, there is a radius mismatch and a recipe for dropping a valve if the engine goes into valve float.

Intake Manifolds

Everyone is very concerned with cylinder-head flow, flow numbers, and cylinder-head performance, but many seem to forget the intake manifold bolted to it. In reality, it is just as important as the cylinder head. The intake-manifold runner is an extension of the intake port. Given that, you have to look at the intake runner as a whole, from the plenum where the runner starts, to the intake valve. The biggest problem with intake manifolds (especially older designs) is that the intake runner cross-sectional area is usually smaller than the intake ports, and this changes volume along the path too much. Current casting technology has come a long way and the runner sizes can be controlled much better than years ago.

One of the reasons Oldsmobile engines have a reputation of producing tremendous torque is because their intake manifolds have very long runners due to the tall deck height of the block. In general, equal-length longer runners help produce more torque in the lower-RPM ranges. This is the reason extended runner dividers inside the manifold plenum often make more power. It seems that you can never get the runners long enough in single 4-barrel manifold designs for any application.

Dual Planes versus Single Planes

I have never been a fan of dual-plane manifolds for performance applications. To me, I see no reason to make the air/fuel mixture make a bunch of twists and turns to get to the valve. These dual-plane designs typically have very long runners, which are conducive to low-end torque. But the bottom line is that if you want a better ET slip at the racetrack, the ET will likely be lower with a single-plane manifold. Some say that the dual-plane manifold is better for the street, but the way I see it in my world, whatever manifold makes the car faster at the racetrack is the one that is better for the street.

Single-plane manifolds have a reputation of losing low-end torque, but I am not sure that is true. I have competed in the *Popular Hot Rodding* magazine's Engine Masters Challenge three times with an Oldsmobile engine, which measures engine performance on a dyno between 2,500 and 6,500 rpm. On this subject, 99 percent of all the entries, including mine, used single-plane manifolds. I found that on these engines, in what I consider a typical street-RPM range,

The W-30 intake manifold is basically the same as all of the other cast-iron intake manifolds of that era. The advantages are the weight and the ability to cut it up, port it, and weld it back together.

Replica W-30 intake manifolds are available through various Oldsmobile vendors.

CHAPTER 7

Cooling System

The cooling system in an Oldsmobile engine is not much different than in any other V-8 engine. The coolant (or water) starts at the inlet of the water pump and forces coolant through the two holes in the front of the block, where it pressurizes the water jackets. Coolant travels to the cylinder head through the deck and is metered by various size restrictor holes in the head gasket so that more or less of the coolant travels to the needed areas of the cylinder head. After the cylinder head transfers its heat to the coolant, the job is done and the coolant is returned to the radiator through the front passage of the cylinder head, which is connected to the thermostat housing in the intake manifold.

When it comes to cooling priorities, the cylinder head is the most important part to keep properly cooled followed by the engine block. This statement is proven by the fact that in hardcore racing applications I completely fill the block with HardBlock (or non-shrink grout); I cool only the cylinder heads.

You can improve the cooling of the cylinder head with a few modifications. The center of the head where the two exhaust valves meet is one of the hottest areas of the head. Modify coolant holes in the head gaskets to direct coolant to this notorious problem area. If you enlarge areas of the gasket to flow more water to a certain area, it is a good idea to shrink or plug other areas that do not need as much water at the same time.

Another simple add-on is to plumb the coolant exits in the rear of the cylinder head ports via the intake manifold that connects to the thermostat housing area. This allows the coolant to exit the cylinder head from the front and the rear so it cools the cylinder head more evenly.

The best improvement you can make to the cooling system is to reverse cool the engine, even though it is a little more complicated. This method simply supplies the coolest fluid straight from the radiator to the cylinder head first. The coolant then drains through the head's deck and block into the water jackets and then is returned to the radiator. I would rather see the cylinder head receive the coolest fluid from the radiator than be at the end of the cycle and receive coolant that is already heated by the block.

Mechanical Water Pumps

Three water pump lengths are available for the 330- to 455-ci Oldsmobile engines. The shortest water pump measures approximately 5.080 inches from the backside of the pump (where it meets the timing cover) to the flange (where it bolts against the inside of the pulley). The medium-length water pump measures 5.550 inches and the long water pump measures approximately 5.950. The longest are generally found on Oldsmobile engines with air conditioning.

Mechanical water pumps work all right, but they actually flow way too much water through the engine. So forget high-flow water pumps because mechanical water pumps seem to always do the job when the engine is running and rarely leave you stranded.

The three Oldsmobile water pumps available are 5.95 inches long for A/C applications, 5.55 inches long for non-A/C, and 5.080-inch long for very early engines.

CYLINDER HEADS AND INDUCTION

After many dyno tests, I have noticed a drawback to the mechanical water pump. As RPM climbs during the pull, the water pump moves so much water that the lower inlet hose collapses shut.

Do you wonder why engines get hot when you beat on them? I have tried lower hoses with support springs inside them but the hoses still collapse. This situation is aggravated when large factory lower crankshaft pulleys are used; they overdrive the speed of the water pump by almost double.

Think about it. With a typical performance Oldsmobile engine, you may run at least 5,500 rpm. Do you really think your water pump needs to spin 10,000 rpm? Probably the only way to fix it is to use a piece of stainless pipe with short pieces of hose at either end; connect it to the radiator and water pump.

With the water pump robbing horsepower and sucking the lower hose shut, you may want to consider an electric water pump.

Electric Water Pumps

You have a few options if you want to use an electric water pump in your Oldsmobile engine. Meziere and CSR make the most versions. I always have a hard time getting CSR pumps because of limited manufacturing, so I use Meziere pumps. I have found them to be high quality and trouble free. I have supplied plenty of street engines to customers over the years without any complaints. They flow plenty of fluid to keep an engine cool for racing or street use.

The only time an electric water pump is an issue is when your Oldsmobile has a lot of accessories, particularly air conditioning. For these situations, it's much easier to use the belt-driven factory water pump.

Coolant

Most street cars use a 50-50 mixture of antifreeze and water, which is the most effective at cooling your engine. One of the best things that using antifreeze does for you is to keep the inside of the water jackets from rusting.

In racing applications for which you must use water, it is highly advisable to use distilled water. I have had many engines apart (that I originally built) in the shop for service and I've seen what tap water from certain areas of the country can do to the block and aluminum heads. Distilled water alleviates that issue.

In addition, Water Wetter from Red Line Synthetic Oil Corporation is a very good additive. For many years I have used a mixture of distilled water and Water Wetter in my racing engines. This is the best non-antifreeze coolant you can use for your Oldsmobile performance engine.

The best electric water pump for your Oldsmobile race car or street car is from Meziere. They are available in a few different colors so that it looks just right for your engine compartment.

In racing applications, use Water Wetter combined with distilled water for the best brew of coolant.

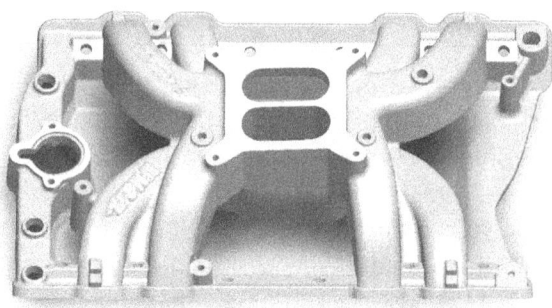

The brand-new Edelbrock Oldsmobile 455 RPM Air Gap Manifold (PN 7551) has a constant cross-sectional area of 2.94 inches and is a good match for an out-of-the-box set of Performer RPM Olds cylinder heads.

The old Edelbrock 04B is still very popular.

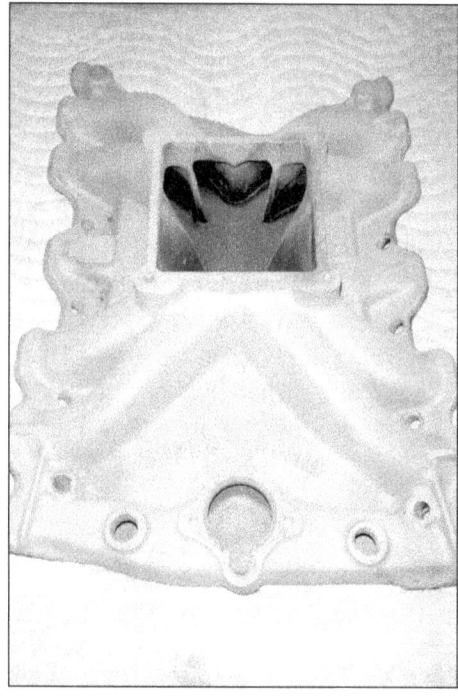

The Edelbrock Torker for the big-block Oldsmobile engine is very popular. This single-plane manifold is about as tall as you can get and still fit under stock hoods. These are very hard to port as the runners are very long. I have extrude-honed a few of them and it appears that doing so is worth about 15 hp.

The Offenhauser Port-O-Sonic accepts a 4150-style carburetor and the Super Sonic intake manifold (shown) accepts a 4500-series carburetor. Although these models are out of date, there are some hard-running Oldsmobile engines out there using them.

The plenum on the Torker has an unusual shape and requires a tremendous amount of work to get it to function almost as good as a new-style Victor manifold.

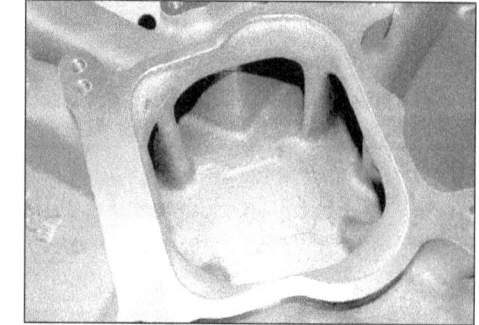

CYLINDER HEADS AND INDUCTION

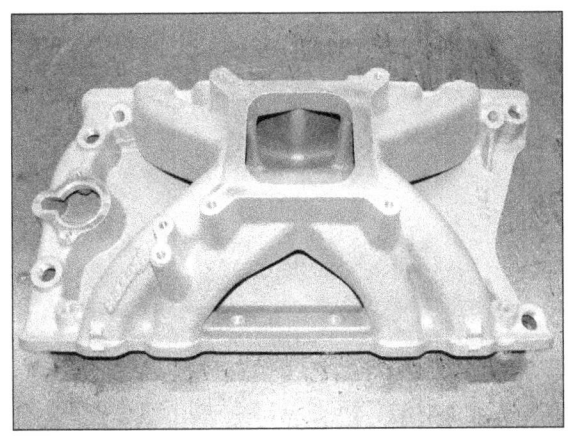

The 2812 Edelbrock Victor is only available with the 4150-style carburetor flange and has a constant cross-sectional area of 3.2 square inches. When using the Performer RPM cylinder head on a small-block Olds engine, this manifold is required; most other manifolds generally do not have enough material at the top of the runners.

When using the W31 factory intake in a hydraulic roller application, you must install some of the roller lifters on the inner cylinders with the tie bar facing the cylinders so that they clear the heat crossover underneath the intake manifold.

the camshaft and header design had more to do with low-speed power than having a dual-plane manifold. Use a single-plane manifold if performance is the goal. If you are concerned with cruising and rarely go above 3,000 rpm, I guess the dual-plane wouldn't hurt.

Porting

Porting an Oldsmobile intake manifold is not a simple operation. The runners are very long and it is difficult, if not impossible, to get even the longest of carbide burrs inside to open up the runner size. If the cross-sectional area of that runner is smaller than the cylinder-head runner, it doesn't matter how much the head flows on the flow bench, the manifold won't feed it.

Think of it this way: Let's say you have a 3-inch-long piece of 2-inch pipe, and on your flow bench it flows 300 cfm for your baseline reading. After you spend days porting it, use some epoxy on the floor, and flow it again, it flows 320 cfm. Great job! Now add a piece of 10-inch-long, 1-inch pipe on top of your great job and see how well it flows. Get the point? Given that, you need to determine if your intake manifold will feed your cylinder head, and chances are it will not.

Older intake-manifold designs like the Edelbrock Torker, the Offenhauser Port O Sonic, the Super Sonic, and even the new Rocket Racing/Wenzler intake manifolds have very small intake runners. The only way you can get inside to open up the cross-sectional port dimension is to cut access passages near the runners, cut the manifold in half (or into sections to be able to get inside), and then weld that manifold back together when done.

The good news is that the latest Edelbrock Victor intake manifolds have a constant cross-sectional area so that you don't have to kill yourself to port the runner of an intake manifold so it can feed the ported cylinder head on which you've spent so much time or money. The big-block Oldsmobile Victor (PN 2810 and PN 2811) manifolds are designed with a constant cross-sectional area of 3.4 square inches, which feeds the largest cylinder heads. The small-block Oldsmobile Victor intake (PN 2812)

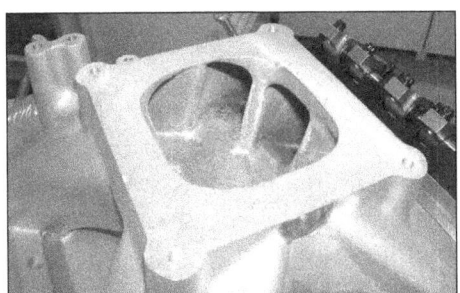

I have milled the carburetor flange on the Edelbrock Victor manifold as much as .625 inch so it fits under a W-30 hood. You have to weld up the vacuum port in the back of the plenum prior to doing so.

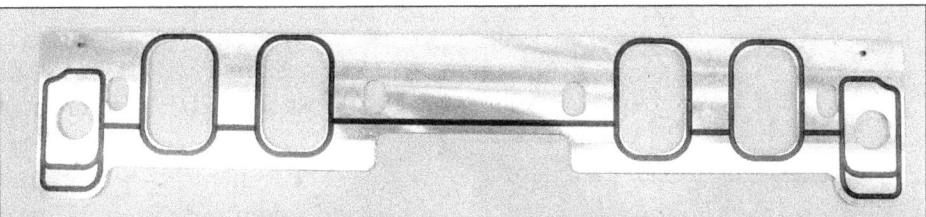

This gasket spacer has O-rings on both sides to allow the intake manifold to fit properly on conventional cylinder heads with intake ports raised to the maximum.

Looking at a big-block Oldsmobile Victor manifold (left) next to a Port-O-Sonic, it is easy to see which one produces more horsepower.

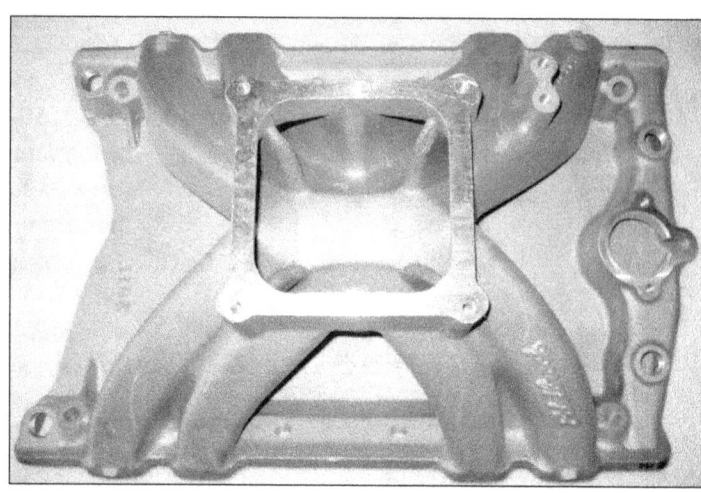

The Edelbrock 2811 Victor Dominator flange manifold has a constant cross-sectional area of 3.4 square inches. The plenum and runner length are about as optimal as possible. If I were to design a manifold for an engine other than an Oldsmobile, it would look very close to this.

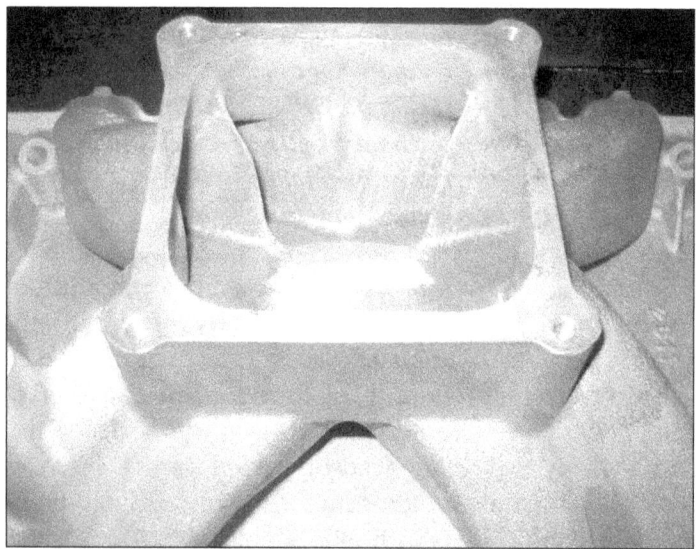

This reworked 2811 Victor made 820 hp and 725 ft-lbs of torque on a 506-ci big-block Olds.

This "Gigantafold" is a highly modified Edelbrock Victor manifold made for a high-RPM application. With its short, even runners, it should be a winner.

is designed with a constant cross-sectional runner area of 3.2 square inches.

The plenum area of the intake manifold is important also, but is a secondary concern to the runner volume. Making all edges inside the plenum smooth and increasing the radius from the carburetor-flange wall to the entrances to the runners increases performance. Changing the plenum shape (with bolt-in geometric shapes sometimes known as turtles) and extending the runners should be done on an engine dyno or a racetrack, unless you have already proved that change to work on that particular manifold. I have seen

CYLINDER HEADS AND INDUCTION

Spacer intake gaskets are available through Flatout Gaskets. They are available in just about any thickness, even for unconventional applications. You simply glue the standard 1/16-thick gasket on both sides of the aluminum spacer. Flatout Gaskets made a set for me that was 5/8 inch thick.

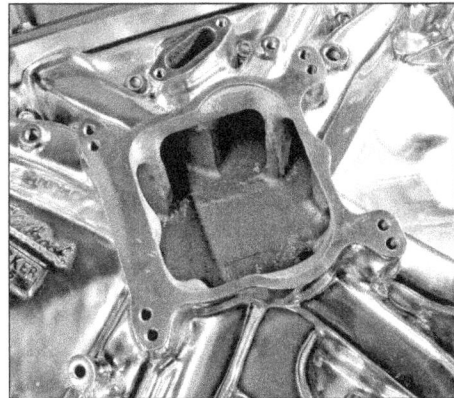

Minor modifications to the plenum of the Edelbrock Torker, such as shown, improves power. Make sure your carburetor gasket seals the largest portion of the plenum. Some carburetor gaskets barely seal that area; some are too small and do not seal at all, which causes a vacuum leak.

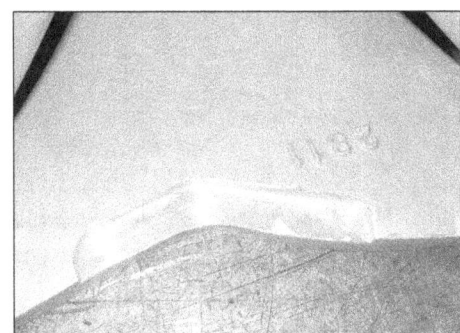

Often the distributor hits this area of the big-block Victor manifold. Make sure you mock it up before you glue on the manifold. It's not the time to find out there is an issue when you are ready to fire up the engine.

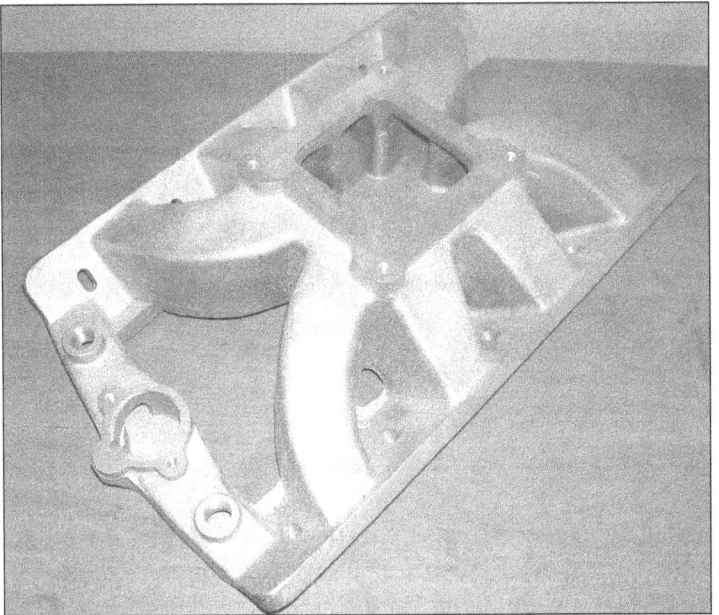

The Rocket Racing/Wenzler intake manifold is low enough to fit under stock hoods.

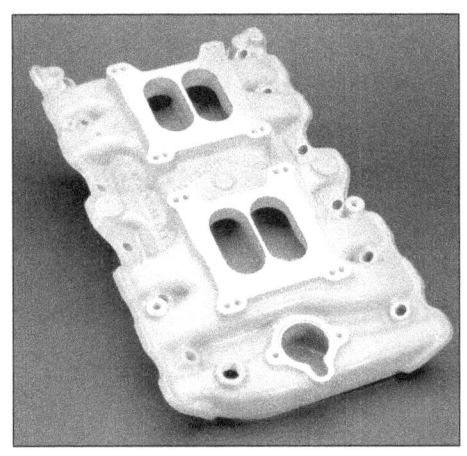

Offenhauser made a wide variety of manifolds such as this low-profile, dual 4-barrel aluminum manifold. It is a good-looking showpiece, but not good for performance.

OLDSMOBILE V-8 ENGINES: HOW TO BUILD MAX PERFORMANCE   119

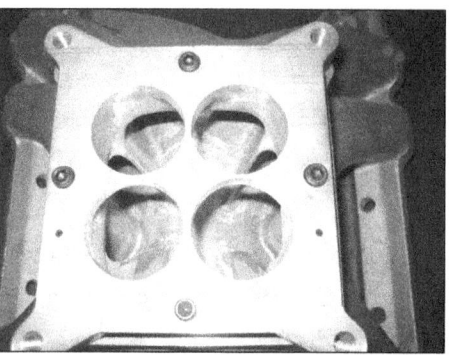

This highly modified 2811 Victor with Dominator flange was converted to a 4150 flange with extended runners and a blended-in four-hole BTR tapered carb spacer. It was the manifold used on the 2008 Popular Hot Rodding Engine Masters Challenge 400-ci engine that finished in the top ten.

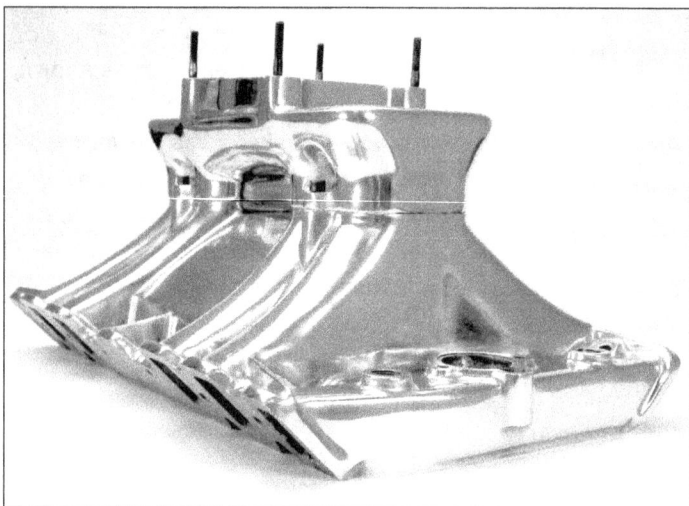

The Offenhauser tunnel ram was only made for the big-block Oldsmobile engine. It is available with a dual-4-barrel top or a single-4-barrel top (shown). You want the long straight runners, but their cross-sectional area is very small and the plenum does not have the best shape for performance. I consider it a show piece more than a performance manifold.

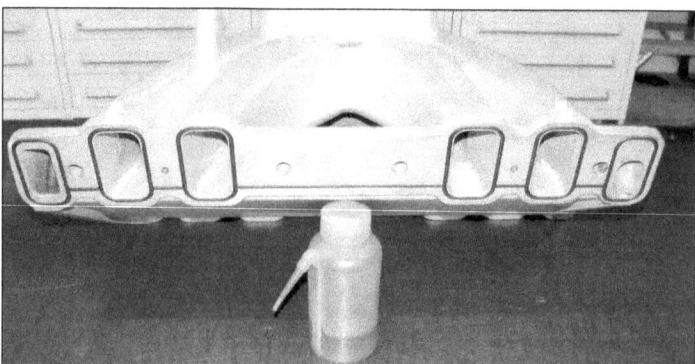

When a manifold needs to be milled severely to fit an engine properly, or in high-boost situations, we fit it with no gaskets and run a CNC program that machines O-ring grooves so that you never have to scrape a set of intake gaskets ever again. I hate scraping gaskets!

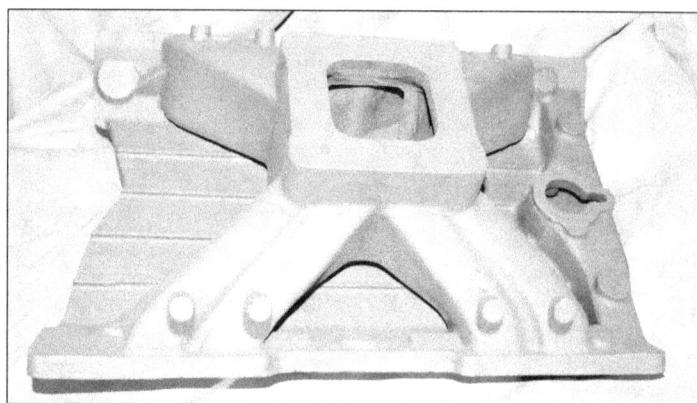

This manifold is a raw, non-machined big-block Batten intake manifold with a 4150 carburetor flange.

This unique, Algon stack-injection manifold was manufactured in the 1960s. You don't see too many of these around nowadays, but Greg Grubel uses this on his 1951 Chevrolet. An interesting tidbit on isolated runner manifolds is that they have wicked throttle response and I have seen them spit fuel like crazy (right out of the top of the stacks) at a certain RPM in a dyno cell.

CYLINDER HEADS AND INDUCTION

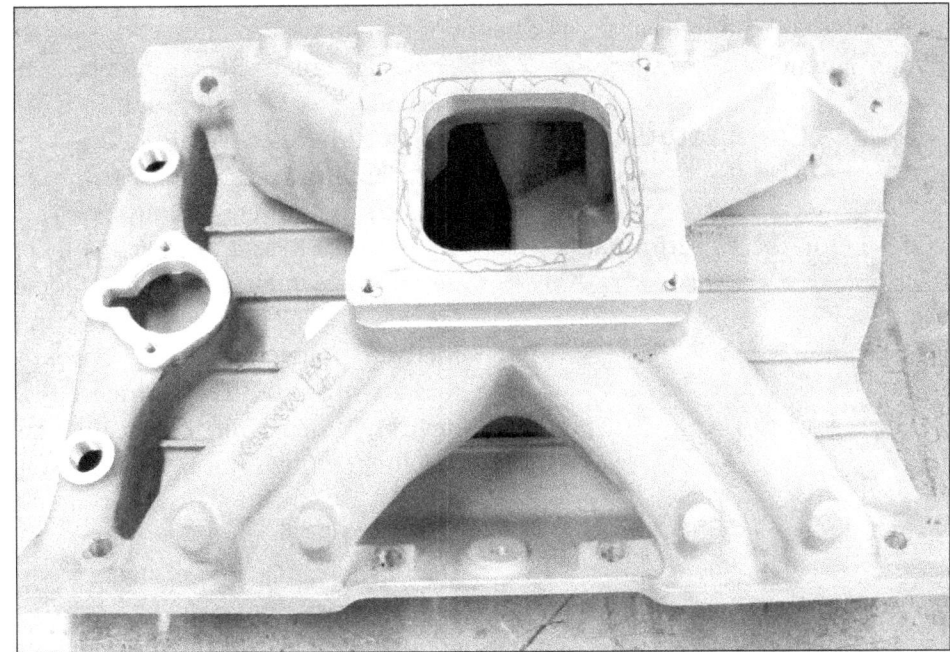

The 4150 flange Batten big-block Olds manifolds can be converted to accept a Holley Dominator-style carburetor with some machining of the plenum opening and relocating the mounting holes.

Steve at BTR is working on John Turner's custom billet tunnel ram.

The finished BTR billet tunnel ram helped make 780 hp out of Turner's 417-ci BTR-prepared DX Olds.

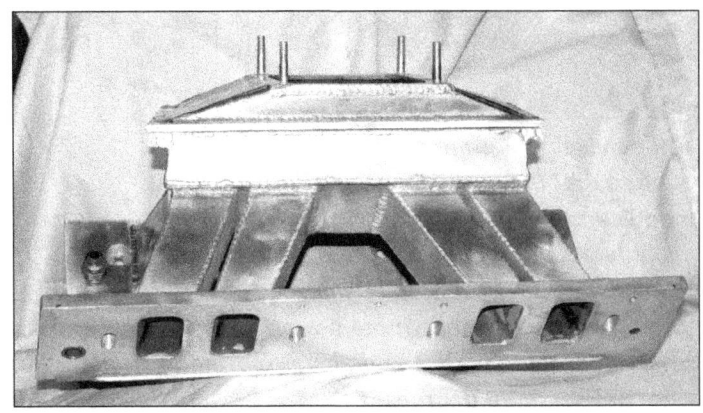

There have been numerous sheet-metal tunnel ram designs over the years for the Oldsmobile. Most of them are on a shelf rather than being used on a race car. The combination of short runners and large plenums are not necessarily a good fit for an Oldsmobile engine with an automatic transmission.

OLDSMOBILE V-8 ENGINES: HOW TO BUILD MAX PERFORMANCE   121

CHAPTER 7

more than one intake manifold with modifications inside the plenum that appeared like it should work well but did not. The modifications you do to the manifold floor affect fuel distribution and you typically cannot predict the outcome. These modifications have to be tested on an engine dynamometer or a racetrack.

Carburetors

What carburetor should you choose for best performance for your high-performance Oldsmobile? There are many books, much technical data, and varied opinions on which carburetor should be used for what application. Most of the technical data out there is many years old and looks at RPM and cubic inches to determine which carburetor should be selected. I am not sure that this method holds true today. Carburetors are ingenious self-compensating devices. When airflow increases, the carburetor flows more fuel. When airflow diminishes, the carburetor

The Rochester Quadrajet was a great carburetor as long as it was large enough for the application. When the Rochester products division stopped making carburetors, it sold the tooling to Weber, which made them for Edelbrock. The original tooling has since been destroyed, so brand-new ones are difficult to find. FYI, the old Rochester Products plant, now used by GM Delphi, just happens to be across the street from my shop.

While messing around on the dyno, I learned that the angle of the throttle blades and the upper air valve make a considerable horsepower difference. The 455 W-30 NHRA Stock Eliminator engine always made more power when the throttle blades and air valve were not set at 90 degrees.

I currently use Cubic Flow Modifications carburetors by Dale Cubic. I don't know what he does to these things, but each one I have tried has made power and had good idling characteristics and drivability.

CYLINDER HEADS AND INDUCTION

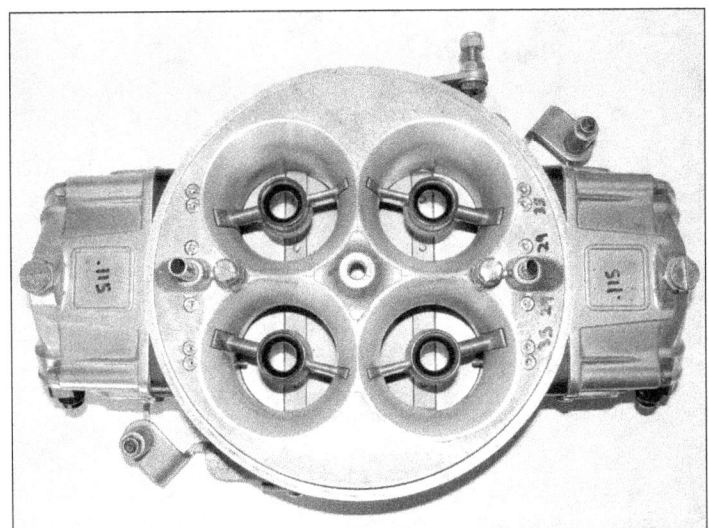

My CFM-prepared Holley Dominator carburetor has been highly modified for my small-cubic-inch nitrous application. This thing is big! Big carburetors can go faster if prepared correctly. I set the record in 2009 at 7.97 at 172 mph at Bradenton Raceway Park in the National Muscle Car Association's Xtreme Street class directly after bolting on this new one.

flows less fuel. To a degree, on whatever size engine a certain size carburetor is used, the ratio of air to fuel remains about the same.

Carburetor Spacers

Whether you have a Holley 4150 or Dominator-style carburetor, I have yet to see a four-hole tapered spacer

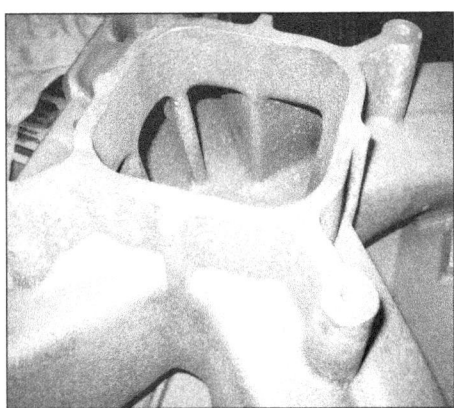

The old Edelbrock Victor small-block manifold for Batten heads only came in a 4150 flange version and needs a considerable amount of work to make good power. It has been unavailable for many years.

Milling off the carburetor flange allows you to get inside the runners to open up certain areas and shape the plenum properly with whatever carburetor flange you desire.

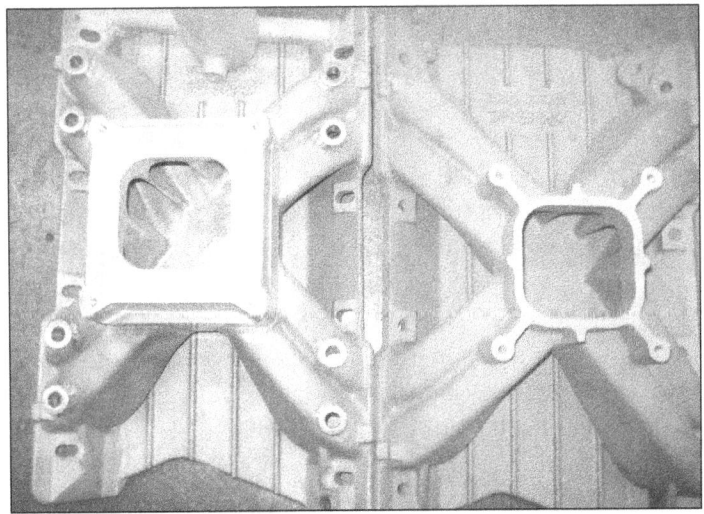

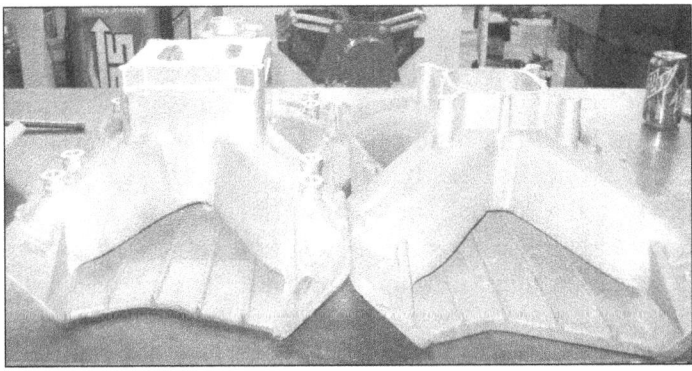

This side-by-side comparison shows an extensive plenum modification (left) on the small-block, old-style Edelbrock Victor for Batten heads for Gene Newton's twin-turbo small-block Olds.

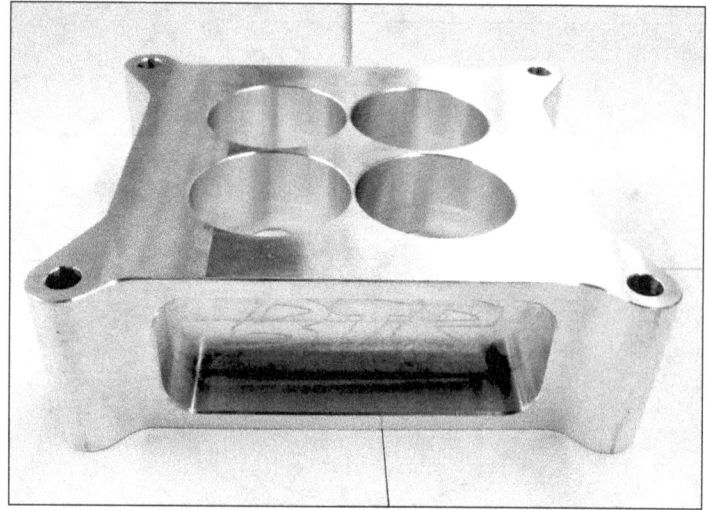

This BTR four-hole tapered spacer almost always helps throttle response and horsepower. Throttle bores slightly larger than the butterfly size on the carburetor make more power.

not increase performance. If you can fit it, use it. I have seen open-plenum spacers pick up power on occasion, but like most items on an engine, you can theorize until you turn blue. The only way to know if there is a net gain from the item you changed is to test it.

Carburetor Jetting

The biggest mistake people make with carburetors is that they select main jets too different from the stock jetting. Carburetor jetting is very simple, but is one of the most misunderstood tuning operations. The main jet in a carburetor is selected according to the size of the venturi, which is defined as the tightest area where the main booster is located. Without getting into a long discussion about how carburetors work, I can tell you that the jetting in a brand-new carburetor is already selected properly for you. This stock jetting is extremely close to being optimum for any engine onto which it is bolted.

When at the racetrack or on the engine dyno in normal air, one or two jet sizes up or down is all that is required to make the best power. It takes an air change of approximately 2,000 feet of density altitude to require you to make a jet change in the carburetor. At the local racetrack, I always see guys fooling with jets from week to week. Remember, the carburetor is self-compensating, and that rule applies to any engine.

Another mistake that people commonly make is in the power valve area. The power valve is simply a valve that opens and closes in front of two passages located in the metering block, allowing added or reduced main fuel (depending on throttle position and engine load). These two orifices in the metering block are equal to a certain size of main jet. For instance, a carburetor has a power valve in the primary side, regardless of that power valve's rating, and the main jet is, let's say, a pair of 80 jets, and the secondary metering block has no power valve and has, let's say, a pair of 90 jets. If you want to remove the primary power valve, and block it with a power valve plug, a pair of 90 jets is required for the primary main jet or the same as the secondary side of the carburetor. If the venturi size is the same, primary to secondary, the jetting should be the same. The common misconception is that when plugging the power-valve passages, you must add 10 jet sizes. Remember, the main jet is selected by venturi size.

Off-the-Shelf Carburetors

The average high-performance Oldsmobile street-and-strip enthusiast uses a 4150-style carburetor. The basic 350 engines with minimal modifications always seem to perform very well with the basic 650- to 750-cfm Holley (PN 4776 and PN 4779, respectively). The same-style 455 engines seem to love the basic 850-cfm Holley (PN 4781). If you have a low budget, you can't beat them. These carburetors work great, until someone puts their hands on them. The Holley HP-series carburetors take the HP Olds engine to the next level if you have extra money in the budget. I have used these in many different applications and they all performed well.

The Holley 950 HP (PN 80496) is the best choice for a 4.25-stroke

CYLINDER HEADS AND INDUCTION

Custom Rebuilt Carburetors restored this old Rochester Quadrajet. It looks great and worked perfectly on David Mendez's 520-hp 496 W30 restoration engine. It even picked up power over my old "best" dyno Quadrajet.

If you choose to run a high-flow mechanical fuel pump, such as the ROBBMC fuel pump, you have to modify the Edelbrock cylinder head. A portion of the front of the cylinder head is milled out into the water jacket and a new piece must be welded in.

455-type street engine that spins 6,000 rpm or the 375-ci stroker small-block. On my ever-so-popular 496 pump-gas street engines, I recommend the Holley 1000 HP (PN 80513). Both of these carburetors have downleg boosters and idle beautifully because their calibration is spot-on for these applications. Don't worry about them not having a choke; you do not need it.

I have dyno tested with these carburetors many times and have found that the calibration is pretty much spot-on straight from Holley. I typically reduce jet size by one number to make it perfect, but it may be different for you.

For the ultimate in Oldsmobile performance, the Holley Dominator carburetor is always the winner. I don't know if I have ever seen a 4150-style carburetor outperform the Dominator-style carburetor, regardless of the application. The box-stock 1,050-cfm Dominator with power valves (PN 8082) is a great choice for the street, and the 1,050-cfm Holley Dominator without power valves (PN 9375) is a pretty good choice for strip applications. Both of these carburetors work excellently on your basic 455, where budget is an important consideration, but a custom carburetor for the application brings performance to the next level.

Quadrajet Carburetors

The Rochester Quadrajet carburetor is a great carburetor in the applications for which it was designed. In more serious performance applications, they have their drawbacks. I recommend the Rochester for a restored Oldsmobile vehicle, or if the engine is going to appear stock, as do my 496 W30 engines.

These carburetors have two major problems. The first is that the main body on almost all of the Quadrajets tends to bend from over-torquing the front two 5/16 bolts that mount it to the intake manifold. Because of this, some of the passages between the main body and the top usually do not seal; the carb will never run well without repairing this situation first and it's not an easy fix.

Some carbs are worse than others, so this would be the first thing to look at when selecting a Quadrajet carburetor for your Oldsmobile build. If you think you are going to keep looking for one with the correct numbers that isn't warped, good luck. It would be very rare to find a perfect one. Some companies can repair, re-plate, rebuild, and recalibrate these carbs, if necessary.

The second issue is that these carbs have only one needle and seat, and a relatively small float bowl. These units have difficulty keeping enough fuel in the bowl for high-horsepower applications that require more fuel flow. Larger needles and seats are available, but that leads to other issues such as flooding because the float is not able to overcome the inlet pressure. The typical Quadrajet carburetor cannot withstand much more than 6 or 7 psi at idle with the largest needle and seat diameters.

One trick to make these carbs work in high-horsepower applications is to install a vacuum port above the diaphragm on your fuel regulator and run manifold vacuum to it. This modification reduces fuel pressure at idle as the negative pressure (vacuum) increases. At wide-open throttle, the manifold pressure is near zero, which gives the carburetor more pressure than the unit can manage at an idle. This setup is generally for racing only because part-throttle operation generates very high manifold vacuum pressure and lowers the fuel pressure considerably.

The diameter of the diaphragm in the fuel regulator and idle vacuum affect how the pressure reacts, so if you are going to try this, you cannot just hook up a vacuum line and drive around or race. You have to experiment to get it to work well.

I can't tell you how many Quadrajet "experts" are out there who screw up these carburetors! Do not despair if you plan to use a Rochester Quadrajet for your Oldsmobile build and need an expert to restore it and make it run well. I have sent numerous Quadrajets to Phil Cancilla at Custom Rebuilt Carburetors. I received every restored carburetor in nearly brand-new condition, and they all performed perfectly. I used to get a pit in my stomach every time I had to fire up a brand-new engine on the dyno with a "reworked by an expert" Quadrajet. I don't have that problem anymore and you don't have to either.

Custom Carburetors

A custom carburetor is a good investment for the serious Oldsmobile racer who would rather be going fast at the racetrack than fooling with a carburetor. Are they expensive? It depends on how you look at it. Everything of quality is expensive. A custom carburetor built for your application does everything it is required to do: make more horsepower and have a fuel curve as good as a properly tuned, and more expensive, electronic fuel injection setup. Yes, I mean more horsepower and less expensive.

A carburetor that is on the small side for an application performs well and does everything required for the racer, such as have crisp throttle response, go onto the trans brake quickly, and recover off the shift. A larger carburetor makes more power, but lacks those other attributes unless you purchase a larger custom carburetor from someone who knows how to make it work for your application.

A handful of carburetor shops are the real deal, but most of the rest are marketing hype. I bet that most people hear or see very little about these good guys; you want to be skeptical of the guys who are advertising all over the place. In my experience, these quality shops include Cubic Flow Modifications (Dale Cubic), Book Racing Enterprises (Bob Book), Braswell, and BLP Products, Inc. (Bo Laws). I have used carburetors from all of these companies and all of them exceeded my expectations. I suggest contacting one of them if you want the best-performing carburetor to complement your high-performance Olds build.

If you want to make maximum power from your Olds for the street, I recommend having Dale Cubic at CFM build you a custom Holley Dominator. It will be custom calibrated for your combination and have excellent street manners, which you won't get from a shelf Dominator-style carburetor.

CHAPTER 8

EXHAUST SYSTEM

Never has such a variety of exhaust solutions been offered for 1964 to 1976 Oldsmobile engines as now. Varieties available include aftermarket cast-iron "factory-style" exhaust manifolds, shorty headers, and stainless-steel headers with merge collectors. Although the factory performance cast-iron manifolds have become scarce, more aftermarket reproductions are now available and there are more Oldsmobile header manufacturers than ever before.

Virtually every mass-produced aftermarket Oldsmobile exhaust manifold and header is designed around the factory cylinder head. If you're using Edelbrock Oldsmobile cylinder heads, you're in luck because they are designed with the same exhaust flange as the factory heads and are compatible with all OEM-style Oldsmobile headers.

Batten cylinder heads require a custom exhaust flange and header and are not compatible with conventional Oldsmobile headers. Others, such as those made by Bulldog, Rocket Racing/Wenzler, and Mondello/Knowlton also use the factory exhaust flange.

Factory Cast-Iron Manifolds

Sometimes the decision is whether to go with factory cast-iron manifolds or aftermarket tubular headers. If yours is a stock restoration, a street-only, or a touring car and you want to hear the stereo and relax with the A/C on, your best choice is to use factory cast-iron exhaust manifolds.

The factory chose heavy cast-iron "log-style" manifolds because the thick, dense cast iron does a great job of dampening the exhaust note. Also, they were easy to manufacture, they were easy to install on the engine in a production line environment, and they made it easy to install the exhaust system in the frame on the assembly line. But there are a couple of downsides to these manifolds.

First, upon exiting the port, the exhaust gases hit the wall of the "log," causing part of the burnt gases to bounce back into the cylinder. This

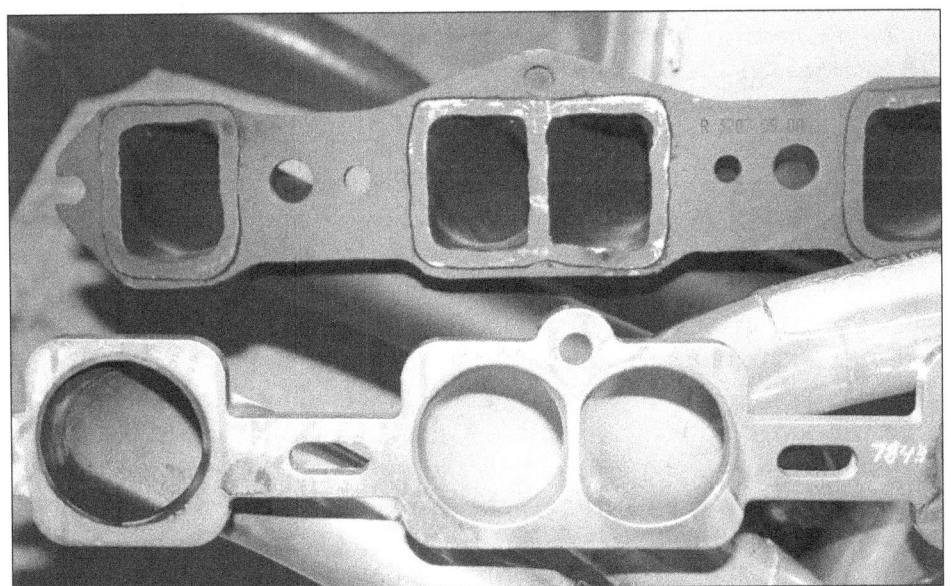

The upper flange is the 2-inch Hooker Super Competition headers, which are sized to match factory exhaust ports; the lower flange is the Zinch Kooks headers, now manufactured by Dick Miller Racing.

CHAPTER 8

This is the factory log-style cast-iron exhaust manifold for the Hurst Olds. This driver-side exhaust manifold has the casting number in the middle.

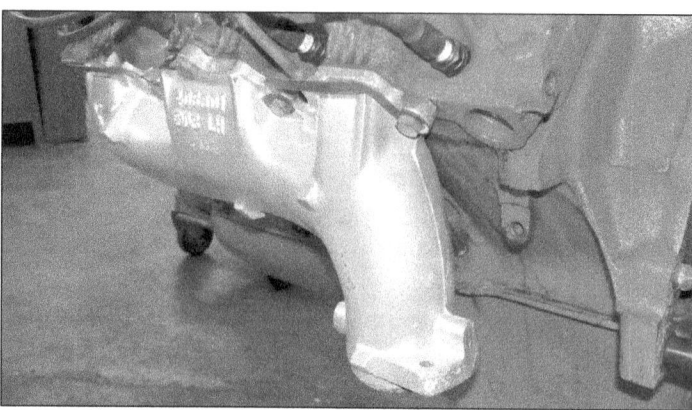
Oldsmobile, like many other manufacturers, used heavy and inefficient cast-iron manifolds. These are desirable for a stock restoration, but they are too restrictive for a max-performance engine.

The passenger-side Hurst Olds manifold is shown. A divider is placed between the middle two exhaust ports on the 1969–1972 exhaust manifolds. If you want to build serious horsepower, you need to replace them with tubular headers.

The casting number for this exhaust manifold appears close to the exhaust outlet.

dilutes the fresh incoming charge on the intake cycle and reduces power. To make matters worse, the cylinders are not isolated from one another in a log style, so you have four cylinders dumping exhaust into a relatively small area. This produces increased pressure in the exhaust system.

Other cylinders with an open valve become affected whenever the pressure in the log is greater than the pressure in the open cylinder, again resulting in a diluted or reduced intake charge and reducing power. If you have a 1973-or-newer-style intake with an exhaust gas recirculation (EGR) valve, you're in an even worse situation, with even more burnt exhaust gases further diluting your intake charge.

Second, you now have a huge hot hunk of cast iron (up to 1,500 degrees F at wide-open throttle) bolted to the side of your cylinder head. Add a crossover port, heating up your intake manifold, and you have two hot hunks of metal bolted to each side of the cylinder head heating it up and promoting detonation, pre-ignition, valveguide wear, and stress on the cooling system. If your application requires factory exhaust manifolds, you should, at the very least, block off the intake riser because your car probably doesn't need to heat up quickly on a cold winter morning, as we rarely drive these cars in the winter anyway.

Only three factory performance exhaust manifold sets were manufactured by Oldsmobile: the X/W manifolds, which came on the 1965 to 1967 442s; the X/Y manifolds, which came on the 1969 442s; and the W/Z manifolds, which came on the 1970 to 1972 442s.

You have the factory reproduction big-block X/W (1965–1967),

W/Z (1970–1972), and B&C Body cast-iron exhaust manifolds. There are also factory-style small-block exhaust manifolds with a passenger-side manifold that does not have the single exhaust port in the bottom of the passenger-side manifold (as all factory small-block passenger-side exhaust manifolds did). These are manufactured by Thornton Muscle Cars and sold through retailers such as Fusick and The Parts Place.

Performance Tips

I performed a couple of back-to-back tests on the dyno to compare these stock exhaust manifolds and tubular headers. In one test on a W-31–style street engine with hydraulic roller cam, stock intake manifold, and Quadrajet, the engine made 350 hp with the factory exhaust manifolds and 375 hp with 1¾-inch tubular headers. The horsepower difference between the exhaust manifolds and headers was not terribly significant, so if you want your W31 ride to look stock, exhaust manifolds certainly keep that sleeper/original appearance.

I also dyno tested one of my 496-ci 500-hp W-30 restoration engines with exhaust manifolds; horsepower levels were so low that I searched for a major problem. I started pulling spark plugs, taking compression tests, and generally looking at the condition of the engine because I knew how much power the engine should make.

I found that the engine was perfect so the only thing that could be killing it was the exhaust manifolds. I just simply refused to believe that the exhaust manifolds could kill torque that much. Then, I bolted on a set of Hooker 2-inch Super Comps and power levels were right where they should be. I believe it was somewhere in the neighborhood of 50 horsepower and about 50 ft-lbs of torque difference.

So, I suggest that you stay away from stock exhaust manifolds if you are looking for all-out performance, especially on big-blocks. And I do not think that porting them fixes anything. To put it simply, the issue is having no header tubes off the head; the exhaust ports basically dump into a big cavity.

Center Divider on Factory Heads

So what do you do with the recessed center divider on factory iron heads? It is this small factory-design characteristic that gives a stock Oldsmobile that unique Oldsmobile idle. Why is that? The short version is that factory engineers intended to combine the exhaust pulse of the four inner cylinders to smooth out the exhaust note. Since the Oldsmobile was marketed as a luxury car, engineers designed the cylinder heads and exhaust manifolds to make Oldsmobile engines smoother and quieter.

Because all headers and the aftermarket cast-iron manifolds have a center divider in them, you must make a decision on how to deal with them. Your options are to leave it alone, mill the exhaust surface down, or weld/braze in a center divider. In performance applications such as the 442, W-30, and H/O, the factory designers decided to leave it alone. Even though the exhaust manifolds have center dividers, they left the recessed center divider alone because the cost to tool separate cylinder head castings with a center divider was not justified by the limited market for high-performance Oldsmobiles at the time.

You have several options if you want to separate the center cylinders. Some suppliers make a cheesy wedge of sheet metal that the manifold or header is supposed to hold in place after you shove it into place to extend the divider. Another option is to mill down the exhaust-flange surface to anywhere from .125 to .150

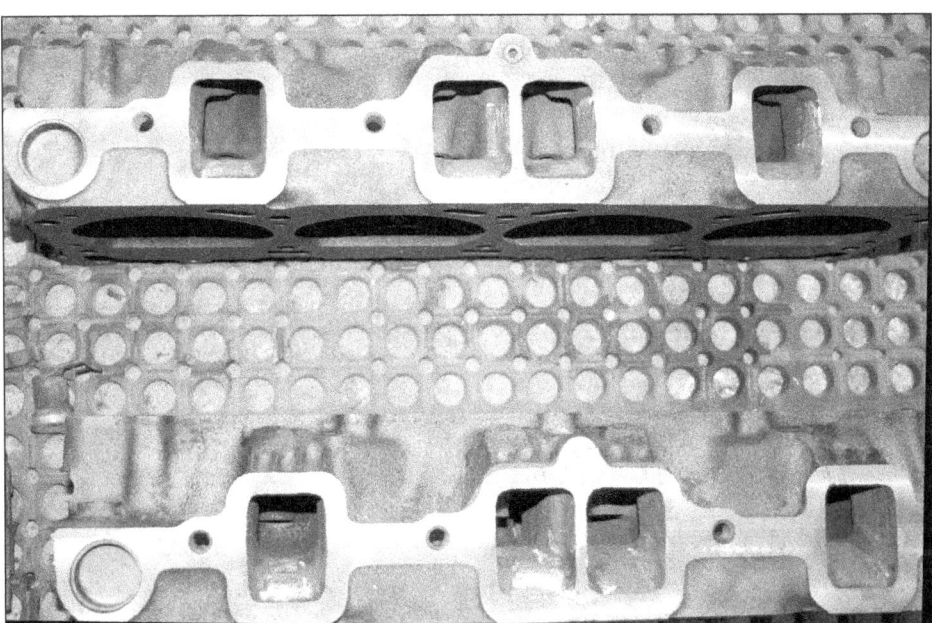
With a little hand work, the center exhaust ports can be made much nicer.

CHAPTER 8

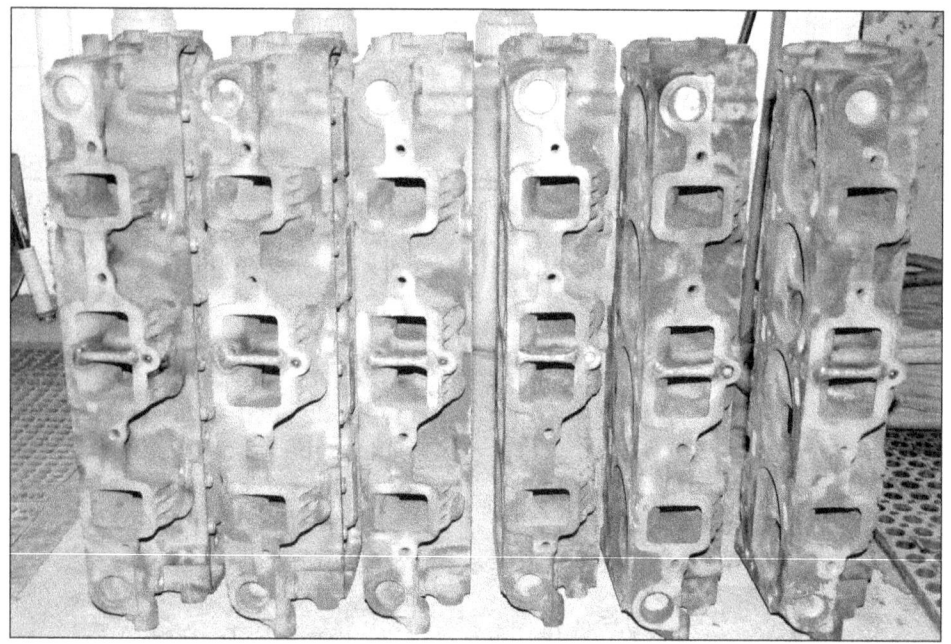

You can carefully MIG-weld the center exhaust divider so that it can be machined flush. Keeping the heat low gives you the best chance of not cracking the divider.

inch until you get down to a flush divider, but this can change the fit of your headers. The header flanges will probably hit the deck of the block, and you have to port the header and raise the roof in it.

The preferred method is to either braze or MIG-weld-in a center divider extension, shape the divider to the gasket with porting tools, and then mill the flange just enough to make a flat surface. My preference is for welding a divider, but it requires an experienced, patient welder with the will to do it right. Some prefer to pre-heat the casting. I do not braze the dividers.

Header Sizing

The basic principle of tubular headers is that, just like an intake manifold, they are an extension of the cylinder head's exhaust runner. And the goal is for them to have a similar cross-sectional area as the cylinder head exhaust runner. You neither want a header primary tube smaller in size than the exhaust port, nor that primary tube considerably larger. In a high-performance Olds cylinder head, the maximum exhaust-valve diameter is in the neighborhood of 1.65 to 1.7 inches. The exhaust port should have a gradual expansion from that valve. You don't want 2¼-inch header tubes right off the port creating a rapid expansion (the goal is for smooth exhaust flow). A 1¾- to 2-inch-diameter primary tube effectively and ideally extends the cylinder-head runner.

In a maximum-effort engine, the header should get larger slowly (referred to as step headers) so that flow isn't disrupted with rapid expansions. The primary tube should closely match the cross-sectional area of the exit of the exhaust runner for the first 9 inches or so of the primary header tube and then step up to the next tube size. Some step headers go up one size, some even go up three tubing sizes.

I think all of these guidelines are on target but are worthless without testing. As many times as I have been correct in my testing of exhaust-header selections, I have lost power on other tests. The bottom line here is that if you follow these guidelines in header sizing and selection, you make reasonably good power. To extract every ounce of horsepower, you have to test your theories.

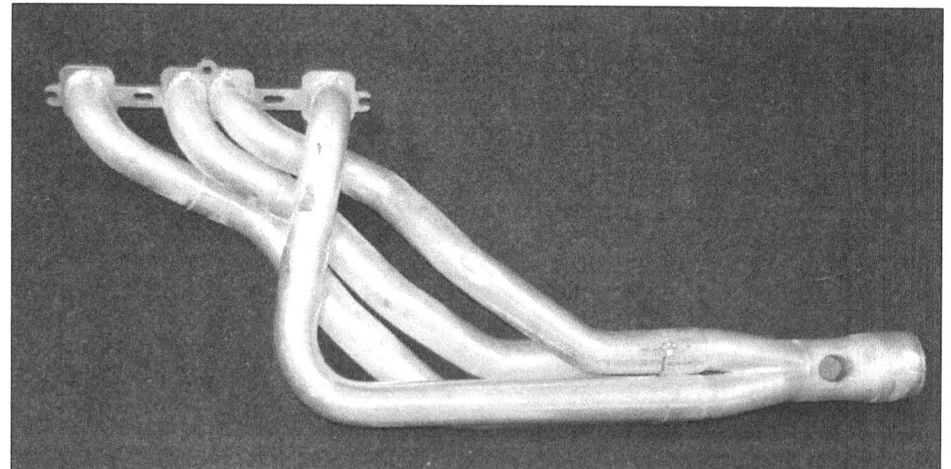

This 2-inch primary Kooks header with merge collector was originally tested on our first Popular Hot Rodding *Engine Masters Challenge 410-ci small-block Olds entry. The engine had a weird torque loss from 2,500 to 3,500 rpm so we didn't use it. We wound up using the 1⅞-inch Hooker Super Competition model for a 1977 Cutlass.*

Full-Size Headers

Today, there are more Oldsmobile header manufacturers than there have ever been.

Hooker Headers

In my experience, if you want good-quality headers that fit, and by that I mean you do not have to dent any tube on the headers with a ball-peen hammer to make them fit, you should be buying a set of Hooker Headers. Hooker has been making them since the 1960s; they fit back then, and they still fit today.

For the 455, the 3101 Super Comps have 1¾- x 32-inch-long primary tubes with a 3-inch collector and are about $500 (painted) at the big speed-parts retailers. The 3202 Super Comps have 1⅞ x 36-inch-long primaries with a 3.5-inch collector and are about $650 (unpainted). Finally, Hooker also makes the 3201, a 2 x 32-inch-long primary tube header. The driver-side header has one tube that passes over the frame rail and requires some minor notching of the inner fender. They are all great headers for general street/strip applications.

American Racing Headers

If you need a good-quality set of headers that make power and are a step up, American Racing Headers can handle the job. It has headers available for G bodies with a primary-tube diameter of up to 1⅞ inch, and the 1964–1977 Cutlass with a primary-tube diameter of up to 2 inches, in regular steel and optional stainless steel if you are sick and tired of rusty headers. All of these headers come standard with merge collectors, and ARH often custom-sizes them for application. I used the G-body headers in the 2008–2010 *Power Hot Rodding* Engine Masters Challenge engine competition and I'm here to tell you that the design of these contributed to the success of that engine.

Other Headers

Several other quality brands are available, including Doug's Headers and Kooks Custom Headers; this last company makes quality headers for big-block Olds applications. As I have not tried them, I can't vouch for their fit.

Visit some of the popular Internet forums and do your research before you buy.

Low-Cost Headers

If you need to go with an inexpensive header, both Hooker and Hedman have offerings in the $200 range and both have been building Oldsmobile headers since the 1960s. Do not buy any other brand of low-cost header unless you hold it in your hand and look at it before you buy. A number of recognizable names sold as low-priced products on the Internet and at the big name retailers are junk. You'll recognize them when you see welds that look as if they were done with a 1950s-era stick welder.

Merge Collectors

I have seen different-shaped collectors make different horsepower readings on many different engines. The largest gains you see with merge collectors are in the low-end torque

These are bolt-on merge-style collectors. These collectors usually increase low-end torque. But when it comes to exhaust headers, nothing seems to be guaranteed. Testing is almost always necessary.

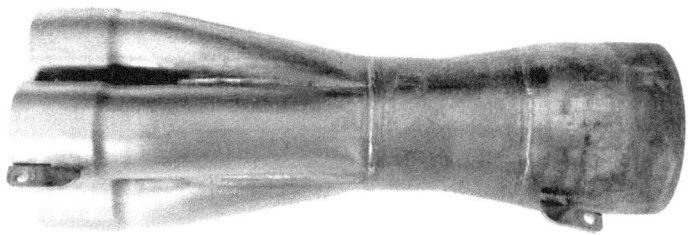

This merge collector is from my 403-ci 1,200-hp Olds Starfire. The headers are 2- to 2⅛-inch Kooks stainless step headers. The merge section necks down from the four 2⅛ primary tubes to 3½ inches, then exits to 4 inches and goes into a 4-inch straight-through muffler.

numbers. I really noticed some very large torque swings with collectors during preliminary dyno testing on my 400-ci Engine Masters Challenge engine at low RPM because the contest required that the dyno pull start at 2,400 rpm. At this low RPM, I saw torque reductions of as much as 100 ft-lbs of torque; in the worst case, it was between 2,500 and 3,500 rpm, depending on collector size and shape. Merge collectors ultimately help these numbers. But with the shape, length, and size of the merge collectors that I tried, all did something different.

Merge collectors are always a good idea, but unless you are dyno testing, let one of the header experts, such as American Racing Headers, choose them for you.

Painted versus Coated versus Stainless

Over the years I have owned many different sets of headers that were painted, coated with various products, and made of stainless steel. Yes, I know the stainless-steel headers are more expensive. I'm here to tell you, after owning every kind of header imaginable, I would never, ever, own another set of headers that were not made of stainless. I hate doing things twice, buying things twice, and looking at rusted headers.

Crank Case Evacuation

I have seen plenty of crankcase evacuation tubes welded in collectors that simply do not work. I played around with this stuff years ago and monitored the negative pressure. What I learned was that the 1/2-inch pipe nipple had to be positioned in exactly the right position to get any kind of negative pressure, and very little at that. Anything other than the exact location didn't do a thing for pulling vacuum. When any kind of muffler was installed in the exhaust system, I could not achieve a negative pressure, no matter what. If you want crank case evacuation, install a vacuum pump on the engine

Exhaust Gaskets

Flatout Gaskets manufactures some killer header gaskets for the Oldsmobile engine. They are available in silicone coated, soft copper, graphite, and steel-clad versions. I personally use the steel-clad header gaskets and find them to seal great,

Flatout Gaskets re-useable exhaust gasket (PN 7186S) for stock Oldsmobile Performer RPM exhaust ports.

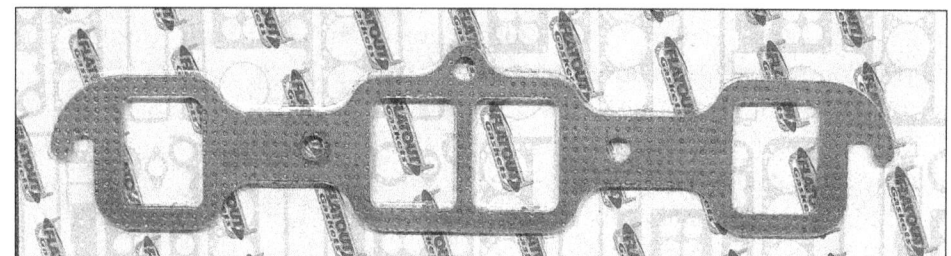
Flatout Gaskets re-useable exhaust gasket (PN 7016S) for stock Oldsmobile factory cast-iron cylinder-head exhaust ports.

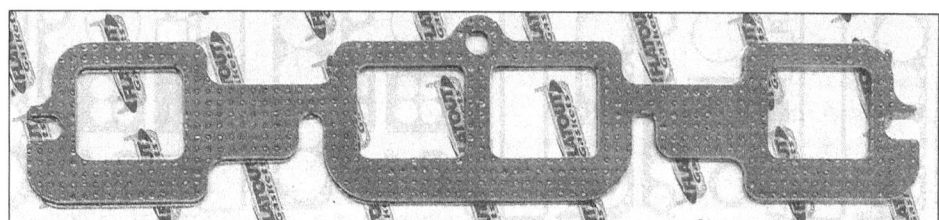
Flatout Gaskets re-useable exhaust gasket (PN 7032S) for Oldsmobile Batten cylinder-head exhaust ports.

Flatout Gaskets re-useable exhaust gasket (PN 7182) for Oldsmobile Edelbrock cylinder head with BTR port/Bulldog.

EXHAUST SYSTEM

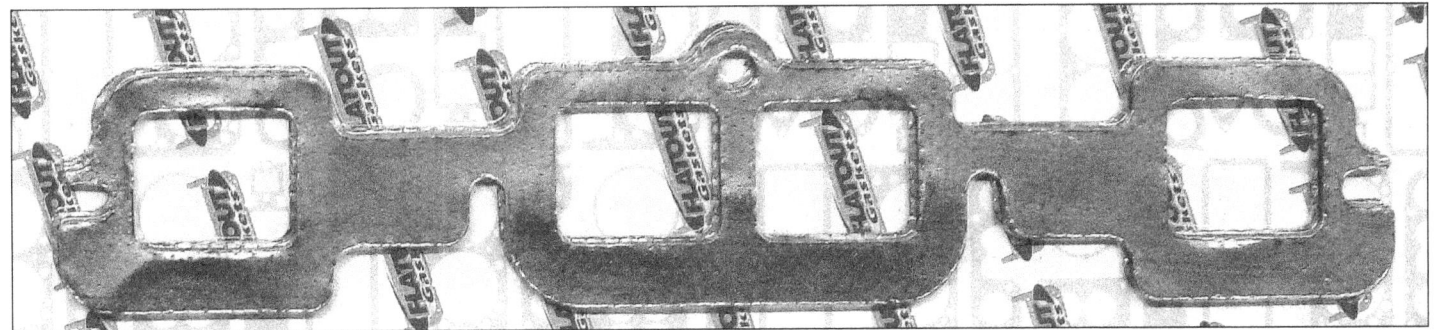

Flatout Gaskets' soft graphite header gasket (PN 7032) for Oldsmobile Batten cylinder-head exhaust ports.

and they can be reused many times. The soft graphite gaskets work great on an application that doesn't get torn apart often and has surface irregularities. All exhaust gaskets are available in all three styles. Order with no suffix for the graphite type, the "S" suffix for the steel-clad reusable style, and the "C" suffix after your part number for a copper exhaust gasket.

Mufflers and Exhaust Pipes

Borla, MagnaFlow, DynoMax, Hooker, and others make very nice straight-through-design mufflers. The larger the volume of the body means the quieter the muffler. A 3.5-inch straight-through bullet has the same performance as a 3.5-inch straight-through big-bodied DynoMax muffler, but that big-bodied DynoMax is quieter. It's that simple.

Back in the day, when I raced my street-driven red 1970 Cutlass, I tried a bunch of different mufflers and ended up with some very-large-bodied, straight-through, 4-inch mufflers mounted in the rear of the car. I think there was only about a .050-inch difference in quarter-mile ET, but the car was extremely quiet. It was a pleasure to race that car with virtually no noise.

I have never been a fan of chambered mufflers and feel that they sacrifice power. Although I have never done any back-to-back testing, I can't be convinced that air flowing around baffles is better than air flowing through a straight tube. Air in; air out. That is what makes power. Flowmaster, Hooker Aero Chamber, Spin Tech, and others manufacture these types of baffled mufflers, which produce a unique sound.

The DynoMax Ultra Flo series of mufflers are a straight-through design, and are a very light stainless muffler, if weight is a consideration.

This 3½-inch MagnaFlow muffler is a straight-through design and has little or no restriction.

Oldsmobile V-8 ENGINES: HOW TO BUILD MAX PERFORMANCE

CHAPTER 9

IGNITION SYSTEM

The ignition system is one of the commonly overlooked areas of an engine build. Everyone wants a reliable, high-horsepower engine that doesn't skip a beat, idles well, doesn't load up spark plugs, and doesn't burn your eyes from unburned fuel coming out of the exhaust. You can achieve this, but not with an old HEI distributor that has rusty weights that hang up or, even worse, a Chinese knock-off that has other issues.

Do not overlook this area. It is just as important as the build itself. I use MSD Ignition Products exclusively to finish off a successful build. MSD has the highest quality and reliability of all ignition systems on the market. If you look at a successful racing operation at any racetrack, 99.9 percent of the competitors have MSD ignition systems products throughout the race car.

Ignition Boxes

A multiple-spark-discharge ignition box, commonly referred to as an MSD box, is mandatory on all of my builds and should be mandatory on your engine builds if you want your project to run well. Two kinds of ignition boxes are currently manufactured. These are the old-style analog boxes and digital boxes that use the latest technology.

Analog Ignition Boxes

The original basic analog MSD box, such as the 6A unit, is by far the most popular ignition box of all time. For the Olds enthusiast on a budget, this unit is your bare minimum. For such a high-quality product, they are very inexpensive when new.

Beware of "great" deals on the Internet because many are actually counterfeit MSD boxes. Buy your ignition box from a reputable dealer; they are already a great deal for what you get in return. The 6A is a simple basic spark box that puts some serious voltage to the spark plugs; the plugs don't "foul" out like the old days.

When I was a young guy playing around with my first Cutlass, I bought an MSD 6A box as one of its first performance upgrades. After the simple installation, the first thing I noticed when I fired up the engine was that my eyes didn't burn when the car sat and idled. I also noticed right away that the spark plugs were no longer black. Before I installed the box, I put in new spark plugs all the time and they always fouled black. With the addition of the 6A box, the plugs stayed clean. It was a simple solution to a simple problem.

If you want an upper-RPM rev limiter, you need an MSD 6AL unit. This

If you're building a max-performance engine, you need a modern high-performance ignition system to keep pace with it. MSD makes some of the best ignition components for Olds V-8 engines.

product has the same features as the 6A box plus a small "chip" that limits the engine to a maximum safe RPM. This feature is generally good to have because there will be a time when your car spins the tires severely, breaks a rear gear (or something else), and the engine's RPM goes to the moon. At that point, something in the valvetrain usually flies apart, and you end up with bent pushrods or worse.

It doesn't cost much more to get an MSD box with the rev limiter, so it's a wise investment that can save you a lot of money when the engine buries the tach. Notice that I said *when* and not *if* the engine buries the tach. It will happen.

The MSD 7A box is probably the most popular bracket racing ignition box. These boxes have been in production for a very long time and many are still in service. This ignition box has increased spark energy for high-compression engines as well as those burning alcohol. It comes with features such as a two-step RPM rev limiter. One rev limiter is for maximum engine RPM and the second rev limiter is so the driver can apply the transbrake and limit engine RPM below converter stall speed to control traction or reaction time.

In addition to these popular analog boxes, MSD also manufactures the 7AL3, MSD 8, and MSD10 for applications that require the absolute most spark energy. All of these analog boxes are being phased out in favor of MSD's digital ignitions.

Digital Ignition Boxes

There are basically two styles of digital ignition boxes from MSD. One is programmable with a laptop computer and the other original designs are not. The programmable ignitions are the only boxes worth discussing in detail.

The programmable MSD ignition has many advantages. It allows the user to set any engine timing anywhere in the curve. The programmable ignition box gives the user full control with a computer keystroke.

I consider the MSD 6AL2 programmable ignition box (PN 6530) mandatory on all of my street Olds builds for numerous reasons. A distributor, or even worse, an old HEI or OEM distributor, with rusty weights does not provide accurate timing. Have you ever seen someone at a racetrack trying to adjust the timing while struggling to see the mark and revving the engine to 9,000 while trying to get the timing to stop moving? Does this make sense to you? Trust me; it's not the way to set your timing.

The way to have accurate timing is with programmable digital ignition boxes from MSD and a distributor with no moving weights. When you have all of the proper components working together you just let the engine idle, set your baseline timing, and have the computer do the rest.

One of the biggest advantages of using this box is that it allows the user to have full timing at idle. This keeps the plugs clean and gives the best idle quality. One of the biggest mistakes you can make is to have low ignition timing at idle.

Have you ever noticed that when you set the ignition timing low (14 degrees at idle, for example), set the idle speed, and then set the timing higher the idle speed increases? What frequently happens is that when you have low ignition timing, the throttle blades have to open up to get to the idle speed you want. That typically uncovers the transfer slots in the carburetor throttle bores too much or allows too much air speed past the idle fuel passage. The result is over-rich idle. You cannot fix this without extensively modifying the carburetor.

By selecting full timing at idle, it's an easy fix for the MSD Digital 6AL. You can easily produce a timing curve so that the engine has full timing at idle and much less at starter cranking speed. The main screen of the MSD Graph View file has a graph called the "run retard curve" file.

The MSD 6530 ignition box is laptop controllable and has a number of features that you need to get your Oldsmobile performance engine running at its peak performance! It is one of the best bolt-on products you can buy.

The MSD 6425 digital 6AL gives the entry-level user a rev limiter and basic high-voltage spark. The upper RPM rev limit is adjustable with a small screwdriver, unlike the different-value chips that had to be purchased for the analog 6ALs of the past.

CHAPTER 9

The MSD Power Grid system is the ultimate in performance applications. It has the ability to control ignition timing in every way. If you are a serious track racer or street racer, you can even control traction in multiple ways with add-on units.

This allows the user to place dots in strategic locations to set the ignition timing at user-selected values and RPM for the ignition. Once you set the ignition timing the first time, you pretty much never need to get the timing light out again. Everything from that point on is done on the laptop screen and transferred into the 6530 box.

Advance Curves

I do not usually find the need for an advance curve in an engine as I did in the old days. The "all in by 3,000 rpm" rule is a thing of the past. If the engine is designed properly, with the right compression for the fuel, there is not much need for reduced timing at low RPM. If you happen to get some bad fuel or you are running the compression on the ragged edge, it is useful to remove a few degrees at cruise RPM between 1,700 and around 2,700. That's a snap with digital programmable boxes from MSD.

Another hot trick from the past that you want to avoid is the infamous top-end retard. In the past, people removed timing in high gear, but this does not increase an ET. I'm not even sure where that trick came from, but I can assure you, it doesn't help. If you want to play with an advance curve, there may be some advantage to adding timing as RPM increases, especially in first gear. In my personal engines, I have found that horsepower and ET increases by adding a few degrees to timing in first gear as RPM increases.

Crank Triggers and Magnetic Pickups

A crank trigger gives you the most accurate ignition timing. Do you need this setup on a street engine? You probably don't if you have a good MSD Pro Billet distributor and programmable digital ignition box, but your ignition timing cannot be too accurate. The following is a quick refresher on the reason for a crank trigger, how they work, and what they do.

The crank trigger wheel, along with the magnetic sensing pickup, is simply an accurate switch. The combination of these two items tells the ignition box to throw a spark at a precise moment; this is the ignition timing. This switch does exactly the same thing as the magnetic pickup or the points inside a distributor. Again, all of these (points, magnetic pickup, the Mallory Unilite, or the crank trigger) are simply switches.

The difference between the switch inside the distributor and the crank trigger is the diameter of the triggering device. The diameter of a typical crank trigger wheel is generally about 8 inches with four magnets at 90-degree intervals. A typical reluctor inside a distributor is about 1 to 2 inches in diameter and the distance between each sensing tip is quite a bit less than on an 8-inch wheel.

At high RPM it is much more accurate to have a larger-diameter wheel with more space between the magnets. You will probably never see a difference with a timing light at low RPM. If you are a serious racer, you run a crank trigger setup.

Distributors

A number of Oldsmobile distributors are on the market. If you want to purchase a high-quality distributor so that you can cross distributor issues off your headache list, just purchase an MSD Pro Billet (PN 8566). Simply put, they work, and I have *never* had an issue with one. (And I have seen various problems through the years with some other brands of aftermarket distributors.)

MSD also manufactures a "ready to run" model (PN 8529 Pro Billet Distributor) that does not require a coil or an ignition box. Everything required to run the engine is self-contained inside the unit. I have never used one, but would not be afraid to because I trust all of their products.

If you want stock appearance, the old-style stock housing works well with a points conversion kit. I have used Pertronix points conversion kits with success. I have used both the lobe sensing kit (PN 1181LS) as well as the kit that has a magnetic wheel that bolts underneath the rotor (PN 1181). Both of these simply bolt in and work well.

The conversion kit is very easy to install and has everything you

IGNITION SYSTEM

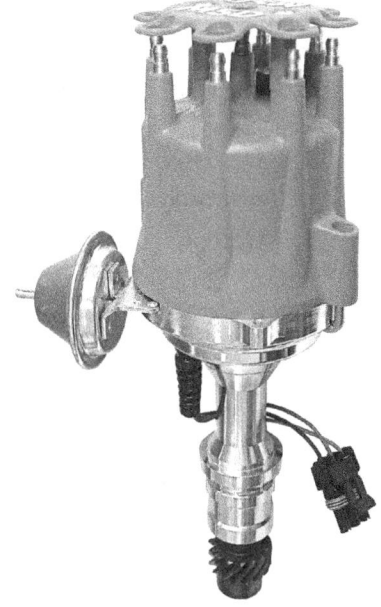

The MSD ready-to-run distributor is designed for the entry-level street enthusiast who needs a distributor to make the engine run with the entire ignition system contained in one unit. This distributor contains the coil and the spark box right inside. Just hook up a few wires and go!

I have not seen any quality HEI caps and rotors in parts stores lately. If you are using an HEI Oldsmobile distributor in your ride, do yourself a favor and purchase the MSD 8416 cap and rotor kit. The kit includes a carbon low-resistance bushing that does not burn up as the auto parts store equivalents do.

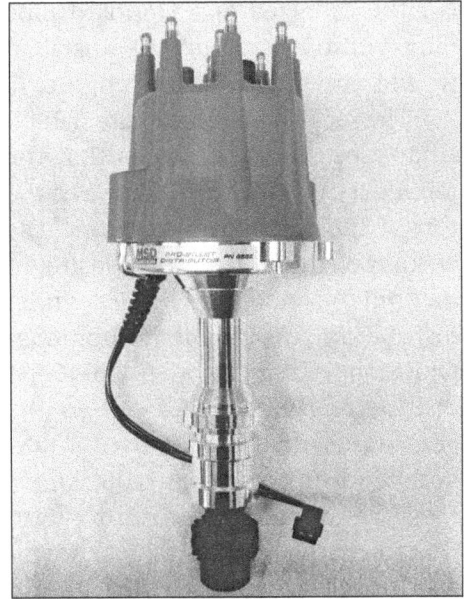

Choosing the MSD 8566 distributor is a no-brainer in Oldsmobile performance applications. It looks like a million bucks, fits well, and performs flawlessly. I always lock the advance mechanism. To do this, remove the gear, remove the nut underneath the weights, rotate the shaft 180 degrees, and reinstall the nut. You don't want to run an advance curve because if you do, your engine idles poorly and loads up with fuel. There is absolutely no reason to run a vacuum advance, which is probably the reason it is not an option.

The Pertronix Ignitor electronic conversion kit works well if you have to run a stock Oldsmobile distributor for restoration purposes.

need. The Pertronix pickup has red and black leads; the red wire hooks up to a 12-volt ignition source and the black wire hooks up to the white triggering wire on the MSD box.

When using the stock GM distributor, it is best to lock the weights with tack welding or pinning them so that they *never* move; use an MSD 6530 programmable box. If you are going to mess around with the stock weights and springs for an advance curve, you are just asking for a headache. Trust me on this.

Distributor Gears

Three types of distributor gears are manufactured: steel, nitrided steel, and bronze. All of the manufactured distributor gears are made for a .491-shaft distributor with the exception of MSD, which only sells a steel gear. These are manufactured for a .500 shaft, which is unique to MSD distributors.

When a bronze or nitrided steel gear is needed for an MSD distributor, the distributor has to be reamed to .501 because they are manufactured at .491 for stock-style distributor shafts.

Oldsmobile performance vendors generally stock the .501-diameter bronze or nitrided steel distributor gears for the MSD distributors if you need one.

The typical steel distributor gears that come standard on all distributors are used on camshaft cores that use a cast-iron gear. These camshaft cores include all flat-tappet camshafts and some special hydraulic-roller models. Typical hydraulic-roller and mechanical-roller camshafts require a bronze or a nitrided steel distributor gear.

I recommend a bronze gear rather than the nitrided steel gear.

CHAPTER 9

The all-too-common worn distributor pad in the engine block. Installing a shim between the distributor gear and the distributor housing (as in a Chevrolet) always causes this. I have used blocks with this worn pad, but if you are selecting a block for your project, it is better to have one that is not worn.

Oldsmobile enthusiasts with street engines and roller cams always seem to worry about wearing out a gear. I have found that if you don't have crazy oil pressure that puts more load on the gears, and you have the spit hole in the rear of the lifter passage spraying oil onto the gears, the bronze distributor gear is not a problem.

The nitrided steel gear from Comp Cams is certainly an option, but if there is an unforeseen issue between the gears, for whatever reason, the nitride gear will take out the camshaft gear and you will be replacing both of them. If you have a bronze gear riding on the camshaft and that unforeseen issue actually happens, it will take out the bronze gear but the situation can be resolved without tearing the engine apart to replace the camshaft.

Distributor gear problems generally have one of two causes. The first is that the spit hole in the 3/8-pipe plug in the rear of the lifter passage is either plugged or a standard pipe plug without a hole was installed when someone rebuilt the engine.

The second possible cause, which I have seen many times, is that the rebuilder installed shims between the top of the distributor gear and the bottom of the distributor housing to take out the endplay as in a Chevrolet distributor. This is a big no-no on an Oldsmobile distributor! A Chevrolet distributor rotates clockwise so the gear wants to climb upward. Oldsmobile distributors, as you know, have a counter-clockwise rotation that forces the distributor gear downward against the machined pad in the engine block.

By taking the endplay out of the distributor, it forces the bottom of the distributor gear into that pad, causing severe wear. This design works in such a way that when the distributor is rotating, the gear has a slight downward force, which allows the bottom of the distributor gear to rest against that machined pad in the block. It sets the gear height so that the relationship of the camshaft gear and distributor gear has proper mesh.

The MSD HVC2 coils (PN 8261) is the highest voltage coil available for power grid ignitions. You find this coil on 90 percent of maximum-performance applications.

The factory designed all this to work properly; don't redesign anything in this area.

Ignition Coils

You need the proper ignition coil to provide spark to your Oldsmobile performance engine. If you are running an MSD box, as you should, it requires a particular ignition coil, depending on which product you are using. Be sure that the ignition coil is compatible with the ignition box.

Spark Plugs

For most Oldsmobile applications I use NGK V power spark plugs. I install BKR7E spark plugs for nearly all street applications with Edelbrock Performer RPM cylinder heads. It's a good all-around heat range that stays clean in 10.5:1 compression engines and does not induce detonation. The "7" in the part number is the heat range. If you want a colder spark plug, select an "8" or higher number. If you want it to be a little hotter

The MSD 8251 coil is the original HVC coil. When I was dyno testing one of the EMC Oldsmobile engines, I performed back-to-back dyno tests with the HVC 1 versus the HVC 2; the HVC 1 coil came out the winner. If someone told me this, I would not have believed it; but I saw it with my own eyes.

IGNITION SYSTEM

in the range, select a lower number, such as a BKR5E.

You always want the hottest-range spark plug that does not induce detonation so that it stays clean. For cast-iron factory heads, I use an NGK XR45 99 percent of the time. The only time I use something else is if I am running nitrous oxide or some sort of power adder. This is usually not the case for an Oldsmobile enthusiast; this person typically uses an aluminum cylinder head.

In high-performance or racing applications requiring a 14-mm .750 reach spark plug, I use Autolite AR series racing spark plugs. On the hotter side of the range, plug number AR3934 is in order. I generally use this heat range on engines with a compression of 13:1 and less that use racing gas or alcohol.

On engines with more compression or small power adders, I use the AR3933 plugs. On serious nitrous oxide, turbocharger, or blower applications, and my own personal nitrous Oldsmobile 1,200-hp small-block, I use an Autolite AR3932 spark plug.

Reading Spark Plugs

You cannot read spark plugs that have been run for a while, so don't try. I cannot tell you how many times I have seen someone looking at old spark plugs and say they look rich or lean, or had someone ask me to read a spark plug that had a lot of time on it.

The only way to properly read a spark plug is to have a brand-new set installed with very little (preferably none) idle time on them. Then, make some full-throttle pulls on an engine dynamometer or make a quarter-mile pass down a dragstrip, shutting off the engine as soon as you can when you get off the throttle.

As a side note, you cannot shut the engine off at high speed and move the transmission to neutral on a TurboHydramatic 400 or a 350 transmission, because it is very likely that you could break the sprag inside the unit. In these applications, slow the car as quickly as possible and kill the ignition as soon as you can.

In general, what you are looking for is clean porcelain with a small amount of coloring on the base all the way down, where it is difficult to see without a good magnifying glass or loupe. In general, clean is not lean. The ground strap on the plug should show some heat discoloration. The amount of heat on the ground strap generally tells you if the heat range, or the ignition timing, is correct.

Spark Plug Wires

Of course, I recommend MSD spark plug wires. Moroso also manufactures a very good spark plug wire. The ends used in either of these sets snap onto the spark plug or cap tightly and stay crimped on the wire during many on and off cycles.

I use the NGK V Power spark plug (PN BKR7ES) in 99 percent of my pump-gas street builds with Edelbrock heads. Another good choice for max compression pump-gas Oldsmobile engines is the Autolite AR3934 spark plug.

Setting Ignition Timing

I cannot stress the importance of setting the ignition timing properly. The quickest way to ruin an engine is improper ignition timing. The absolute first thing you should do when you fire up a new engine or change an ignition box is to check your timing. Ignition boxes of the same model can differ.

You can ruin an engine by assuming that the timing was proper because when the engine ran on a dyno it was off-the-charts advanced (but was installed with a different ignition box).

Retarded ignition timing is nearly as bad. I have had customers who break-in camshafts with retarded ignition timing and then stick valves in valveguides into the center cylinders. These center cylinders, with the adjacent exhaust ports, become a little hotter than the rest. The combination of that along with retarded timing is a perfect recipe for disaster, even though there was enough stem-to-guide clearance.

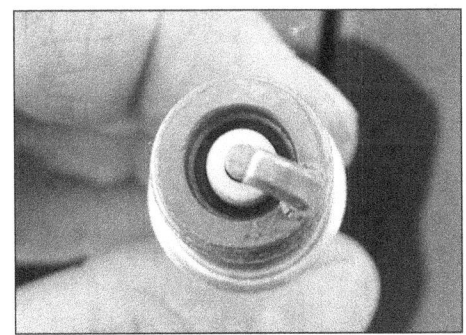

This is what a spark plug should look like in a properly tuned engine. It does not look this way after multiple passes down a dragstrip or a number of street miles, but if you look at your brand-new spark plugs after a full-throttle hit and they look like this, you are good to go. Don't waste your time trying to read old spark plugs.

APPENDIX A

Assembly Tips and Techniques

Oldsmobile engines are different from other V-8 engines in the GM engine family. These engines have different assembly requirements than Chevy, Pontiac, or Buick V-8s. When assembling an Oldsmobile small- or big-block engine, follow the assembly tips and directions provided below. Although these recommendations are not comprehensive, it is important to complete the procedures so that you have the strongest-running engine possible.

Number 1

You can never achieve 100-percent-clean status when cleaning the engine block, so spend as much time as you can and use a small flashlight to look in all the holes.

Number 2

When installing the cam bearings it is a good idea to deburr them and lubricate the housing bore and cam bearings before installation. Do not use Loctite or install dry. Install one cam bearing at a time and insert the camshaft so that if the camshaft does not fit properly, you will know exactly which cam bearing is giving you the problem.

Number 3

For crankshaft installation, use 30-weight oil on cam bearings instead of assembly lube or heavy oil and no rear seal; this allows you to rotate the shaft to ensure that it feels friction-free. Then you can reinstall the crankshaft with the rear main seal. It is okay to use the thin oil for final assembly but, at this point, it's acceptable to use whatever you want. Oil works for me.

Number 4

When installing the rings on the pistons and then assembling the pistons onto the connecting rods, assemble all eight completely so that you can look over everything one more time before final assembly into the bores. The definition of "10 on the suckometer" is when you are installing the oil pan and you see a single spirolock on the workbench.

Number 5

The only acceptable way to check for interference between the connecting rod chamfer or bearing and the radius of a questionable rod journal is to measure the width of the rod journal with a gauge block, measure the two connecting rods with a micrometer, and then calculate the amount of clearance you want.

Then, with the rods installed, use a feeler gauge to measure that calculated clearance. You have a problem that needs to be resolved if, for example, you calculate .016 inch and you cannot place a .012-inch feeler gauge in the space between. The issue is not having machined the flat portion of the big end of the connecting rods.

Number 6

Torquing fasteners is not necessarily straightforward. The way you pull on the torque wrench, how fast you pull on the torque wrench, the brand and type of torque wrench, the lubricant you use on the fastener, the length of the fastener, the material into which you are installing the fastener, and I could keep going; all of these things affect torque specs. The goal is to torque a fastener to 75 to 80 percent of its yield point, which is the point at which the fastener does not return to its original length. Measuring the stretch of a fastener is fairly difficult and requires special tools.

When assembling your high-performance Oldsmobile engine my advice is to use a good lubricant and make sure all friction points are well lubricated when installing the fasteners. Every different-diameter fastener requires a different torque depending on its tensile strength. With that said, you have to sneak up on the torque setting until it *feels* correct and is in the range that the fastener requires.

Here is one example that applies to all: Between 90 and 110 ft-lbs of torque is required when torquing a 1/2-inch ARP main stud. Start at 85 ft-lbs and get a feel for it. When you hear an instant click on your torque wrench the fastener is not getting much stretch. Back the nut off, increase by 5 ft-lbs, and try again.

You will get to the point at which you can feel when you are over-stretching the fastener. Then you can make an educated guess as to what the "spec" is at that point.

Number 7

When installing the oil pump, make sure that the housing is not hitting the nut when using main studs. When the pump is installed with the bolts, try inserting a .001-in-thick feeler gauge between the pump and the cap.

Number 8

When installing the main or any other studs, bottom them out and back them off approximately a half turn before you install the nut. The goal is to prevent a stress point caused by the threads bottoming out.

Number 9

Use the intake-opening method to degree your camshaft; it is the least time consuming. If you do not have the cam card but know the duration and lobe separation, you can calculate the intake opening point by using this formula: duration ÷ 2 − required intake centerline.

Number 10

Verify the relationship of the TDC mark on the harmonic balancer and the pointer before you install the cylinder heads.

Number 11

If your Oldsmobile engine is equipped with an ATI harmonic balancer and a mechanical water pump, you must not forget to grind or machine the bottom of the water pump. The time to remember isn't when you have the gasket on and you're ready to bolt it together.

Number 12

Torque the cylinder head's inner bolts to the outside bolts. It's not critical and you don't need to follow a particular sequence. Start with half the torque value and then apply the final torque. It is usually a good idea to re-torque once during the installation; back off one bolt at a time completely and then go right to the final torque setting.

Number 13

An easy way to set rocker geometry on a stud-type rocker arm is with the cylinder head on the workbench. Properly set rocker arm height and geometry changes with the amount of valve lift used.

With no valvespring or retainer in place, add a piece of masking tape to the valvestem so that the valve can go up and down. The tape stops the valve at maximum valve lift. Lock the rocker arm at a set height and look at the sweep of the roller tip from zero to max lift. At those two positions, the roller tip should be in the same spot on the face of the valvestem if the so-called rocker arm geometry is correct.

Once you have the rocker arm locked in the spot where the rocker needs to be, install the cylinder head and use an adjustable pushrod to fill in the distance between the rocker and lifter. Add about .050 for hydraulic-lifter applications to give proper preload; in solid-lifter applications, adjust the length of the adjustable pushrod until the required lash is set. That is the length of the pushrod you should order.

Number 14

Soaking lifters and rocker arms in oil is a good idea, but they only need to be soaked long enough for air bubbles to stop coming out of the parts. It usually takes 5 minutes or so; don't soak overnight or for several days.

Number 15

Blow through the hole on brand-new pushrods to ensure that there is no leftover manufacturing debris inside. I had that issue once with a pushrod. It is highly unlikely that you will have an issue, but it doesn't hurt to check.

Number 16

When setting valve lash or adjusting hydraulic-lifter preload, start in the front and work your way to the back, one cylinder at a time. The rule is to adjust the exhaust rocker arm just after full lift when the intake rocker starts to close. When the exhaust rocker arm begins to open, adjust the intake rocker.

Number 17

Glue the valvecover gaskets to the valvecovers with Permatex The Right Stuff. It is very aggressive and holds the gasket in place. You will be able to remove and reinstall the valvecovers many times without replacing the gaskets.

APPENDIX B

POPULAR *BTR* PERFORMANCE COMBINATIONS

Throughout the years I have built numerous different Oldsmobile Max Performance engines, but the following combinations are the most basic and are by far the most popular.

Build No. 1

375-ci Stroker Pump-Gas Small-Block Street Engine
- CP Bullet flat-top piston kit
- 4.125 bore
- Chevrolet 6 x 2-inch rod journal, H-beam connecting rods
- Gasoline 350 N crankshaft, machined to 3.5-inch stroke
- Comp Cams/BTR custom hydraulic roller camshaft
- ATI harmonic balancer
- Harland Sharp 5016 or 5017 roller rockers
- Trend .135 wall pushrods
- Edelbrock Performer RPM aluminum cylinder heads, unported milled for desired compression
- 10.7:1 compression
- Edelbrock Victor intake
- Holley 950-hp carburetor

Output: 475 hp

Build No. 2

375-ci W31 Restoration Stroker Pump-Gas Small-Block Street Engine
- CP Bullet flat-top piston kit
- 4.125 bore
- Chevrolet 6 x 2-inch rod journal, H-beam connecting rods
- Gasoline 350 N crankshaft, machined to 3.5-inch stroke
- Comp Cams/BTR custom hydraulic roller camshaft
- ATI harmonic balancer
- Harland Sharp 5016 or 5017 roller rockers
- Trend .135 wall pushrods
- Factory iron cylinder heads with 2.000/1.625 valves, mild bowl porting
- 10.7:1 compression
- W31 intake manifold
- Rochester Quadrajet

Output: 410 hp

Build No. 3

468-ci Pump-Gas Big-Block Street Engine
- CP Bullet dished piston kit
- 4.185 bore
- Eagle H-beam 455 Oldsmobile connecting rods
- 455 crankshaft ground with stock stroke
- Comp Cams/BTR custom hydraulic roller camshaft
- ATI harmonic balancer
- Harland Sharp 5016 or 5017 roller rockers
- Trend .135 wall pushrods
- Edelbrock Performer RPM aluminum cylinder heads, unported
- 10.7:1 compression
- Edelbrock Performer RPM or Torker
- Holley 950-hp carburetor

Output: 520 hp

Build No. 4

496-ci W30 Restoration Stroker Pump-Gas Big-Block Street Engine
- CP bullet dished piston kit
- 4.185 bore
- BTR 7.100 long H-beam connecting rods
- 455 crankshaft machined for 4.500 stroke with 2.200 rod journals
- Comp Cams/BTR custom hydraulic roller camshaft
- ATI harmonic balancer
- Harland Sharp 5016 roller rockers

- Trend .135 wall pushrods
- Factory iron cylinder heads with 2.071/1.625 valves, mild bowl porting
- W30 intake manifold, factory original or replica
- Rochester Quadrajet

Output: 430 hp with exhaust manifolds
Output: 475 hp with headers

Build No. 5

Engine: 496-ci Stroker Pump-Gas Big-Block Street Engine
- CP bullet dished piston kit
- 4.185 bore
- BTR 7.100 long H-beam connecting rods
- 455 crankshaft machined for 4.500 stroke with 2.200 rod journals
- Comp Cams/BTR custom hydraulic roller camshaft
- ATI harmonic balancer
- Harland Sharp 5016 roller rockers
- Trend .135 wall pushrods
- Edelbrock Performer RPM aluminum cylinder heads, unported
- 10.7:1 compression
- Edelbrock Performer RPM or Torker
- Holley 1,000-hp carburetor

Output: 570 hp, 640 ft-lbs torque

Build No. 6

506-ci Stroker Race-Gas Big-Block Street Engine
- Custom CP flat-top pistons
- 4.185 bore
- GRP custom aluminum connecting rods
- Bryant Racing billet 4.600 stroke with 2.000 rod journals
- Comp Cams/BTR custom mechanical roller camshaft
- ATI harmonic balancer
- T&D custom offset roller rockers
- Trend .135 wall pushrods
- BTR/Edelbrock Performer RPM aluminum cylinder heads, max ported with 2.165/1.680 valves
- 15:1 compression
- Edelbrock Victor intake manifold
- Dale Cubic Dominator carburetor

Output: 750 to 830 hp, 700 ft-lbs torque

Source Guide

American Racing Headers
880 Grand Blvd.
Deer Park, NY 11729
631-608-1986
americanracingheaders.com

Bryant Racing
1600 E. Winston Rd.
Anaheim, CA 92805
714-535-2695
bryantracing.com

BTR Performance
1517 Mount Read Blvd.
Rochester, NY 14606
585-303-7560
btrperformance.com

Cloyes Gear & Products
7800 Ball Rd.
Fort Smith, AR 72908
479-646-1662
cloyes.com

Comp Cams
3406 Democrat Rd.
Memphis, TN 38118
800-365-9145
compcams.com

CP Pistons
1902 McGaw Ave.
Irvine, CA 92614
949-567-9000
cp-carillo.com

CSR Performance Products
16936 Cty. Rd. 252
McAlpin, FL 32062
386-776-1476
csr-performance.com

CFM Performance Carburetors
3337 Yost Rd.
Litchfield, OH 44253
330-723-5688
cfmperfcarbs.com

Cometic Gasket
8090 Auburn Rd.
Concord, OH 44077
440-354-0777
cometic.com

SOURCE GUIDE

Custom Rebuilt Carburetors
200A Wood Ave.
Middlesex, NJ 08846
732-356-4333
customrebuiltcarbs.com

Custom Speed Parts
Harland Sharp
19769 Progress Dr.
Strongsville, OH 44149
440-238-3260
harlandsharp.com

Dakota Parts Warehouse
Ferrea Valves
405 12th St.
Rapid City, SD 57701
877-235-2832
dpwferreavalves.com

Dick Miller Racing
5930 Hwy. 305
Hernando, MS 38632
662-233-2301
dickmillerracing.com

Eagle Specialty Products
8530 Aaron Ln.
Southaven, MS 38671
662-796-7373
eaglerod.com

Edelbrock
2700 California St.
Torrance, CA 90503
310-781-2222
edelbrock.com

Flatout Gaskets
668 Tower Rd.
Mundelein, IL 660060
877-837-9200
flatoutgroup.com

JE Pistons
15312 Connector Ln.
Huntington Beach, CA 92649
714-895-9594
jepistons.com

GRP Connecting Rods
333 W. 48th Ave.
Denver, CO 80216
303-935-7565
grpconrods.com

Holley Performance Products
1801 Russellville Rd.
Bowling Green, KY 42101
270 781-9741 (Tech Service)
holley.com

Kooks Headers
141 Advantage Pl.
Statesville, NC 28677
1-866-586-KOOK
kooksheaders.com

M&J ProFormance
4444 Meese Rd.
Louisville, OH 44641
330-875-8096
mjproformance.com

Manton Pushrods
601 Crane St., Bldg. C
Lake Elsinore, CA 92530
951-245-6565
mantonpushrods.com

Melling Engine Parts
2620 Saradan Dr.
Jackson, MI 49204
517-787-8172
melling.com

Meziere Enterprises
220 S. Hale Ave.
Escondido, CA 92029
800-208-1755
meziere.com

Mondello Performance Products
1103 Paso Robles St.
Paso Robles, CA 93446
805-237-8808
mondellotwister.com

Moroso Performance
80 Carter Dr.
Guilford, CT 06437
203-458-0542
moroso.com

MSD Ignition
1490 Henry Brennan Dr.
El Paso, TX 79936
951-857-5200
msdignition.com

Olds Performance Products
4 Executive Blvd., Ste. 100
Suffern, NY 10901
845-369-9602
oldsperformanceproducts.com

PerTronix Performance Products
440 E. Arrow Hwy.
San Dimas, CA 91773
909-547-9058
pertronix.com

RocketRacing Performance
8207A Big Bend Rd.
Waterford, WI 53185
262-706-3277
rocketracingperformance.com

Red Line Synthetic Oil Corporation
6100 Egret Ct.
Benicia, CA 94510
707-745-6100
redlineoil.com

Racing Engine Valves
2610 Windsor Ave.
West Palm Beach, FL 33407
800-398-6348
revvalves.com

Swain Tech Coatings
963 North Rd.
Scottsville, NY 14546
585-889-2786
swaintech.com

T&D Machine Products
4859 Convair Dr.
Carson City, NV 89706
775-884-2292
tdmach.com

Total Seal
22642 N. 15th Ave.
Phoenix, AZ 85027
623-587-7400
totalseal.com

Titan Speed Engineering
13001 Tree Ranch Rd.
Ojai, CA 93023
805-525-8660
titanspeed.com

Wix Filters
P.O. Box 1967
Gastonia, NC 28053
704-864-6748
wixfilters.com

www.ingramcontent.com/pod-product-compliance
Lightning Source LLC
Chambersburg PA
CBHW081451070526
44586CB00019B/2311